CIMA

PRACTICE & REVISION KIT

Stage 4 Paper 15

Information Management

BPP Publishing
January 2000

First edition 1994
Sixth edition January 2000

ISBN 0 7517 3859 X (previous edition 0 7517 3878 6)

British Library Cataloguing-in-Publication Data
A catalogue record for this book
is available from the British Library

Published by

BPP Publishing Limited
Aldine House, Aldine Place
London W12 8AW

www.bpp.com

Printed in Great Britain by
WM Print Ltd
Frederick Street
Walsall
West Midlands WS2 9NE

We are grateful to the Chartered Institute of Management Accountants for permission to reproduce past examination questions. The answers to past examination questions have been prepared by BPP Publishing Limited.

CONTENTS

The headings indicate the main topics of questions, but questions often cover several different topics.

Tutorial questions, listed in italics, are followed by advice on how to **approach the question,** thus easing the transition from study to examination practice.

A date alone (5/99, say) or 'specimen paper' after the question title refers to a current syllabus paper.

After current syllabus questions we also indicate whether the question was compulsory.

Questions preceded by * are **key questions** which we think you must attempt in order to pass the exam. Tick them off on this list as you complete them.

REVISION

This is a very important time as you approach the exam. You must remember three things.

Use time sensibly
Set realistic goals
Believe in yourself

Use time sensibly

1 **How much study time do you have?** Remember that you must EAT, SLEEP, and of course, RELAX.

2 **How will you split that available time between each subject?** What are your weaker subjects? They need more time.

3 **What is your learning style?** AM/PM? Little and often/long sessions? Evenings/ weekends?

4 **Are you taking regular breaks?** Most people absorb more if they do not attempt to study for long uninterrupted periods of time. A five minute break every hour (to make coffee, watch the news headlines) can make all the difference.

5 **Do you have quality study time?** Unplug the phone. Let everybody know that you're studying and shouldn't be disturbed.

Set realistic goals

1 Have you set a **clearly defined objective** for each study period?

2 Is the objective **achievable**?

3 Will you **stick to your plan**? Will you make up for any **lost time**?

4 Are you **rewarding yourself** for your hard work?

5 Are you leading a **healthy lifestyle**?

Believe in yourself

Are you cultivating the right attitude of mind? There is absolutely no reason why you should not pass this exam if you adopt the correct approach.

- **Be confident** - you've passed exams before, you can pass them again
- **Be calm** - plenty of adrenaline but no panicking
- **Be focused** - commit yourself to passing the exam

QUESTION PRACTICE

There is little point in simply opening this Kit and, beginning with question 1, attempting all of the questions. You need to ask yourself three questions.

Am I ready to answer questions?
Do I know which questions to do first?
How should I use this Kit?

Am I ready to answer questions?

1 Try to fill in the blanks on the **Do you know? checklist** for a particular syllabus area. Compare your answers with the corresponding **Did you know? checklist**.

2 If you are happy with what you have written, you can go ahead and start answering questions. **Do not attempt questions if you could not fill in any of the blanks**. Go back to your BPP Study Text and revise first.

Do I know which questions to do first?

1 **Start with tutorial questions**. They warm you up for key and difficult areas of the syllabus. Try to produce at least a plan for these questions, using the guidance notes following the question to ensure your answer is structured so as to gain a good pass mark.

2 Don't worry about the time it takes to answer these questions. Concentrate on producing good answers.

How should I use this Kit?

1 Once you are confident with the Do you know? checklists and the tutorial questions, you should try as many as possible of the exam-standard questions; at the very least you should attempt the **key questions,** which are highlighted in the **question and answer checklist/index** at the front of the Kit.

2 Try to **produce full answers under timed conditions**; you are practising exam technique as much as knowledge recall here. Don't look at the answer, your BPP Study Text or your notes for any help at all.

3 **Mark your answers to the non-tutorial questions as if you were the examiner**. Only give yourself marks for what you have written, not for what you meant to put down, or would have put down if you had had more time. If you did badly, try another question.

4 Read the **Pass marks** in the answers very carefully and take note of the advice given and any **comments by the examiner**. Don't worry if you found something difficult; **Prizewinners' points** indicate parts of questions that only a prizewinner might get right in an exam.

5 When you have practised the whole syllabus, go back to the areas you had problems with and **practise further questions**.

6 Finally, when you think you really understand the entire subject, **attempt the mock exam** at the end of the Kit. Sit the paper under strict exam conditions, so that you gain experience of selecting and sequencing your questions, and managing your time, as well as of writing answers.

EXAM TECHNIQUE

Passing professional examinations is half about having the knowledge, and half about doing yourself full justice in the examination. You must have the right approach to two things.

The day of the exam
Your time in the exam hall

The day of the exam

1 Set at least one **alarm** (or get an alarm call) for a morning exam.

2 Have **something to eat** but beware of eating too much; you may feel sleepy if your system is digesting a large meal.

3 Allow plenty of **time to get to the exam hall**; have your route worked out in advance and listen to news bulletins to check for potential travel problems.

4 **Don't forget** pens, pencils, rulers, erasers.

5 **Avoid discussion** about the exam with other candidates outside the exam hall.

Your time in the exam hall

1 ***Read the instructions (the 'rubric') on the front of the exam paper carefully***

Check that the exam format hasn't changed. It is surprising how often examiners' reports remark on the number of students who attempt too few - or too many - questions, or who attempt the wrong number of questions from different parts of the paper. Make sure that you are planning to answer the **right number of questions**.

2 ***Select questions carefully***

Read through the paper once, then quickly jot down key points against each question in a second read through. Select those questions where you could latch on to 'what the question is about' - but remember to check carefully that you have got the right end of the stick before putting pen to paper.

3 ***Plan your attack carefully***

Consider the **order** in which you are going to tackle questions. It is a good idea to start with your best question to boost your morale and get some easy marks 'in the bag'.

4 ***Check the time allocation for each question***

Each mark carries with it a **time allocation** of 1.8 minutes (including time for selecting and reading questions). A 20 mark question therefore should be completed in 36 minutes. A 60 mark case study should take 108 minutes. (Just over 1¾ hours). When time is up, you *must* go on to the next question or part. Going even one minute over the time allowed brings you a lot closer to failure.

5 ***Read the question carefully and plan your answer***

Read through the question again very carefully when you come to answer it. Plan your answer to ensure that you **keep to the point**. Two minutes of planning plus eight minutes of writing is virtually certain to earn you more marks than ten minutes of writing.

6 ***Produce relevant answers***

Particularly with written answers, make sure you **answer the question set**, and not the question you would have preferred to have been set.

7 ***Gain the easy marks***

Include the obvious if it answers the question and don't try to produce the perfect answer.

Don't get bogged down in small parts of questions. If you find a part of a question difficult, get on with the rest of the question. If you are having problems with something, the chances are that everyone else is too.

8 ***Produce an answer in the correct format***

The examiner will **state in the requirements** the format in which the question should be answered, for example in a report or memorandum.

9 ***Follow the examiner's instructions***

You will annoy the examiner if you ignore him or her. The **examiner will state** whether he or she wishes you to 'discuss', 'comment', 'evaluate' or 'recommend' (see the section on examiners' instructions on page (xx).)

10 ***Present a tidy paper***

You are a professional, and it should show in the **presentation of your work**. Students are penalised for poor presentation and so you should make sure that you write legibly, label diagrams clearly and lay out your work neatly. Markers of scripts each have hundreds of papers to mark; a badly written scrawl is unlikely to receive the same attention as a neat and well laid out paper.

11 ***Stay until the end of the exam***

Use any spare time **checking and rechecking** your script.

12 ***Don't worry if you feel you have performed badly in the exam***

It is more than likely that the other candidates will have found the exam difficult too. Don't forget that there is a competitive element in these exams. As soon as you get up to leave the exam hall, ***forget* that exam** and think about the next - or, if it is the last one, celebrate!

13 ***Don't discuss an exam with other candidates***

This is particularly the case if you **still have other exams to sit**. Even if you have finished, you should put it out of your mind until the day of the results. Forget about exams and relax!

THE EXAM PAPER

Format of the Year 2000 exams

		Number of marks
Section A	Case study with one compulsory question (4 to 5 parts)	60
Section B	two questions from three	40
		100

Time allowed : 3 hours

> **Recent pass rate**
>
> The UK and overseas combined pass rate for the May 1999 exam was 38.2%.

Analysis of past papers 1995-1999

The analysis below shows the topics which have been examined in the ten sittings of the syllabus and the CIMA Specimen paper for *Information Management.*

November 1999

Section A

1 Case study based around a telecommunications service provider: information sources for price setting, effects on employment and society, aligning systems and strategy, EIS and decision making

Section B

2 Intranet and information sharing

3 Outsourcing / hardware and software maintenance agreement,

4 Verifying information, Cost-benefit analysis

This paper forms the mock exam at the end of the Kit.

May 1999	*Question number in this Kit*
Section A	
1 Case study based around the development of international software in a service organisation: reasons for project failure, SDLC, Human Information Processor, local information needs, data transfer risks and controls	59
Section B	
2 Website v paper-based catalogue; website as a support tool	49
3 Good quality information	10
4 Information system inputs and outputs	36

Examiner's comments

The overall standard of scripts in this examination appeared to be lower than in previous diets. The main reasons for this fall in standard are:

- A lack of application of knowledge to the specific situations outlined in the questions (especially question 1(a) and (b)).
- Not always explaining points being made or simply asking rhetorical questions rather than showing why the point was actually relevant to the question asked.
- Some lack of planning of answers. In particular, the writing of lengthy introductions to answers which provided little of relevance to the question asked.
- Too many answers tended to end with either a detailed summary of the points made, wasting time for the candidates because nothing new was added.
- The addition of new information in a conclusion, almost as an after-thought. While this did obtain some credit, the inclusion of the comment in the main body of the answer with full explanation would gain more marks.

The overall standard of presentation and legibility was much improved. Many candidates who did not pass at this attempt will need to concentrate on providing **more detailed content** in their answers.

November 1998

		Question number in this Kit
1	Case study concerning supplier of office and stationery products: comparison of new systems; information requirements; leasing or purchase; human issues	58
Section B		
2	E-mail: impact on work practices and situations when inappropriate	42
3	IT department costs: chargeout methods	32
4	MIS and expert system: characteristics, hardware and software requirement	31

Examiner's comments

Many candidates produced a high standard of answer by:

- Planning their answers and providing clear formats and presentation
- Having a reasonable knowledge of the IFM syllabus
- Applying knowledge to specific situations.

Questions where candidates tended to obtain good marks were 1(a), 1(c), 2(a) and 4(a).

The general standard in other questions was poorer, with the answers to 4(b) in particular being very weak. Reasons for this appeared to be:

- Almost all candidates spent too much time on Question 1(a) which frequently meant Question 4 was answered under severe time pressure.
- Not explaining the points made. In quite a few situations, candidates provided a list of points without showing why those points were relevant to the question being asked. Very few marks can be awarded for this type of answer.
- Not providing sufficient analysis of the situations in the case study. A significant minority of candidates provided very superficial answers which failed to address the key issues being raised in each question.

In Section B, Question 2 on e-mail was the most popular, followed by Question 4; very few candidates attempted Question 3.

May 1998	*Question number in this Kit*
Section A	
1 Case study concerning a theme park operator: sources of information; analysis and design; changes required to EIS; back-up options; Internet bookings	57
Section B	
2 IT strategy: reasons for and examples	15
3 Human problems and human and IT solutions	50
4 Quality of information; information centre	34

Examiner's comments

Candidates should not be surprised by the lack of detailed questions about computer hardware or software, as the Information Management exam is looking at the use of information and not how the systems that provide that information actually work.

Most candidates could have obtained additional marks by planning their answers to ensure that a sufficient number of points are included in the answer; explaining why the points being made are relevant to the question, and not repeating question information without showing the relevance of this to the question being asked.

November 1997	*Question number in this Kit*
Section A	
1 Case study concerning a car manufacturer: qualities of information; importance of IT; data security; human-computer interface	56
Section B	
2 Evaluating software suppliers	25
3 Strategic and operational benefits of a proposed EPOS	30
4 Internet services; charging for information provision	44

Examiner's comments

The standard of a substantial number of answers was quite poor, indicating that candidates were insufficiently prepared for the examination.

Many poorer answers included lengthy sections concerning the hardware or software that candidates thought would be appropriate. The IFM exam focuses on the use of information and not necessarily on the technology which enables the use of that information.

Characteristics of scripts that did not achieve a pass standard were the following.

Question 1 was answered last, and candidates failed to complete it.

Lack of any evidence of planning.

A failure to use the question information to support comments being made in answers.

May 1997	*Question number in this Kit*
Section A	
1 Case study concerning a food processing business: sources of information; the limitations of a closed loop system; limitations of market research information; CSFs and performance indicators; computerised bulletin boards	55
Section B	
2 JH Ltd and its working group for IT strategy formulation	14
3 Glue manufacturer and its MIS: weaknesses of information provision and how to improve it; MIS and strategic information	6
4 Insurance company and homeworking	47

Examiner's comments

Many answers show that candidates are applying their knowledge to questions, although some 'classic' examination problems such as not reading the question and lack of time management still plague a significant minority of candidates.

The examiner has stated that the IFM examination will continue to examine new technology and its applications in the information area, and this will continue to be the case. The inclusion in this examination of questions on homeworking and investigation of the problems of information itself are markers in this direction.

There are still many scripts which show little evidence of planning. The need for planning cannot be stressed enough, especially given the poor quality of some of the answers to question 2(b). There was also an interesting trend in this examination of many candidates answering the main 60-mark scenario question last. While this may give candidates the benefit of getting two questions 'under the belt' early in the examination, it does have the problem that an insufficient amount of time may be left to complete the scenario. Good time allocation continues to be a major requirement in passing the IFM examination.

November 1996	*Question number in this Kit*
Section A	
1 Case study concerning an international airline operator: strategy, information characteristics, upgrading, the Internet and security	54
Section B	
2 Problems and benefits of using e-mail in a dairy product manufacturing company operating 20 factories	46
3 Plastic mouldings manufacturer: Merits of departmental information compared with a centralised database; problems of creating the database	7
4 Local authority: introducing a DSS	8

Examiner's comments

Positive features of candidates' answers noted during the marking process were:

- candidates thinking about company strategy in some detail whilst attempting to apply theory from other Stage 4 examination syllabuses
- good use of memory joggers such as BPP's ACCURATE acronym
- attempts at applying knowledge to unknown or more difficult areas

A potential weakness of many examination scripts was the lack of any evidence of answer planning. for example:

- points were repeated within an answer
- poor time allocation resulted in later parts of an answer being rushed.

Time spent planning is not wasted. In the majority of situations, adequate planning will enhance the quality of answers.

The IFM examination has now completed the two year 'introduction'. Future IFM examinations will tend to use this examination as a 'model' or indicator of the style of the paper.

May 1996	*Question number in this Kit*
Section A	
1 Industrial chemicals manufacturer – information and process-related problems. Includes CSFs, BPR, reporting, decision making, change and HIPs	53
Section B	
2 System changeover and the Systems Development Life Cycle.	19
3 Small retail chain - central information storage; the Data Protection Act	43
4 Freight forwarding company - the use of an information centre	14

Examiner's comments

The standard of answers in the May 1996 examination was still below what is expected at this level, but there was some evidence that the overall standard is improving. In particular the examiner was pleased to note that:

(a) some candidates are spending more time planning answers before writing them out,

(b) there is more evidence of candidates using the case study material in the question as a basis for their answers, and

(c) there are fewer answers that go for some 'technology fix' in response to every problem.

The majority of answers still showed considerable room for improvement. In particular, most scripts would have benefited from:

(a) not simply stating the company name in answers to try and disguise 'general' comments. The case study information has to be used wherever possible

(b) providing sufficient detail in answers and not lists of points. For example, 'the benefits of centralisation include cost, access, compatible hardware' etc as a list is not sufficient. An explanation of each of these items must be included in the answer.

To continue the improvement candidates must:

(a) read the question

(b) apply their knowledge to question information

(c) avoid repeating knowledge without reference to the case study

November 1995	*Question number in this Kit*
Section A	
1 Travel agency - installation of new computer system	52
Section B	
2 Supermarket chain - specification for MIS	33
3 Manufacturing company - key indicators	9
4 Railway company - use and presentation of information	5

Examiner's comments

The main reasons for failure in this examination include:

(a) failing to produce answers that are worthy of a good Stage 4 student who is shortly to be a Chartered Management Accountant

(b) failing to apply knowledge to scenarios and case studies

(c) having an inadequate knowledge of key areas of the syllabus, and

(d) relying too much on knowledge of computer systems and repetition of basic theory

The standard of scripts was lowered by candidates doing the following.

(a) Not considering what they wanted to write before putting pen to paper. In some scripts, a lot of time was wasted by candidates repeating the same point or emphasising the same point again and again. Some time spent in planning would enable candidates to identify exactly what points they wanted in their answers and then ensure that all points were included (once) in their answers.

(b) Writing all they knew about a subject without considering whether it was relevant to the question being asked. The result was long and verbose answers with little mark-earning ability.

(c) Using poor handwriting, and writing with poor quality fine nib pens which made scripts very difficult to read.

(d) Using highlighters unnecessarily, which tends to distract markers from other, sometimes more important, information in the scripts.

A little more effort spent in ensuring good presentation and planning of answers would be worthwhile. In many cases some planning would enhance the quality of answers considerably and would increase their mark-earning potential.

Unless tutors and candidates can get to grips with such key concepts as Human Information Processors and good screen design in the very near future, then this examination will prove to be a major stumbling block to many potential Chartered Management Accountants.

May 1995

Section A

1 Police force - information deficiencies; hardware and software solution; critical success factors and performance indicators; outsourcing

Section B

2 Industrial explosives - systems access and data integrity; daily order process and MIS outputs

3 Cost of operating an EIS; focus on internally-produced information

4 Bookshop chain - pre-requisites for a VAN; benefits of VANs; staff reaction

Examiner's comments

The first examination was designed to lead candidates into the realm of IFM. The trend in future exams would be away from the SSADM type of answer and further into the rigour of the IFM syllabus.

Specimen paper

Section A

1 Delivery company - information problems; critical success factors; system proposal; systems design steps

Section B

2 Executive information system - characteristics; assessing information requirements

3 Staff concerns about networking; role of IS manager

4 Security procedures; data communication system

How the syllabus has been examined - an overview

	11/99	5/99	11/98	5/98	11/97	5/97	11/96	5/96	11/95	5/95	Specimen
(a) Information resource management											
Information and communication	✓	✓			✓	✓	✓	✓	✓	✓	✓
Information theory		✓			✓						
Information for decision making	✓	✓	✓	✓	✓	✓	✓	✓	✓	✓	✓
(b) Information strategy and systems development											
Matching IT to business strategy and structure	✓		✓	✓			✓		✓		
Development and implementation of strategy	✓	✓				✓	✓	✓			
Systems development lifecycle		✓	✓	✓	✓			✓	✓	✓	✓
End use participation								✓			
(c) Management of information systems and technology											
Role and structure of Management Information Systems	✓	✓	✓	✓	✓	✓	✓		✓	✓	✓
Distributed systems and central control			✓	✓	✓	✓		✓			✓
Audit and security of systems		✓		✓	✓		✓	✓		✓	
(d) Social dimensions of information											
Societal	✓	✓	✓	✓		✓	✓	✓	✓	✓	
Organisational power and privacy											
Employment	✓		✓	✓	✓	✓		✓	✓	✓	

(The full syllabus is on pages (xxi) to (xxiii).)

CURRENT ISSUES

The Internet and e-commerce

The influence of the Internet economy is spreading rapidly, on a global scale. In the last year, electronic commerce (e-commerce) has grown beyond almost everyone's expectations. People are finding new ways to provide innovative products and services electronically. The Internet is changing the way businesses do business, from the acquisition and servicing of customers, to the management of their relations with suppliers. It is revolutionising our access to information and the way we communicate, shop and entertain ourselves. The development of a 'digital economy', based upon virtual trading and electronic markets, and the application of computing power to exchange and analyse information should be to the benefit of all. Many observers believe this 'information revolution' will have an impact as profound as the industrial revolution. Even though the value of e-commerce transactions is still small relative to the size of the economy, it continues to grow at a rapid rate. Both the new Internet-based companies and the traditional producers of goods and services are transforming their business processes into e-commerce processes in an effort to lower costs, improve customer service, and increase productivity. At the same time, the digital economy makes possible a truly global marketplace.

Viruses

Macro viruses are now regarded as amongst the most dangerous type of security risks faced by modern organisations. A macro virus is a piece of self-replicating code written in an application's 'macro' language.

The distinguishing factor which makes it possible to create a virus with a macro is the existence of **auto-execute events**. Auto-execute events are opening a file, closing a file, and starting an application. Once a macro is running, it can copy itself to other documents, delete files, and create general havoc. Viruses are increasingly spreading via e-mail attachments.

Summary of recent articles

A list of useful articles published recently in *Management Accounting* are noted briefly below.

Technology makes paper return to the fold, Anthea Ballam, Management Accounting, May 1999, page 50

The millennium bug: Accident, negligence or cynical manoeuvre?, Richard Blake, Management Accounting, May 1999, page 28

Digital versatile disk drives, Terry Corbitt, Management Accounting, June 1999, page 36

Implementing a new accounting system, John Tate, Management Accounting, July/August1999, page 41

Searching the net, Terry Corbitt, Management Accounting, September 1999, page 52

Using the internet for business information, Terry Corbitt, Management Accounting, October 1999, page 54

International software development, Alan Lewin, Management Accounting, October 1999, page 68 (Alan Lewin is the examiner. This article is a commentary on the May 1999 case study - see Q59 in this kit.)

Systems implementation: some practical guidance, John Tate, Management Accounting, November 1999, page 37

Tax evasion and the internet, Terry Corbitt, Management Accounting, November 1999, page 42

E-commerce: Dispelling the myths and exploiting the opportunities, Martin Corboy, Management Accounting, December 1999, p 38

Going virtual, Trevor Bentley, Management Accounting, December 1999, p 44

EXAMINERS' INSTRUCTIONS

The examinations department of the CIMA has asked the Institute's examiners to be precise when drafting questions. In particular, examiners have been asked to use precise instruction words. It will probably help you to know what instruction words may be used, and what they mean. With the Institute's permission, their list of recommended requirement words, and their meaning, is shown below.

Recommended requirement words

Advise/recommend	Present information, opinions or recommendations to someone to enable that recipient to take action
Amplify	Expand or enlarge upon the meaning of (a statement or quotation)
Analyse	Determine and explain the constituent parts of
Appraise/assess/evaluate	Judge the importance or value of
Assess	See 'appraise'
Clarify	Explain more clearly the meaning of
Comment (critically)	Explain
Compare (with)	Explain similarities and differences between
Contrast	Place in opposition to bring out difference(s)
Criticise	Present the faults in a theory or policy or opinion
Demonstrate	Show by reasoning the truth of
Describe	Present the details and characteristics of
Discuss	Explain the opposing arguments
Distinguish	Specify the differences between
Evaluate	See 'appraise'
Explain/interpret	Set out in detail the meaning of
Illustrate	Use an example - chart, diagram, graph or figure as appropriate - to explain something
Interpret	See 'explain'
Justify	State adequate grounds for
List (and explain)	Itemise (and detail meaning of)
Prove	Show by testing the accuracy of
Recommend	See 'advise'
Reconcile	Make compatible apparently conflicting statements or theories
Relate	Show connections between separate matters
State	Express
Summarise	State briefly the essential points (dispensing with examples and details)
Tabulate	Set out facts or figures in a table

Requirement words which will be avoided

Examiners have been asked to avoid instructions which are imprecise or which may not specifically elicit an answer. The following words will not be used.

Consider	As candidates could do this without writing a word
Define	In the sense of stating exactly what a thing is, as CIMA wishes to avoid requiring evidence of rote learning
Examine	As this is what the examiner is doing, not the examinee
Enumerate	'List' is preferred
Identify	
Justify	When the requirement is not 'to state adequate grounds for' but 'to state the advantage of'
List	On its own, without an additional requirement such as 'list and explain'
Outline	As its meaning is imprecise. The addition of the word 'briefly' to any of the suggested action words is more satisfactory
Review	
Specify	
Trace	

SYLLABUS

The syllabus contains a weighting for each syllabus area, and a ranking of the level of ability required in each topic. The Institute has published the following explanatory notes on these points.

Study weightings

A percentage weighting is shown against each topic in the syllabus; this is intended as a guide to the amount of study time each topic requires.

All topics in a syllabus must be studied, as a question may examine more than one topic, or carry a higher proportion of marks than the percentage study time suggested.

The weightings do not specify the number of marks which will be allocated to topics in the examination.

Abilities required in the examination

Each examination paper contains a number of topics. Each topic has been given a number to indicate the level of ability required of the candidate.

The numbers range from 1 to 4 and represent the following ability levels:

Appreciation (1)
To understand a knowledge area at an early stage of learning, or outside the core of management accounting, at a level which enables the accountant to communicate and work with other members of the management team.

Knowledge (2)
To have detailed knowledge of such matters as laws, standards, facts and techniques so as to advise at a level appropriate to a management accounting specialist.

Skill (3)
To apply theoretical knowledge, concepts and techniques to the solutions of problems where it is clear what technique has to be used and the information needed is clearly indicated.

Application (4)
To apply knowledge and skills where candidates have to determine from a number of techniques which is the most appropriate and select the information required from a fairly wide range of data, some of which might not be relevant; to exercise professional judgement and to communicate and work with members of the management team and other recipients of financial reports.

Syllabus overview

This syllabus contains the two complementary areas of cost accounting and quantitative methods. In each area great importance will be attached to fundamental numeracy, analytical techniques and computer literacy. Students will be expected to understand the basic methods and techniques of cost accounting, and when and why they are used in practice. They should also have the ability to understand and interpret statistical and mathematical information.

The syllabus as a whole provides the essential background techniques for *Information Management* at Stage 4.

Aims

To test the candidate's ability to

- understand how component elements of cost make up the total cost of an activity, service or product
- prepare cost accounting records and statements of profit for management from cost accounting records in particular operational environments
- explain the purpose of various cost accounting methods and activities; explain their relevance to management and decision making
- recognise when a quantitative approach is applicable
- use quantitative methods to obtain accurate and reliable management information; explain and present results

Content and ability required

	Ability required
15(a) Information resource management *(study weighting 20%)*	
Information and communication: data capture and reporting; communications and information meaning; effective communication and choice of media; knowledge building and learning; learning cycles; auditing and quality assurance of information and communication	4
Information theory: systems theory - application of entropy, requisite variety; information economics; cost and value; consumption and usage; redundancy and requisite variety; attributes of data and information; data and file structures	4
Information for decision making: critical success factors and performance indicators; internal data sources and structure (Electronic Data Interchange, client server, distributed systems); external data sources (market and competitor intelligence); perfect information; uncertainty and risk; expected values	4
15(b) Information strategy and systems development *(study weighting 35%)*	
Matching information technology to business strategy and structure: vision and reality; technological and operational architecture; standards and protocols; communications and networks; identifying the costs and benefits of information strategies	4
Development and implementation of strategy: methods and processes; innovation and organisational development; timing the change; costs of conversion and change	4
Systems development life cycle: establishing user requirements; production of a business case; systems design and selection; stages and methods; project and team management; project life cycles; alternative processing methods; systems implementation; managing change; software selection; maintenance and documentation; testing and training; quality assurance	4
Selecting and acquiring systems; lease or buy, facilities or dedicated; contracting for services; responsibility and technical support	4
End-user participation: consultation; commitment and training; acceptance and empowerment	4

	Ability required
15(c) Management of information systems and technology *(study weighting 25%)*	
Role and structure of management information systems (MIS): data processing and operational systems; planning forecasting and external systems; internal control; decision support and executive information systems (EIS); formal and informal; information centres and services	4
Distributed systems and central control: personal computer networks and file servers; data and network administrators; systems control and maintenance; charging for services	4
Audit and security of systems: security, auditability and quality systems; physical security and systems integrity; disaster planning; back-up procedures and recovery; confidentiality and legal responsibilities; data protection legislation	4
15(d) Social dimensions of information *(study weighting 20%)*	
Societal: social and economic impact of information and communication technology; distributed and networked systems; value added networks; information markets; technological change and developments	4
Organisational: power and privacy; sharing and consumption; organisational and management learning; decision support systems; office automation; electronic data interchange (EDI)	4
Employment: restructuring of departments and tasks; human factors in systems development; designing the human computer interface; human information processor capacities and limitations	4

CIMA SYLLABUS GUIDANCE NOTES 1999-2000

The following Guidance Notes were published by CIMA as an aid to students and lecturers.

'*The following guidance notes have been drafted by the Chief Examiner for each of the subjects. They are intended to inform candidates and lecturers about the scope of the syllabus, the emphasis that should be placed on various topics and the approach which the examination papers will adopt.*'

General guidance note (Stage 4)

As the final test of professional competence in management accountancy, Stage 4 has certain unique characteristics. It is the culmination of the whole examination and requires from candidates the highest level of ability.

From Stage 2 onwards, candidates should remember that the syllabus content of subjects at earlier Stages is re-examinable. This does not imply that a Stage 2 question will appear in a Stage 4 question paper. However, it does mean that candidates need the ability to build on knowledge and skills including numerical skills, learned originally for an earlier stage.

Candidates will be required to integrate new material with that learned earlier, and to use the combined knowledge at a higher level of ability. Revision of earlier material, particularly by those who have been credited with exemptions, must form part of the studying process. The majority of the topics in the four papers are ranked at ability level 4 (Application). This means that candidates must not only be able to select the relevant data and apply the appropriate technique; they must also be able to communicate to others the results obtained. There is, thus, an emphasis on the practical application of knowledge and skill. To test this, the Examiners rely heavily on case study questions and scenario-based questions.

A case study is simply a history or description of an organisation, firm or industry facing a particular set of circumstances which could be a problem of some sort, or perhaps an opportunity. There is usually some discussion of how the organisation's current situation developed, and there is often a number of central characters charged with the task of resolving the problem, or exploiting the opportunity. Such characters are invariably senior members of management, eg the managing director, because it is at this level where policy and strategic decisions are made.

Cases will be between one and three pages long. They may be based around activities of real people and organisations (although candidates do *not* require any specialist knowledge of any particular organisation), or they may be fictitious.

The essential function of the case study is to test a candidate's ability to resolve relatively complex, unstructured problems. There may be several feasible solutions and candidates should not necessarily expect there to be a single definitive answer. The solution will involve the selection and use of techniques which have been learned, but usually also requires the exercise of judgement and creative thinking. This means that study and examination techniques which might have been suitable at earlier Stages need to become more sophisticated and directed when preparing for Stage 4. Preparation to answer case study/scenario-based questions cannot be reliant on reading alone, but must be heavily supplemented by question practice under examination conditions.

It is important to realise that in case study questions marks are earned by the quality of the reasoning and exposition displayed. The ability to structure a coherent report which leads logically to its conclusion is regarded as essential. Recommendations are often required. Acceptable recommendations may vary, but must be sensible and fully justified.

As candidates advance through the examination Stages, their career progress can restrict their available study time. Fewer find it possible to obtain contact with a teacher or tutor as part of a class. Yet the nature of the examination makes that contact highly desirable - perhaps more so than at earlier Stages.

However, candidates will be gaining a greater breadth of experience in the workplace. This valuable practical experience can be drawn on when answering practical-based questions.

Candidates' chances of success will be significantly enhanced if they are familiar with the current business environment. An easy way to achieve this is to read selectively from the *Financial Times* which analyses companies' published accounts, comments on marketing and strategy, and publishes a management page on an almost daily basis. There are also other international newspapers which carry out the same sort of analysis. It is quite clear that answers are enhanced by examples drawn from press articles and that such answers are given credit by the markers.

Stage 4 involves the integration of all subjects. There is inevitably, and deliberately, some overlap between papers as topics are dealt with from the different perspectives of strategy, marketing, information management, control and financial management. The following guidance notes give more information on the syllabuses for the subjects, but candidates should be continually aware of the integrative nature of Stage 4 and should not view each of the syllabuses in isolation.

Information resource management

Syllabus reference 15 (a)

Study weighting 20%

This section investigates how information as a resource is managed in different types of entities. Candidates will therefore need to know about information itself, and the differing structures within entities that can help or hinder the use of that information. For example, the Anthony hierarchy could be used to explain 7how information format and usage differ within the various organisational tiers of a company.

For this section of the syllabus, candidates will need an understand of the following:

- the relationship between data and information
- methods of data capture, that is how data gets into a system
- how data and information are communicated within a system.

In the examination, candidates may be required to:

- demonstrate an understanding of the effective transmission of information within a company and how to check that the information has been properly received and understood by the recipient
- show an appreciation of the requirement of the company to have certain types of data. For example, a chartered management accountant could be asked to justify IT investment by demonstrating the information value to the business of that investment. Alternatively the cost to the company of obtaining and using the wrong data, or of processing data in a way that is not beneficial, could be investigated
- appreciate the effect of uncertainty and risk on decision making. This will be in the form of recommending alternative courses of action or suggesting ways of decreasing the risk of information being incorrect.

Information strategy and systems development

Syllabus reference 15 (b)

Study weighting 35%

This section tends to be more technical in nature, compared to section (a). It looks at how IT (both hardware and software) can be used to assist the strategy of a company. The overriding consideration here is that IT is the enabler that helps companies to do what they want. Companies do not, therefore, implement IT systems and then look at what to do with them - IT does not drive the business entity. The approach to this section is to identify what business entities actually want to do (which could be achieved, for example, by looking at Johnson and Scholes or Porter's models) and then to see how IT fits into these systems. Questions on this section will be practical in nature.

In the examination, candidates may be required to display knowledge in a number of different areas including:

- how businesses support their overall strategy and structure with appropriate IT systems
- how IT strategies are developed and implemented
- explaining and applying the 'classical' systems development life cycle
- how to choose between competing systems, showing clearly the reasons for the choice
- how, and to what extent, end-users should be included in the decision to acquire systems
- an understanding of LANs, WANs and other communication systems. This will normally be subsidiary to an explanation of how these systems will meet or help meet the company's overall strategy and vision
- how to spot future opportunities for the company. Candidates should not expect to provide old or trusted solutions to business problems. In this area, as in others, suggestions for innovation that is possible given the state of technology will be rewarded in the examination
- how to apply knowledge to specific circumstances rather than producing a straight repetition of knowledge on any part of the systems development life cycle
- how to produce a report for management on the options for equipment selection, based on some constraints already noted within a question
- how to ensure that the needs of the user are met within the context of any systems change.
- interpreting diagrams provided in the examination paper, eg system flowcharts, GANTT charts, decision trees, network diagrams and data flow diagrams.

The following item is *not* examinable:

- the production of system flowcharts, GANTT charts, decision trees, network diagrams, data flow diagrams and similar presentation mediums.

Management of information systems and technology

Syllabus reference 15 (c)

Study weighting 25%

This section examines the ways in which IT systems process and present information to individuals within different business entities. This is likely to be the syllabus area where the background knowledge, which candidates need to understand, will change the quickest. Executive Information Systems tend to be updated annually; candidates will therefore need to keep up-to-date with the more recent changes to hardware and software, so that they can explain these adequately in an examination question. However, it is the *use* of technology that is important in this section and in the examination as a whole.

In the examination candidates may required to:

- explain how MISs and Executive Information Systems (EIS) are set up, how they function, how they are controlled and what they are used for
- explain what distributed systems are and how these are established. More recent system concepts will be examined, bearing in mind the eighteen month technology rule of IFM
- explain how computer systems can be kept secure, including the statutory requirements in this area
- answer questions on the provision and use of information. In particular candidates should understand the importance of ensuring that the correct level of management is receiving the right level of information. Questions may also be asked about the features of these information systems, especially as those systems develop over time
- answer questions on the acquisition and establishment of distributed systems to meet the needs of the company
- apply specific controls and techniques to a given situation to ensure that a company's computer system is not compromised. For example, candidates are much more likely to be asked 'what procedures should a company have to ensure that it meets the requirements of the Data Protection Act 1998 on the accessibility of data', than to be asked to state the data protection principles that are found in the Act.

The following item is *not* examinable:

- detailed explanation of how different parts of IT hardware and software work.

Social dimensions of information

Syllabus reference 15 (d)

Study weighting 20%

This section draws on the work of theorists such as Mintzberg and Kolb and investigates the impact that computer systems have on individuals, companies and society as a whole. The pace of change in the knowledge required for this section will be determined by how the theory develops, rather than by the change in the IT systems themselves.

Questions in this section will normally be based around case studies involving a company experiencing change. The ability of the company to adapt to this change could be questioned, or the effect of the change on staff. Again, whatever the situation, candidates should expect application of knowledge to be important and not merely simple definitions or lists of facts.

In the examination, candidates may be required to display knowledge in the following areas:

- the effect of information on society
- how computer systems provide the ability to increase the power of individuals, whilst at the same time potentially decreasing the amount of privacy
- how computers can affect the level of employment in a company and cause company restructuring in certain cases.
- the problems facing human informatiprocessors and the design and rise of the human computer interface.

Question bank

DO YOU KNOW? - INFORMATION RESOURCE MANAGEMENT

- *Check that you can fill in the blanks in the statements below before you attempt any questions. If in doubt, you should go back to your BPP Study Text and revise first.*
- Data can be collected from .... Management information systems are used to convert this data into information and to .... Many management information systems are not designed, but .... An MIS which develops without formal planning is likely to be inefficient. Environmental scanning is a process of obtaining information from .... Externally generated information may be more difficult to assimilate or to input into an information system, but is just as important to management as internal information.
- Different types of system are required for gathering information from each source. Much internal information can be generated by a company's .... systems. External information can be collected from a range of sources, some formal (perhaps subscription-based) and some informal.
- Information must be presented in such a way as to support its .... and .... This will help to ensure that it is used effectively in the ....

TRY QUESTION 5

- Most tasks in an organisation include some level of knowledge work. Knowledge work tasks involve the use of information. Knowledge is acquired by .... Many modern approaches to training emphasise the importance of learning via ....
- Systems theory is relevant to the study of information technology because general system principles apply to any type of system, including an information system such as a computer system. A system receives .... which it processes and generates into .... Any system can be thought of in terms of ...., ..., and ....
- Information can be said to have value to the extent that .... has value. The cost of collecting information bears no relation to its value. In order to minimise the cost of information, the information system should be designed to collect only ....

TRY QUESTIONS 6 AND 7

- One of the key uses of information is in decision making. The making of a decision has a number of identifiable stages. Decisions must be taken in response to choices and options regarding how an organisation responds to its .... and runs its ....

TRY QUESTION 8

- The use of critical success factors can help to determine the .... of senior management which in turn assists in identifying the ....required by an organisation. Critical success factors are ....where .... for the organisation to flourish.

TRY QUESTION 9

- Decision making almost invariably involves .... The information used to make a decision may be .... or ....and the consequences of a decision cannot be known with certainty. There are a number of methods of taking .... and ......into consideration when reaching a decision.

TRY QUESTION 10

- *Possible pitfalls*

  Write down the mistakes you know you should avoid.

DID YOU KNOW? - INFORMATION RESOURCE MANAGEMENT

- *Could you fill in the blanks? The answers are in bold. Use this page for revision purposes as you approach the exam.*
- Data can be collected from **within and beyond an organisation**. Management information systems are used to convert this data into information and to **communicate it to management at all levels**. Many management information systems are not designed, but **develop informally.** An MIS which develops without formal planning is likely to be inefficient. Environmental scanning is a process of obtaining information from **external sources**. Externally generated information may be more difficult to assimilate or to input into an information system, but is just as important to management as internal information.
- Different types of system are required for gathering information from each source. Much internal information can be generated by a company's **formal transactions processing systems**. External information can be collected from a range of sources, some formal (perhaps subscription-based) and some informal.
- Information must be presented in such a way as to support its **effective communication** and **correct interpretation**. This will help to ensure that it is used effectively in the **decision-making process**.

  TRY QUESTION 5
- Most tasks in an organisation include some level of knowledge work. Knowledge work tasks involve the use of information. Knowledge is acquired by **a process of learning**. Many modern approaches to training emphasise the importance of learning via **practical experience**.
- Systems theory is relevant to the study of information technology because general system principles apply to any type of system, including an information system such as a computer system. A system receives **inputs** which it processes and generates into **outputs**. Any system can be thought of in terms of **inputs, processing** and **outputs**.
- Information can be said to have value to the extent that **a decision making use of that information** has value. The cost of collecting information bears no relation to its value. In order to minimise the cost of information, the information system should be designed to collect only **the information which is required**.

  TRY QUESTIONS 6 AND 7
- One of the key uses of information is in decision making. The making of a decision has a number of identifiable stages. Decisions must be taken in response to choices and options regarding how an organisation responds to its **environment** and runs its **internal activities**.

  TRY QUESTION 8
- The use of critical success factors can help to determine the **information requirements** of senior management which in turn assists in identifying the **information systems** required by an organisation. Critical success factors are **the few key areas of each executive's job** where **things must go right** for the organisation to flourish.

  TRY QUESTION 9
- Decision making almost invariably involves **risk and uncertainty**. The information used to make a decision may be **inaccurate** or **incomplete** and the consequences of a decision cannot be known with certainty. There are a number of methods of taking **uncertainty** and **risk** into consideration when reaching a decision.

  TRY QUESTION 10
- *Possible pitfalls*
  - **Assuming that the Information Management exam is about technology. It is not, it is about the MANAGEMENT of information in an organisation, by all means available.**
  - **The examiner will not award many marks to answers that simply show that the candidate is a computer expert, with no understanding of management issues.**

1 TUTORIAL QUESTION: LEVELS OF INFORMATION

An effective management information system should support decision making at all levels of management. Each level of management requires information with different characteristics. The information within an organisation can typically be classified into three levels.

Required

(a) Using a typical manufacturing company as background, define the three levels and give examples of the information which would be provided at each level. In what ways does the destination level influence the presentation of the information?

(b) Discuss the features of deterministic, probabilistic and adaptive systems, giving a practical example of each.

Approaching the question

1 To ensure that you satisfy all the requirements of part (a) of this question, divide your answer into (at least) four parts. The first three should identify and define each of the three levels of information. This should be second nature to you by now.

2 The levels into which information can be analysed are strategic, tactical and operational. Remember to give an example of information at each level.

3 Finally, do not overlook the final part of the question on destination levels. Like the rest of the question, this relates to information requirements within an organisation, not outside it.

4 If you are not sure about the relevance of part (b), this suggests that you have failed to come up with a practical example of each.

2 TUTORIAL QUESTION: INFORMATION THEORY

FBK Ltd is a manufacturer of office stationery. Most products are made from paper or card and the company operates from a new purpose-built site where it has developed an advanced manufacturing environment. Production and financial systems are designed around feedback control and exception reporting principles and each major system has its own control system.

Required

(a) A system must be controlled to keep it steady or to enable it to change safely. Explain the major features of a control system.

(b) The development of many management information systems involves the computerisation of management reporting or 'feedback' systems. Describe how the following systems based on feedback control might operate in a company such as FBK Ltd.

(i) Standard costing.
(ii) Credit control.
(iii) Stock control.

Approaching the question

1 Our answer to (a) explains why control is necessary and deals with terms such as sensor, entropy, requisite variety and so on.

2 Our answer to (b) attempts to relate the well-known concepts to FBK Ltd, so far as the small amount of information given will allow. Award yourself *no* marks for this question unless you make some attempt to do this yourself.

3 TUTORIAL QUESTION: LOGICAL DATABASE MODELS

Traders plc, a large manufacturing company, is considering implementing a large-scale corporate database. The Chief Executive has been told that the company must carry out a data analysis exercise and choose a logical database model.

Required

Identify the main features of the following logical database models.

(a) The hierarchical model
(b) The network model
(c) The relational model

Approaching the question

1 These early tutorial questions are designed to get you 'warmed up'. The IFM examiner has indicated that straight repetition of facts will not be a normal feature of this examination.

2 Again, award yourself *no* marks at all unless your answer mentions Traders plc and any manufacturing examples that are appropriate for a large manufacturing company, even though you know about nothing about it.

3 In these early questions we are trying a deprivation strategy to make you hungry for *more* case study information! Using the case study information means much more than just mentioning the name of the company, as you will find when you tackle the next question.

4 TUTORIAL QUESTION: CRITICAL SUCCESS FACTORS

SEC LEA is a local education authority responsible for the education and training of young people. The region which it covers contains 23 secondary schools each with average pupil numbers of 800. It also has responsibility for primary and tertiary education.

The mission statement of SEC is 'to provide a quality education to the young people of the region by encouraging as many as possible to undertake tertiary education and by maintaining acceptable examination pass rates'. The objectives of the authority include:

(a) a pass rate in final secondary school examinations of 75%;

(b) 40% of all secondary school leavers continuing with further education;

(c) increasing public satisfaction with the authority's provision of education by 1% per annum.

Pass rates in the final secondary exams are running at 64%, while 62% of candidates for these exams then leave full-time education altogether. The authority does not know how to measure public satisfaction.

Required

(a) Describe the critical success factors that apply to SEC. State the data sources that will be required to ensure that these CSFs have been met.

(b) Comment on any limitations in the use of the performance indicators described.

Approaching the question

1 We identify and describe four CSFs derived from the mission and objectives stated in the scenario. Don't just copy the information you are given: you must interpret it.

2 Suggesting data sources is a bigger test of your application skills. Just use your common sense: what information would *you* want to enable you to judge the success of a LEA, and where would you find it? Our answer has seven suggestions.

3 For part (b), explain how performance measures used to judge an LEA (such as comparisons) may be unfair or misleading.

5 WR RAILWAY CO: INFORMATION EXCHANGES (11/95) *36 mins*

The WR Railway Co owns and operates train services in a large country.

It has approximately 75,000 kilometres of track joining the 13 major towns in the country with another 176 minor stations. Trains are run each day in accordance with a pre-determined timetable.

Four of the classes of employees on the railway are

(1) Ticket office clerk - issues tickets to customers for their train journeys to any point on the railway network in the country using a cumbersome manual system. Tickets are normally purchased for travel on specified trains. A summary of the day's transactions is produced at the end of each day, although this is normally collated in a hurry and mistakes are common.

(2) Analyst - produces information on the profitability of each train. This information, which is produced for each train for each day without any summarisation, is then sent to the senior manager.

(3) Senior manager - reviews results of the railway to decide whether to change the number or frequency of trains being run and makes decisions on new lines and capital investment in rolling stock for the railway.

(4) Planner - reviews daily train information and makes recommendations on changing the frequency of trains on existing lines. The planner also produces feasibility studies for new lines as requested by the senior managers. Feasibility studies are required within two weeks of a request being sent to the planner. The studies normally run into 50 pages and show details of population densities, alternative transport possibilities such as buses, and estimates of extra passenger journeys generated by the new line.

Required

(a) Evaluate the effectiveness of the information exchanges between the four classes of employees noted above, and propose any changes that you consider necessary to enhance the accuracy of information being exchanged. **12 Marks**

(b) Explain, and justify with examples, the most effective method of presenting information to each of the classes of employees mentioned above.

Explain how the information received enables each employee to do his/her job. **8 Marks**

Total Marks = 20

6 RG LTD: INFORMATION NEEDS (5/97) *36 mins*

RG Ltd manufactures industrial glues and solvents in a single large factory. Approximately 400 different inputs are used to produce the 35 specialist outputs, which range from ultra-strong glues used in aircraft manufacture to high-impact adhesives that are required on construction sites.

Two years ago, with the company only just breaking even, the directors recognised the need for more information to control the business. To assist them with their strategic control of the business, they decided to establish a MIS. This is now operational but provides only the following limited range of information to the directors via their networked computer system.

(a) A summary business plan for this and the next two years. The plan includes details of the expected future incomes and expenditure on existing product lines. It was produced by a new member of the accounting department without reference to past production data.

(b) Stock balances on individual items of raw materials, finished goods etc. This report is at a very detailed level and comprises 80% of the output from the MIS itself.

(c) A summary of changes in total demand for glues and solvents in the market place for the last five years. This information is presented as a numerical summary in six different sections. Each section takes up one computer screen so only one section can be viewed at a time.

Required

(a) (i) Comment on the weaknesses in the information currently being provided to the directors of the company. **8 Marks**

(ii) Suggest how the information may be improved, with particular reference to other outputs which the MIS might usefully provide to the directors. **6 Marks**

(b) Explain what strategic information any MIS is unlikely to be able to provide. **6 Marks**

Total Marks = 20

7 KN COMPANY: CENTRAL DATABASE (11/96) *36 mins*

The KN company manufactures a wide range of plastic mouldings. The mouldings are used in such diverse products as motor vehicles, garden furniture and children's toys. As a result of this variety, there are six different sales departments, a single manufacturing department and an ordering department. There is a separate IT service department which provides basic IT services to all the other departments.

The company has established its IT systems within each individual department. Each department has its own computerised records and databases. The IT department of KN has been very successful in previous years in meeting IT systems requirements and in providing a high quality of service to each user department.

KN now wishes to set up one central sales database that can be used by all departments. The database will include, amongst other things, details of goods, customers and debtor analysis. This will mean that the individual databases in each department will be amalgamated into this central database.

Required

(a) Explain the relative merits of the KN company concentrating its data and information on individual departments compared with centralising its database. **14 Marks**

(b) Evaluate the problems that the IT department may experience in amalgamating the company's data into one central database.

Note: Your answer must concentrate on the data held by the company. Comments concerning hardware or the physical location of the database are NOT required. **6 Marks**

Total Marks = 20

8 JBCC: DECISION SUPPORT SYSTEM (11/96) *36 mins*

JBCC, a local administrative authority, provides a range of services to individuals including welfare provision. JBCC has a total workforce of 2,450.

In the welfare department, JBCC employs 30 staff who visit individuals to assess their welfare requirements. This job means visiting individuals, who are normally low paid or facing difficult family circumstances, to find out whether they should receive financial assistance (sometimes termed 'benefits') from JBCC.

The area covered by JBCC has a very low population density. Staff may have to travel many kilometres between each appointment and may not return to their central office for days at a time.

Rules which determine whether people are entitled to financial assistance are complicated, with over 6,500 separate rules and 170 different forms to complete. These rules change frequently; three rules changing each week is not uncommon. Consistent application of rules is difficult because of benefit fraud, human error, constant changing of rules and time delays inherent in the system itself. Staff retention is low because of poor morale.

The existing IT system is a mainframe located at the headquarters of JBCC. The mainframe contains a database showing which benefits are due to which individuals. A list of the benefits due is printed out weekly and benefits are paid out according to the information on this list. The database is accessed and updated from 10 terminals located in the computer room itself. Staff normally update the database when they return from their visits to individuals requiring benefits.

JBCC has decided to establish a Decision Support System to assist its staff in the application of benefit rules to the situations of individuals. JBCC requires that staff should have access to the Decision Support System at any time during their working day.

Required

(a) Describe the essential hardware and software necessary to establish the Decision Support System, explaining why each part is relevant in meeting the aims of JBCC.

12 Marks

(b) Explain how the new Decision Support System may enable JBCC to improve staff retention.

8 Marks

Total Marks = 20

9 EF LTD: KEY INDICATORS (11/95) *36 mins*

EF Ltd is a long-established company which manufactures a large range of computers, from mainframe to portable, on a single site. Its turnover is about £500 million per annum. The company has recently undergone a major information systems change involving the following.

(a) Capital expenditure of £50 million over three years (the NPV will be £7 million)

(b) Workforce change from 10,000 to 7,000 employees.

(c) Radical changes to work practices, both in the manufacturing systems (use of CAD/CAM) and reorganisation of managerial and administrative functions.

The new Managing Director needs to identify and understand some indicators which can be used to evaluate the success or otherwise of this change.

Required

Recommend to the Managing Director up to five key indicators that he can use and explain why each is relevant to his requirements.

20 Marks

DO YOU KNOW? - INFORMATION STRATEGY

- *Check that you can fill in the blanks in the statements below before you attempt any questions. If in doubt, you should go back to your BPP Study Text and revise first.*
- Strategic planning is the formulation, evaluation and selection of strategies for the purpose of preparing a .... The process involves taking a number of steps, from setting strategic objectives right through to ....
- A strategy is a general statement of .... and the ways by which these will be achieved. A strategy needs to be managed; this is a process involving ...., ... and ....
- An organisation may appoint an information director, whose role is ....An information director can ensure that IT activities support ....
- A strategy typically deals with three basic issues: the organisation's overall business objectives and in consequence its ...., the organisation's ....and the ....
- In analysing its current position, an organisation must perform an internal appraisal, to ascertain its ...., and an .... analysis.
- The value chain is .... All of the activities in the value chain have a potential to enhance or impede the organisation's success in adding value. Value chain analysis can be used to identify activities and processes where IT can be used. IT can be used in .... and in ....
- The success of any change must be reviewed to see that it .... Monitoring change is a part of the strategic management process. The key is to find .... of monitoring the success of a strategy.

  TRY QUESTIONS 14 AND 15
- *Possible pitfalls*

  Write down the mistakes you know you should avoid.

DID YOU KNOW? - INFORMATION STRATEGY

- *Check that you know the following basic points before you attempt any questions. If in doubt, you should go back to your BPP Study Text and revise first.*
- Strategic planning is the formulation, evaluation and selection of strategies for the purpose of preparing a **long-term plan of action to attain objectives**. The process involves taking a number of steps, from setting strategic objectives right through to **evaluating actual performance**.
- A strategy is a general statement of **long-term objectives and goals** and the ways by which these will be achieved. A strategy needs to be managed; this is a process involving **strategic analysis, choice of a strategy** and **implementation of the strategy**.
- An organisation may appoint an information director, whose role is **to ensure that IT issues relating to strategic planning are considered at board level**. An information director can ensure that IT activities support overall **organisational strategy and objectives**.
- A strategy typically deals with three basic issues: the organisation's overall business objectives and in consequence its **IT needs**, the organisation's **current IT usage** and the **potential opportunities that IT can bring**.
- In analysing its current position, an organisation must perform an internal appraisal, to ascertain its **existing strengths and weaknesses**, and an **environmental** analysis.
- The value chain is **a model of the activities which need to be linked successfully for an organisation to add value**. All of the activities in the value chain have a potential to enhance or impede the organisation's success in adding value. Value chain analysis can be used to identify activities and processes where IT can be used. IT can be used in **primary activities** and in **support activities**.
- The success of any change must be reviewed to see that it **meets, and is continuing to meet, the objectives which it was supposed to achieve**. Monitoring change is a part of the strategic management process. The key is to find **an appropriate means** of monitoring the success of a strategy.

  TRY QUESTIONS 14 AND 15
- *Possible pitfalls*
  - **Not taking a sufficiently strategic view when asked to do so but concentrating on tactical or operational matters.**
  - **Answering questions without referring to the organisation described in the question, and the issues it faces.**

10 GOOD QUALITY INFORMATION (5/99) *36 mins*

To be effective, operational decision-makers require information that is of good quality.

Required

Explain why information provided to operational decision-makers may not be of good quality. Provide examples from your own experience and/or a business situation with which you are familiar. **20 Marks**

11 TUTORIAL QUESTION: INFORMATION SYSTEMS STRATEGY

Many major organisations use formal strategies to identify development priorities for information systems (IS).

(a) Discuss the reason for this.
(b) What are the major stages in the development of an IS strategy?

Approaching the question

1 Information strategies are at the heart of this part of the syllabus. You should be able to write a lucid and well-argued answer to this type of question without too much difficulty.

2 Remember that an organisation must *match* IT to its business strategy and structure. The vision should be based on reality.

12 TUTORIAL QUESTION: COST LEADERSHIP

(a) What factors are important in achieving 'overall cost leadership'?
(b) Identify the risks to an organisation of adopting this strategy.
(c) Identify two other generic strategies.

Approaching the question

1 We have answered this tutorial question in point form rather than in essay style. You should have at least a passing awareness of the work of Michael Porter.

2 Most corporate strategies include some element of competitive strategy. The competitive environment inevitably affects the strategic context, even in the case of former monopolies such as British Telecom. You should note too that deregulation is not solely a British phenomenon.

3 It is important to remember that a choice of competitive strategy cannot be made without considering the choices made by competing organisations.

4 The Stage 4 general guidance note reproduced at the start of this kit notes that 'Stage 4 examinations involve the integration of all subjects'. There is inevitably and deliberately some overlap between papers and this tutorial question is equally applicable to the *Strategic Management Accountancy and Marketing* syllabus.

13 TUTORIAL QUESTION: THE STAGE HYPOTHESIS

Research has established that organisations go through six stages of computing development, and has provided information regarding the nature of each stage. Such knowledge has resulted in a better understanding of both the impact of computer-based information systems and the need for improved organising, planning and control.

The 'stage hypothesis', developed by Richard Nolan is particularly relevant here.

Describe and comment upon each of these six stages and the uses to which the stage hypothesis might be put.

Approaching the question

1. The six stages are, in order, initiation, contagion, control, integration, data administration and maturity.
2. The stage hypothesis is useful because it encourages a fairly practical analysis and consideration of the systems development process, with due appreciation of the drawbacks. (The systems development life cycle is a *model,* rather than a hypothesis, and views the process from more of a close-up position.)
3. If you find this easy, see if you can write your *own* mini-scenario describing a company that is just reaching the end of one of the stages. Constructing *DIY exam questions* will help you to understand the mind of an examiner.

14 JH LTD: IT STRATEGY (5/97) *36 mins*

The board of JH Ltd has become aware that there is no IT strategy in place within the company. A decision has therefore been made to establish a working group to produce an outline IT strategy. The group members are as follows.

Senior manager	He does not have much knowledge of IT because he has avoided IT in general as he sees it as not providing him with any benefits for his particular job. He is actually quite fearful of IT. He is very task-orientated and dislikes wasting time on non-essential work. He is very good at producing overall policy directives.
IT professional	She has an excellent knowledge of mainframe computers and enjoys being in charge of a large IT department. Her knowledge has arisen from 20 years in computing. She has tended to ignore the recent shift towards end-user computing, believing that 'IT' is best handled by specialists. Although she has some knowledge of PCs, this is not complete. She has very little contact with the users of the information that the IT department produces. She believes that users should accept the information given and not make difficult demands on the department.
IT user: trainee accountant	He is a CIMA Stage 4 student, who has been working in various roles within the accounts function: this is his first major assignment. His agenda is to try and ensure that IT is used effectively and that all staff within the company can therefore use PC applications to support their work. He is already well-read on IT matters and is now looking to advance rapidly in the company by being the IT 'champion'.

Required

(a) Comment on the disadvantages that could arise for JH Ltd by not having an overall IT strategy in place. **8 Marks**

(b) Explain how the background of each individual in the working group may present barriers to the production of an IT strategy as required by the board.

Suggest how these barriers may be overcome. **12 Marks**

Total Marks = 20

15 IT STRATEGY (5/98) *36 mins*

Explain *five* reasons why it is essential for a modern organisation to have an IT strategy.

Illustrate your answer with examples of these reasons drawn from your own knowledge and experience. **20 Marks**

DO YOU KNOW? - SYSTEMS DEVELOPMENT LIFE CYCLE

- *Check that you can fill in the blanks in the statements below before you attempt any questions. If in doubt, you should go back to your BPP Study Text and revise first.*
- The systems development life cycle was developed to .... It is a model of how systems should be developed. It has a number of drawbacks, among which is the criticism that it fails to recognise ....
- A methodology is a collection of ...., ..., ... and .... which are designed to help systems developers in their efforts to implement a new system. Methodologies are usually broken down into phases.
- Methodologies may be process-driven or data-driven. Process-driven methodologies, such as SSADM, are based on the ...., rather than .... Data-driven methodologies focus on data, the rationale being that the .... in a system is less likely to change than ....
- Good management of projects is vital because many systems ...., ... and .... Project management is concerned with the detailed management of the development of a new system.
- In recent years the role of the .... in all aspects of systems development has been recognised and ....has proliferated.
- During the systems investigation, users may be consulted by the systems analyst, who uses a variety of techniques as appropriate, including ....

  TRY QUESTIONS 19, 20 AND 21
- *Possible pitfalls*

  Write down the mistakes you know you should avoid.

DID YOU KNOW? - SYSTEMS DEVELOPMENT LIFE CYCLE

- *Could you fill in the blanks? The answers are in bold. Use this page for revision purposes as you approach the exam.*
- The systems development life cycle was developed to **add discipline to many organisations' approach to system development**. It is a model of how systems should be developed. It has a number of drawbacks, among which is the criticism that it fails to recognise **the importance of the user**.
- A methodology is a collection of **procedures, techniques, tools and documentation aids** which are designed to help systems developers in their efforts to implement a new system. Methodologies are usually broken down into phases.
- Methodologies may be process-driven or data-driven. Process-driven methodologies, such as SSADM, are based on the **processes which are performed**, rather than the **data which is the subject of the processing**. Data-driven methodologies focus on data, the rationale being that the **type of data** in a system is less likely to change than the **processes through which it passes**.
- Good management of projects is vital. Many systems **arrive late, cost more than was budgeted** and **do not meet user requirements**. Project management is concerned with the detailed management of the development of a new system.
- In recent years the role of the **end-user** in all aspects of systems development has been recognised and **end-user computing** has proliferated. Modern approaches to development tend to emphasise the importance of this role.
- During the systems investigation, users may be consulted by the systems analyst, who uses a variety of techniques as appropriate, including **interviews and questionnaires**.

  TRY QUESTIONS 19, 20 AND 21
- *Possible pitfalls*
  - **Regurgitating everything you know about a methodology in abstract terms rather than applying your knowledge to the situation described in the question.**
  - **Ignoring the importance of users**

16 TUTORIAL QUESTION: COSTS AND BENEFITS

A project feasibility study presented to senior management must always contain a detailed 'cost justification' for any proposed computer system.

Categorise and give examples of the costs and benefits which would appear in such a report, including those which might indicate why a project showing a high net present value is not necessarily of greatest benefit to the company.

Approaching the question

1 Costs can be categorised as one-off or recurring. Explain why the distinction is important.

2 Benefits may be measurable or may be intangible. Explain how a financial value may be placed on benefits If you can, refer to the IFM Assessor's recent article, reproduced at the front of this kit.

3 This question addresses one aspect of costs and benefits. It is important that the IS professional is able to choose between competing systems by comparison of costs and benefits. The system must also, of course, meet the business's overall strategy.

4 Another aspect of cost justification is the valuation of *information*. You probably addressed this in your studies for the first part of this syllabus, under the title of information economics.

17 TUTORIAL QUESTION: PROTOTYPING

It has become apparent in recent years that excessive reliance on existing functional specifications and detailed design can increase the risk that a system will be rejected by its users. Additionally, IT is increasingly being applied to business activities for which no written sets of procedures exists.

Describe what is meant by prototyping and explain how it is used in systems design.

Approaching the question

1 A straightforward question and one which you will not be asked in the IFM examination! It is important though that you can answer this and similar questions on, for example, computer-aided software engineering and fourth-generation languages, as these types of techniques may well suggest themselves as valid responses to case study situations in the examination.

2 Prototyping of computer systems has a number of features in common with any other kind of prototyping, for example vehicle design.

3 The unwritten requirement of this question is that you should discuss some of the benefits of prototyping. Explain too *when* you would recommend prototyping.

4 The key to success in the IFM exam is knowing when various techniques might be used. In the suggested solution to this question you will observe phrases such as 'applications backlog', 'time spent on existing system maintenance' and 'encourage the user': these are just the sort of things which might appear in a scenario and need to be dealt with.

18 TUTORIAL QUESTION: STRUCTURED ANALYSIS AND DESIGN

The management of SND Ltd is keen to adopt SSADM as the standard framework for information systems development within the company, as an alternative to the unstructured development which has taken place in the past. SSADM is a structured systems analysis and design methodology used in project development. It consists of a hierarchy of phases, stages and steps, which can be represented by dataflow diagrams. These separate logical descriptions from physical ones, which are generally removed from the initial analysis of the problem, to be re-introduced after the logical design of the system.

(a) Explain the difference between logical and physical elements of systems design.

(b) Describe the purpose of levelled dataflow diagrams.

Approaching the question

1 The examiner has stated clearly that he wants candidates to move away from a focus on SSADM and to embrace the concepts of information management. However, early papers have still had some degree of operational bias and you should be able to apply knowledge of, for example, elements of systems implementation as appropriate.

2 Logical elements deal with what the system is to do, while physical elements deal with how the system accomplishes its task.

19 WRF INC: SYSTEMS DEVELOPMENT LIFECYCLE (5/96) *36 mins*

WRF Inc trades in a dynamic environment where it is essential that information is presented quickly and clearly to its staff. The information can come from the company's database or from other staff members. Significant processing of the information is also required on each individual's Personal Computer (PC) before effective decisions can be made.

WRF Inc intends to upgrade its computer system to improve speed and clarity of information. Each member of staff will have a PC linked to a Local Area Network (LAN). Each PC will run *Windows 98* and a word processor and spreadsheet on its local hard disk. The network will be used for centralised backup, access to a central database, and storage of data files. The LAN will also be used for communication within the office by E-mail.

The system analyst in charge of the project thinks that users will require a Pentium processor running at 75 megahertz with 16 megabytes of RAM. The network will incorporate a central file server and run at a low baud rate. He is pleased that the system will cost only $US 1,500 per user (about £1,000). The systems analyst is on a fixed term contract which terminates when the system installation is complete.

Users have broadly welcomed the move although they have not been formally told of the system change. The requisitioning department of WRF Inc has now questioned the order for the computer hardware and software because of lack of authorisation from the Board.

Required

Write a report to the Board:

(a) briefly explaining the Systems Development Life Cycle (SDLC); and

(b) explaining why it is preferred to the situation outlined above as a means of providing a system changeover for WRF Inc. **20 Marks**

20 BKL PLC: NEW SYSTEMS BACKLOG *36 mins*

BKL is a large electronics group, with interests ranging from large defence projects through to manufacture of civil telecommunications components. There are in total 18 separate manufacturing sites across the country. The computer services department is based at the group's headquarters and provides a wide range of IS support throughout the group. Costs of the computer services department are recovered from internal 'customers' depending on usage. All departmental heads have been told that, even when they expect external expertise to be necessary, they must contact computer services prior to authorising any hardware expenditure in excess of £5,000 and where any writing or modification of non-packaged software is expected.

The group has now reached a position where there is a considerable backlog of possible new applications awaiting computerisation. Demands on the computer services department mean that implementation of a new sales order processing system, which is to be standardised across all group companies, has already slipped by six months. Other systems which are regarded by individual divisions or departments as core have in some cases been waiting for months if not years for attention.

Required

Describe the ways and means available to the group to increase the rate at which new computer based systems are introduced. **20 Marks**

21 MFS LTD: PROJECTS *108 mins*

You are called to the office of the managing director of Metropolitan Financial Services, a large company employing 1,200 staff based in your own country. As a new trainee, you are presently assigned to the computer services section for one month as part of your induction programme. The managing director asks you to look into ways to reduce the time spent on systems development, 'we have highly trained staff with excellent technical skills but we still get behind schedule with our projects', she tells you.

Current systems development

You are told that the main problem at present is that nine months ago it was agreed to centralise the management information systems for the three operational units by the installation of a new computer and the creation of a new computer department at head office. It was planned that the programme would be completed within eighteen months. Transitional arrangements were introduced, so that, for example, one unit would deal with all payroll processing, one with all customer ledger activities and so on, using existing systems.

Problems encountered

At the end of nine months it has become apparent that the project is far from complete and that the eighteen month programme looks increasingly to have been over optimistic.

The installation work on the new computer at head office has progressed steadily, but little progress has been made on the software. As a result the introduction of the new computer system has now had to be deferred for six months, extending the transitional period to two years.

The redistribution of much of the back office and administrative work between units has caused many problems and has left no opportunity to develop the new computer system. At the same time, publication of routine information is being delayed and there are concerns that breaches of regulatory rules may occur without the company realising it.

Staff concerns

Senior management has been aware of the generally slow progress, and is now also becoming aware of the problems arising from the transitional arrangements.

In addition, users are concerned that a great deal of effort is going into development of their new systems without them being given any opportunity to influence the development process. Many staff refer to two or three screens at once, for example:

(a) output from the company's own MIS;
(b) a personal spreadsheet analysing specific aspects of operations;
(c) output from a third party on-line information service.

In the past, the first of these, although logically the easiest to adapt, has proved to be the least user-friendly. In particular, staff involved in dealing activities are thoroughly unhappy with the way they have to navigate between screens when working in a high pressure and fast moving environment. Attitudes to proprietary spreadsheet packages (running under Windows 98) and to state-of-the-art third party systems are satisfactory.

Further discussion reveals that the company still uses a traditional systems development cycle and there is minimal user involvement until the implementation stage.

(a) What advantages could the use of a methodology bring to MFS Ltd? **12 Marks**

(b) Consider why projects at MFS may be unduly time consuming. **16 Marks**

(c) In the form of a memorandum to the managing director, suggest ways to reduce the time spent, increase user participation and develop quality systems. **16 Marks**

(d) Set out the main principles of project management and explain how you would review the effectiveness of the project management techniques used. **16 Marks**

Total Marks = 60

DO YOU KNOW? - IMPLEMENTATION, SELECTION, MAINTENANCE AND REVIEW

- *Check that you can fill in the blanks in the statements below before you attempt any questions. If in doubt, you should go back to your BPP Study Text and revise first.*
- The main stages in the systems implementation process are ...., ..., ..., and ....
- Facilities management is becoming increasingly popular, particularly in the public sector. This involves the use of .... to take over all aspects of an organisation's IT activities.
- Technological change has a marked effect on the working environment. Staff are likely to have a number of concerns, raising from fear of .... to dislike of .... There are many ways in which systems analysts can try to overcome such concerns.
- There are three types of systems maintenance. .... maintenance is carried out following a systems failure, ...maintenance aims to make enhancements to systems and .... maintenance takes account of anticipated changes in the processing environment.
- A system should be reviewed after ...., and periodically, so that any unforeseen problems may be solved and to confirm that it is .... A post-implementation review should establish whether the ....and ....have been met, and if not, why not.

  TRY QUESTIONS 25 AND 26
- *Possible pitfalls*

  Write down the mistakes you know you should avoid.

DID YOU KNOW? - IMPLEMENTATION, SELECTION, MAINTENANCE AND REVIEW

- *Could you fill in the blanks? The answers are in bold. Use this page for revision purposes as you approach the exam.*
- The main stages in the systems implementation process are **installation of hardware and software, staff training, system testing, file creation and changeover**.
- Facilities management is becoming increasingly popular, particularly in the public sector. This involves the use of **external organisations** to take over all aspects of an organisation's IT activities.
- Technological change has a marked effect on the working environment. Staff are likely to have a number of concerns, raising from fear of **redundancy** to dislike of **new working patterns and methods**. There are many ways in which systems analysts can try to overcome such concerns.
- There are three types of systems maintenance. **Corrective** maintenance is carried out following a systems failure, **perfective** maintenance aims to make enhancements to systems and **adaptive** maintenance takes account of anticipated changes in the processing environment.
- A system should be reviewed after **testing**, and periodically, so that any unforeseen problems may be solved and to confirm that it is **achieving and will continue to achieve the desired results**. A post-implementation review should establish whether the **objectives** and **targeted performance criteria** have been met, and if not, why not.

  TRY QUESTIONS 25 AND 26
- Possible pitfalls
  - **Giving too little emphasis to human issues in your recommended solutions to problems**

22 TUTORIAL QUESTION: TRAINING

You are required to design a one-day introduction course for clerical staff who have no previous data processing experience. The company is about to install a PC-based computer system and the clerical staff will be receiving instructions and information from the PCs and inputting transaction data. Explain the following.

(a) What you expect such a course to achieve.

(b) The topics to be covered.

(c) What follow-up action you would advise for staff who will have specialised functions in the new computer system such as, for example, inputting data.

Approaching the question

1 Training may not seem like the most interesting aspect of systems development, but it is of course vital if the system is to be used with any degree of success. Training will not only improve users' skills, but will also encourage users to accept the system. This will empower users to contribute to the continuing operation and future development of the system.

2 You may be able to call on practical experience here. Note that this is an introductory course and the system has not yet been installed. This means that detailed operational training will follow later.

3 Only one day is available. If there is to be time for typical activities such as question sessions and feedback this will probably leave at most three or four main sessions in which information can be imparted. Do not attempt to cram too much into the course.

4 Keep an eye out for articles about IT training. This is an area where classroom delivery is not necessarily the most appropriate medium and hands-on experience is to be preferred. Much software comes with on-line tutorials.

23 TUTORIAL QUESTION: SOFTWARE AND HARDWARE

The Newtown Health Centre is situated in the town of Newtown and provides the general medical services for a population of approximately 30,000. The nearest hospital and regional health centre is at Metrotown some fifteen miles away. The Newtown Centre is staffed by six doctors who are supported by thirteen medical and secretarial staff.

The Centre has a number of administrative requirements which include: an appointments system for the doctors, patient medical records, general correspondence, staff records, including pay and tax details. Health Centre accounts and the collection of statistical material for the regional health centre.

Required

(a) Identify the possible areas for computerisation in the Newtown Health Centre.
(b) Suggest the types and range of software which might be used.
(c) Suggest a possible hardware configuration.

Approaching the question

1 In a question like this, where your ability to apply your knowledge to a practical situation is under scrutiny, make full use of the information given in the question itself. The Health Centre has 19 staff and so, on the hardware side, a mainframe is not likely to be required. Similarly on the software side, a specialist payroll package may not be worthwhile for so few personnel, and in any case you are given a wide range of 'administrative requirements' in the question.

2 The examiner has indicated that a typical question might involve the preparation of a report to management on options for system selection in a given situation where certain constraints exist.

24 TUTORIAL QUESTION: MAINTENANCE OF SOFTWARE

(a) Describe 'maintenance' in the software context, giving reasons why the need for it arises.

(b) State what can be done both to reduce the requirement for maintenance and to carry out the maintenance efficiently should it be necessary. (Assume that off-the-shelf software is not under consideration.)

Approaching the question

1 Maintenance is often categorised as one of three types. Corrective maintenance is carried out when there is a systems failure of some kind, for example in processing or in an implementation procedure. Perfective maintenance is carried out in order to perfect the software, or to improve software so that the processing inefficiencies are eliminated and performance is enhanced. Adaptive maintenance is carried out to take account of anticipated changes in the processing environment.

2 Moving on, you might find it worthwhile checking up on your knowledge of the main pieces of systems documentation. While you will not be asked to describe documentation, you may have to explain why it is necessary. Remember that, for users, on-line help and tutorials form a very real alternative to printed manuals. In fact, on-line help is now considered comprehensive enough for many PC manufacturers and resellers to charge extra for manuals to accompany bundled software, suggesting that many users of popular packages will never open a software manual. Of course, bespoke systems are still likely to be accompanied by ring-binder files full of useful information.

25 LDS: EVALUATING SUPPLIERS (11/97) *36 mins*

Library Direct Services (LDS) is an organisation providing data to central and local government personnel. It maintains a database of

- all laws, both statue and case law,
- reports of proceedings in central government,
- comparative data on the services provided by local government in each region of the country, and
- some comparative data on services provided in different countries.

LDS allows access to this database 24 hours a day, 365 days a year. LDS is contractually obliged to provide this information within 30 minutes of receiving a request. All requests are received by telephone or e-mail.

The existing database is accessed primarily via command line input at DOS, which the database administrators can use quickly and efficiently. Any perceived or actual decrease in the usefulness of the database will mean that the administrators are unlikely to accept the system.

Over the years, a number of small, but significant modifications have been made to the original 'off the shelf' database software. It is essential to retain these if the database is to be used, although the programmer who made these changes has left the company and has not been replaced. Program changes are not fully documented.

LDS is now asking for tenders from database suppliers to upgrade the database to Windows functionality. This is likely to involve re-writing the database itself and implementing a new database management system. LDS needs to make a decision on which company to choose to make this change for them. For budgetary reasons, any proposed change must be completed within the next six months.

Required

Provide six questions that LDS can use to help evaluate potential suppliers for the systems change contract explained above.

Explain why each of these questions is relevant to the specific circumstances of LDS.

20 Marks

26 SWM LTD: IMPLEMENTATION *108 mins*

SWM Ltd is a manufacturing company with three divisions, all of which operate from the same site. The company's main finished goods warehouse is located about one mile away. The main manufacturing site is the location for all other functions, including the IT department.

The company runs a corporate database on a mainframe computer with networked terminals. The terminals do not at present have any independent processing capacity. Departmental managers have become concerned at the speed of processing when several applications or users require computer time at the same time. The chief executive has also expressed concern about the high cost of software maintenance.

The warehouse stock records are maintained on a minicomputer in the warehouse. Each morning, details of the previous day's sales orders taken are sent by courier to the warehouse. The data, which is stored on a floppy disk, is downloaded to the warehouse system, which generates despatch documentation, including invoices, and picking lists. The warehouse's 'free' and 'allocated' stock records are updated.

At the end of each day, details of stock movements are sent to the main site and the mainframe's stock records are updated. These are referred to by sales order processing staff to ensure goods are in stock when booking orders. Copy invoices are also sent to the accounts department for posting to customer ledgers.

A recent review of software maintenance costs by the chief accountant has revealed the following.

(a) The mainframe has limited reporting capabilities. Recent requests for the provision of reports of sales by region and by product group have resulted in substantial reprogramming effort in order to add the required fields and routines.

(b) It is not possible to produce reports containing summary level information at the same time as routine reports are generated. This has meant that senior managers either content themselves with working with the long transactions listings used by operational staff in the relevant department or ask subordinates to prepare summaries 'manually', which the latter usually do with spreadsheet packages.

Required

(a) Write a report to the IS department identifying any information deficiencies in the current system and recommending ways in which the processing of data could be speeded up. **18 Marks**

(b) What controls should be adopted to retain the integrity and the security of the data in the system? **16 Marks**

(c) Draft a report to the chief executive describing the types of software maintenance encountered in computer systems. **14 Marks**

(d) Assume that a new information system is to be installed using database software such as Oracle. Describe the elements that training on the new system should cover and who should undergo such training. What advantages, if any, would additional training in the use of Oracle itself give to the company? **12 Marks**

Total Marks = 60

DO YOU KNOW? - INFORMATION SYSTEMS

- *Check that you can fill in the blanks in the statements below before you attempt any questions. If in doubt, you should go back to your BPP Study Text and revise first.*
- Transaction processing systems are used for .... They provide the raw material used more extensively in ....
- A management information system can be described as ....
- Decision support systems are a form of management information system. They are used by management to .... A DSS does not make decisions itself. An example of a DSS is ....
- Executive information systems are a form of management information system designed to .... They typically include ...., ...and ....for rapid and simple retrieval of the required data.

  TRY QUESTIONS 30 AND 33
- Expert systems use artificial intelligence, the concept that computers can be programmed to .... Expert systems can be used where problems are .... and can be solved by reference to ....
- Some organisations have introduced an .... to support and streamline end-user computing. An .... is a small unit manned by staff with a good technical knowledge. Its task is to provide a link between .... and ....

  TRY QUESTIONS 31,34 AND 35
- .... is processing done by a system containing a number of separate but connected processors, in which some centralised processing is possible.
- A *local area network* is a system of PCs and other devices, such as .... which are connected by .... LANs have a .... computer holding files used by more than one computer, and providing storage capacity to the other computers in the network. In a LAN, data processing tasks can be ...., and single items of peripheral equipment can be ....
- A .... is a network of computers which are dispersed on a wider geographical scale than LANs. They usually are connected over the ....
- .... allows the use of a single set of files and affords better security and control. Disadvantages are ....on head office and a central computer and the risk of ....
- IT costs may be treated as an .... , charged out .... or charged out using a .... chargeout method. Costs may be recouped by providing services or software to third parties in the manner of an FM company.

  TRY QUESTIONS 32, 36, AND 37
- *Possible pitfalls*

  Write down the mistakes you know you should avoid.

DID YOU KNOW? - INFORMATION SYSTEMS

- *Could you fill in the blanks? The answers are in bold. Use this page for revision purposes as you approach the exam.*
- Transaction processing systems are used for **routine operational information processing**. They provide the raw material used more extensively in **management information systems**.
- A management information system can be described as **a system which provides information to management to assist them in decision-making in their roles of planning and controlling**.
- Decision support systems are a form of management information system. They are used by management to **provide assistance in decision making**. A DSS does not make decisions itself. An example of a DSS is **the spreadsheet**.
- Executive information systems are a form of management information system designed to **give senior executives easy access to data**. They typically include a **'drill-down' facility, graphics** and **data manipulation facilities** for rapid and simple retrieval of the required data.

  TRY QUESTIONS 30 AND 33
- Expert systems use artificial intelligence, the concept that computers can be programmed to **imitate certain features of human reasoning**. Expert systems can be used where problems are **reasonably well defined** and can be solved by reference to **a set of rules**.
- Some organisations have introduced an **information centre** to support and streamline end-user computing. An **information centre** is a small unit manned by staff with a good technical knowledge. Its task is to provide a link between **users** and **computer operations**.

  TRY QUESTIONS 31, 34 AND 35
- **Distributed data processing** is processing done by a distributed system, a system containing a number of separate but connected processors, in which some centralised processing is possible.
- A **local area network** is a system of PCs and other devices, such as **printers** which are connected by **cable**. LANs have a **server** computer holding files used by more than one computer, and providing storage capacity to the other computers in the network. In a LAN, data processing tasks can be **shared between a number of PCs**, and single items of peripheral equipment can be **accessed by all of them**.
- A **wide area network** is a network of computers which are dispersed on a wider geographical scale than LANs. They usually are connected over the **public telecommunications network**.
- **Centralisation** allows the use of a single set of files and affords better security and control. Disadvantages are **the extent of local office reliance** on head office and a central computer and the **risk of delays in processing**.
- IT costs may be treated as an **overhead**, charged out **at cost** or charged out using a **market-based** chargeout method. Costs may be recouped by providing services or software to third parties in the manner of an FM company.

  TRY QUESTIONS 32, 36, AND 37
- *Possible pitfalls*
  - **Recommending the equipment or software that could be used in an information system purely in technological terms (eg '450 MHz') without saying WHY that sort of power is necessary, or what the advantages of that sort of software are.**
  - **Not appreciating the differences in purpose, and in the information used and provided by, say, an Expert System as opposed to an EIS.**

27 TUTORIAL QUESTION: ON-LINE REAL-TIME SYSTEMS

A new management trainee tells you that batch processing systems are outdated, and that businesses should use on-line, real-time systems for all business applications if they are to remain competitive.

Required

(a) Describe the operation of batch processing and real-time processing systems.

(b) Describe an application which might be appropriate for each of the following combinations, giving reasons for your choice.

(i) On-line input, real-time processing, and on-line enquiry.

(ii) Batch input, batch processing, and batch output (of the whole file at once).

Approaching the question

1 A question on a topic which has appeared several times in exams, albeit at a lower level than Stage 4. In part (b) you should not simply give an example of each system, you should also explain why that example is appropriate. This will demonstrate that you understand the topic.

2 In the IFM paper, you are more likely to be asked to propose a suitable system for a particular scenario, in which case a knowledge of real-time systems is essential, together with an appreciation of when they are and are not appropriate.

28 TUTORIAL QUESTION: REVIEW OF THE EFFECTIVENESS OF AN MIS

A medium sized manufacturer of domestic equipment has a well established management information system (MIS) which is computer based. Although the computer equipment has been updated recently and has been found to be entirely satisfactory, the design of the MIS has remained virtually unchanged for eight years.

As systems consultant you have been requested to carry out a review of the effectiveness of the MIS with the object of recommending changes where appropriate.

How would you carry out such a review and to what matters would you direct your attention?

Approaching the question

1 The wording of the question makes it clear that you do not need to address *technical* issues such as response times or processing speeds. Start by considering the purpose of an MIS.

2 Over a period of eight years, it is likely that the company's structure and procedures have changed and developed. Consider how this might have changed management's demands of the MIS.

3 Your review should focus particularly on output; consider for example frequency of reporting and cost of reports.

29 TUTORIAL QUESTION: MANAGEMENT SUPPORT

(a) Management support systems are aids to the decision-making process.

Describe the phases, which, according to Simon, constitute that process.

(b) A decision support system is a type of management support system.

Produce a definition of a decision support system, suggest what facilities it might offer, and what its essential components might consist of.

Approaching the question

1 There are two broad categories of information system in most organisations. The *transaction processing system* performs day-to-day processing for operational purposes. The *management information system,* which may be fed by the TPS, provides, as its name suggests, information to management.

2 Beaumont and Sutherland identify the following.

(a) Management information systems, used to process ordinary transactions and from which information for regular and exception reports can be analysed.

(b) Office information systems, a 'toolbox' of facilities such as WP and e-mail.

(c) Decision support systems, such as spreadsheets and EIS.

(d) Knowledge-based systems, such as expert systems.

(e) Inter-organisational systems, such as EDI and airline booking systems.

3 Whatever categories of systems you prefer to identify, you should be familiar with the workings of all the systems identified above and be able to identify situations where each might be appropriate.

30 HS PLC: EPOS AND DATABASE (11/97) *36 mins*

HS plc is a large quoted company which owns and maintains 42 large supermarkets in the country in which it operates. Each supermarket sells a very wide range of food and household goods to the general public.

There is a high level of competition from other supermarket groups.

HS plc has tended to be the industry leader in computerisation and has a corporate objective to offer the best computerised sales service to its customers. HS plc has introduced some computerisation in the stock and ordering systems, although there is no integrated system. Stock levels are high, being three days for perishable goods like milk and up to 28 days for tinned goods. This has resulted in a high stock-holding cost for the company.

HS plc is now considering an investment of over £50 million in the latest Electronic Point of Sale (EPOS) systems to maintain its competitive advantage. The databases associated with the system will be able to store information relating to stock levels of each product line, cash and bankings and even sales by individual customers. Information on HS plc's competitors indicate that they are also considering similar systems, but it will take at least two years to implement them. Because HS Plc has already produced the initial feasibility study and systems specification, the company could have its system running within 10 months.

The board of HS plc is meeting tomorrow to make the final decision on the investment. The managing director has indicated that he expects the investment to take place, but he would like to see a list of the benefits of the EPOS system, from both the strategic and operational viewpoints.

Required

Produce the report requested by the managing director which can be used at the board meeting. The report must show clearly the strategic and operational benefits of the proposed EPOS and database systems and how these relate to HS plc.

20 Marks

31 MIS AND EXPERT SYSTEM (11/98) *36 mins*

The HZ hospital has recently investigated the most up-to-date computer systems to assist its doctors in making assessments of patients' illnesses. Two of the software packages now available to doctors are:

- a Management Information System which provides information on the medical history of each patient. It includes detailed factual information on past illnesses and any recurring symptoms as well as the patient's name, address and other personal information.
- an Expert System which is used to assist in the diagnosis of current illnesses. The Expert System is linked to the MIS to obtain details on each patient's medical

history. From this information, and symptoms of the current illness, the Expert System provides an initial diagnosis, which the doctor uses in making his recommendation for the treatment of the patient. The diagnosis is stated in terms of probabilities of what the illness could be, rather than giving definite conclusions.

Required

(a) Explain the differences in the characteristics of information being provided by the two systems. **12 Marks**

(b) Explain the hardware and software requirement for an Expert System, showing why each item of hardware and software is necessary for the HZ hospital. **8 Marks**

Total Marks = 20

32 IT DEPARTMENT COSTS: CHARGEOUT METHODS (11/98) *36 mins*

JHD Inc manufactures a wide range of products in a large number of different departments. Each department is a cost centre. IT is extensively integrated into the company with departments relying heavily on IT systems for their operational activities. The IT department's work includes the implementation and servicing of equipment as well as central file maintenance.

The IT department is therefore viewed as an essential service: its costs are charged to other departments as part of company general overhead. No other charge is levied on any department for its use of computer services.

The size of the IT overhead cost (approximately 10% of the total wages bill and 15% of indirect expenditure costs) has been concerning the board of JHD plc. Furthermore, some departments have implied that their overhead apportionment is too high for their use of the service and have been obtaining third-party quotes for providing this service. The board is now re-considering the charging method used.

Required

(a) Contrast, from the point of view of the departmental managers, the alternative policies of charging the costs of the IT department

- as part of company overheads, *and*
- on the basis of individual department usage. **12 Marks**

(b) It is proposed that the basis on which usage of the IT department is determined will be the amount of network traffic generated by each department. Network traffic relates to the amount of data transferred across the network each day in megabytes.

Required

Explain the problems associated with the proposal to charge the IT department's cost on the basis of network traffic, and suggest an alternative approach that would solve these problems. **8 Marks**

Total Marks = 20

33 10F GROUP: MIS AND OBJECTIVES (11/95) *36 mins*

The 10F Group runs a chain of small supermarkets selling groceries, newspapers, magazines, drinks and sweets to the general public. Each shop is located in an area of high population density and is open 24 hours a day. Stock can be easily re-arranged on the shelves to take account of different items being demanded at different times of the day or on different days of the week.

Some of the 10F Group's objectives for its next trading year are:

(a) re-stock a shop from its chain of warehouses within four hours of the shop placing an order;

(b) ensure that goods customers require are in stock 98% of the time (this implies that two customers in 100 will not find one particular item they are looking for per visit).

Required

(a) Recommend to the Group the information that must be provided by each shop's MIS, explaining its relevance to meeting the two objectives above. **12 Marks**

(b) State the hardware and software elements required to run the Group's MIS at each shop and at the warehouse. Explain why each element of hardware or software is necessary. **8 Marks**

Total Marks = 20

34 JH PLC: INFORMATION CENTRE (5/96) *36 mins*

JH plc trades in an overseas country, arranging freight forwarding contracts for up to 2,000 corporate clients. The company's mission is to be the most profitable freight forwarder in that country. The company is very profitable, partly due to its high investment in modern IT systems, and its narrow focus on its corporate mission.

The company's IT systems are supported by its Information Centre, which has a staff of 20. Although large, the centre is always well utilised.

In a recent corporate review, the Board of JH plc noted that the Information Centre was costing the company £4,000,000 per annum with no discernible income. The Board is therefore considering whether to close the Information Centre to improve the company's profitability.

The most recent addition to the computer system is a network that links all departments. It is anticipated that an increasing number of clients will send their requirements direct to the company via the company's gateway to the Internet.

Required

(a) Write a memo to the Board to justify the continuance of the Information Centre on non-financial grounds. **12 Marks**

(b) Explain how JH plc's Information Centre can provide an enhanced service to the staff of JH plc using the recently installed computer network within the company. **8 Marks**

Total Marks = 20

35 JS PLC: AN ACCEPTABLE STANDARD OF INFORMATION (5/98) *36 mins*

JS plc is a large manufacturing company. It operates from 10 different sites and produces a wide range of consumer goods. Within each site, each department (eg sales, production, stock control) maintains its own independent computer-based Transaction Processing and Management Information Systems. The computer systems within a site, or on different sites, cannot communicate with each other. The lack of communication is a result of different system implementation dates, operating systems, hardware platforms and substantial amendment by users of the software being used in each individual department.

JS plc is now experiencing significant increased demand for its products, and all systems, computerised and manual, are working excessively. A number of very large orders have recently been lost because managers made incorrect pricing and production decisions. This was surprising because managers obtained what they thought was up-to-date and accurate information from the company's computer systems when they were making the decisions. Subsequent investigation showed that the managers' decision-making process was not at fault: it was the information in the computer system itself that was incorrect.

Required

(a) Explain why the information being provided by the computer systems could be incorrect. Make reference in your answer to the problems in JS plc's computer systems and the information being provided by the systems. **12 Marks**

(b) Discuss how an information centre could help the company provide an acceptable standard of information to its managers. **8 Marks**

Total Marks = 20

36 INFORMATION SYSTEM INPUTS AND OUTPUTS (5/99) *36 mins*

The SFA Company manufactures clothing and operates from one location in a major city. It purchases cotton and other raw materials and manufactures these into garments of clothing, such as sweatshirts, T-shirts and similar articles in its factory. There are approximately 20 administration staff, 30 sales staff and 300 production workers. Although the company is profitable, three major concerns were raised at a recent Board meeting about the operations of the company:

1 The company does not always appear to obtain the best prices for raw materials, which has decreased gross profit in the last few years of trading.

2 Many garments are made to order for large retail shops, but the company has spare capacity and so it maintains an active salesforce to try and increase its total sales. However, the salesforce does not seem to be making many sales because of lack of information about the garments in production and stocks of finished garments.

3 Some production is carried out using Computer Assisted Design and manufacture although the company has found limited use for this application to date. The system was purchased in a hurry two years ago with the objective of keeping up with competitors who had purchased similar systems. The Board believes that greater use could be made of this technology.

The Value Chain model produced by Porter provides a good summary of the primary and support activities of the company. An adaptation of Porter's general model is shown on the following page:

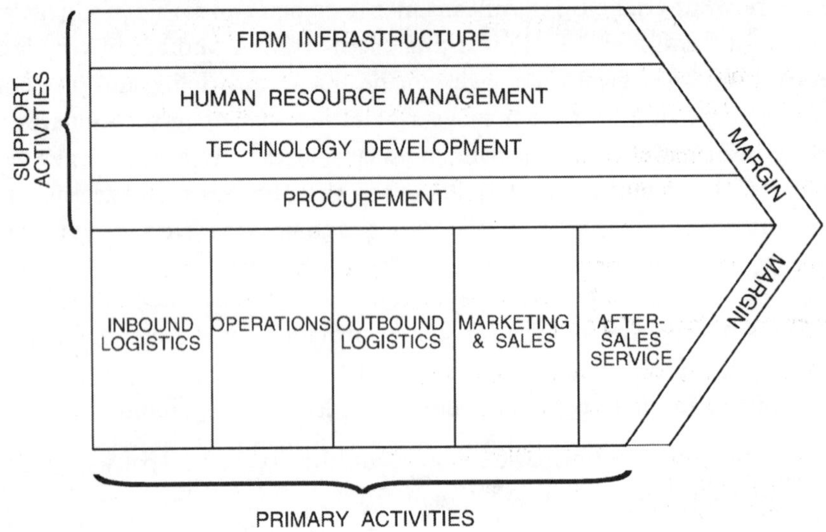

The Board of SFA is currently considering implementing some form of information system or systems, such as a MIS, into the company for all staff to use. Because of the perceived weaknesses in the current systems already mentioned, the directors are particularly interested in the areas of

1 inbound logistics,
2 marketing and sales, and
3 technology development

Required

Explain

(a) what inputs will be needed for the information systems designed to support the operations of the business in the three areas mentioned above; **14 Marks**

(b) what outputs will be required from those information systems. **6 Marks**

Note: Do NOT describe Porter's general model.

Total Marks = 20

37 OKR PLC: ACHIEVING OBJECTIVES *36 mins*

OKR plc has a central computer department which works solely for other departments within the company. Its current charge-out rate is £250 per hour. The rate is the same whatever task is being performed. The manager of the computer department has been given a single objective - to recover her department's costs.

Some of the users are dissatisfied with the computer service, and have observed that external agencies often charge as little as £75 an hour. The users are not allowed to use such external agencies.

Required

(a) Recommend what you consider to be a suitable set of objectives for the computer department. **8 Marks**

(b) Describe control procedures which could assist in achieving the objectives which you have recommended. **8 Marks**

(c) Explain how the computer department could develop a marketing orientation towards its customers. **4 Marks**

Total Marks = 20

DO YOU KNOW? - SECURITY OF SYSTEMS

- *Check that you can fill in the blanks in the statements below before you attempt any questions. If in doubt, you should go back to your BPP Study Text and revise first.*
- Security is the protection of data from .... and the protection of an information system from .... Privacy is the right of the individual ....
- The first steps in developing a security policy are the .... Controls .... to develop and operate, and so the response to risk will not always be the implementation of a control.
- The risks to data may be classified as ...., ..., ..., ..., ..., ... and ....
- .... are appointed by management to maintain the clerical, administrative and financial controls of an organisation. They monitor and report on selected aspects of the organisation's operations.
- Computer audit is a necessary element of the review of many computer systems. Computer assisted audit techniques can be used to ...., ...and ....
- A logical access system is concerned with preventing those persons who have gained physical access from ....
- ....permit a system to continue to be operated in the event of a major breakdown.
- Back-up procedures are necessary to ....
- The Data Protection Act 1998 (and the earlier 1984 Act) is a piece of UK legislation which protects .... about whom data is held. Data users must .... and .... to which the data will be put. The Act contains the ...., to which all data users must adhere.

  TRY QUESTION 39
- *Possible pitfalls*

  Write down the mistakes you know you should avoid.

DID YOU KNOW? - SECURITY OF SYSTEMS

- *Could you fill in the blanks? The answers are in bold. Use this page for revision purposes as you approach the exam.*
- Security is the protection of data from **accidental or deliberate threats** and the protection of an information system from **such threats**. Privacy is the right of the individual **not to have information about him or her disclosed in an unauthorised manner**.
- The first steps in developing a security policy are the **identification and quantification of risks**. Controls **cost money** to develop and operate, and so the response to risk will not always be the implementation of a control.
- The risks to data may be classified as **human error, technical error, natural disaster, deliberate action, commercial espionage, malicious damage** and **industrial action**.
- **Internal auditors** are appointed by management to maintain the clerical, administrative and financial controls of an organisation. They monitor and report on selected aspects of the organisation's operations.
- Computer audit is a necessary element of the review of many computer systems. Computer assisted audit techniques can be used to **read files, extract information** and **carry out audit work**.
- A logical access system is concerned with preventing those persons who have gained physical access from **gaining unauthorised access to data or software**.
- **Standby facilities** permit a system to continue to be operated in the event of a major breakdown.
- Back-up procedures are necessary to **enable file data to be recreated when a file is lost or corrupted.**
- The Data Protection Act 1988 (and the earlier 1984 Act) is a piece of UK legislation which protects **individuals** about whom data is held. Data users must **register** and **announce the uses** to which the data will be put. The Act contains the **data protection principles**, to which all data users must adhere.

  TRY QUESTION 39
- *Possible pitfalls*
  - **Neglecting to mention security aspects that need to be considered when proposing a solution.**
  - **Proposing levels of control that are so high that the system cannot be operated effectively by authorised users.**

38 TUTORIAL QUESTION: COMPUTER MISUSE

What are the three offences which the Computer Misuse Act 1990 defines and the penalties permitted for each?

Approaching the question

1. The Computer Misuse Act 1990 is designed to address the problems raised by hacking by making hacking a criminal offence. By its nature it can only (apart form any value which it has as a deterrent) be of use *after* an offence has been committed.
2. Remember that the Act cannot prevent hacking, and you may well be asked what steps a company should take to minimise the risks in this area in order to *prevent* such an offence taking place.

39 SCP LTD: THREATS *36 mins*

SCP Ltd is an engineering company which is about to implement a new production planning and control system. Following a strategic level review of the business, the board have decided that one of the company's critical success factors is the production of up-to-date and accurate information on internal (eg customer orders) and external (eg raw materials availability) factors, so that the company can respond quickly to changes in demand and other external circumstances. The new system will enable a rapid response to such information and will provide output for a range of production operations including machine loading, control of raw materials, production set-up, batch control, planned downtime and machine utilisation.

The system is seen as a 'mission-critical' one and the company is setting up a new computer centre, which will take responsibility for this system and also take over existing systems currently under the auspices of the finance, sales and personnel departments.

You have been asked to advise the company on the security aspects of the new computer centre.

Required

(a) What potential physical threats would you make your client aware of, what precautionary measures would you suggest, and what techniques would you propose be implemented to control access to the computer centre? **10 Marks**

(b) You also feel that a contingency plan is an essential aspect of the new computing facility.

Explain to the client the purpose of such a plan, how it might be developed, and the standby options which are available. **10 Marks**

Total Marks = 20

DO YOU KNOW? - SOCIAL DIMENSIONS OF INFORMATION

- *Check that you can fill in the blanks in the statements below before you attempt any questions. If in doubt, you should go back to your BPP Study Text and revise first.*
- IT is a major contributor to the increasing pace of change in the business environment. It increases the speed at which information is processed and distributed, permitting .... and ....
- The .... connects millions of computers worldwide and is having a major impact on ways of communicating and doing business. Companies are setting up their own .... using similar technology.

  TRY QUESTIONS 42, 44 AND 49
- Individuals can be affected by change in a number of areas. The effects can be described as ...., ... and .... Resistance to change can manifest itself in different ways, both active and passive.
- The computer environment should be designed to support employee satisfaction. This can range over a wide area of subjects, from ...., for example to eliminate tedium or monotony from what may be essentially repetitive tasks, through to ...., for example in design of chairs and other .... features of the system.

  TRY QUESTIONS 45 AND 50
- Both 'hard-copy' printouts and the screen display must be well designed, because ....p... Dialogue design is a related area which addresses not the *appearance* of the output, but ....
- Input design is concerned with achieving the most efficient input processes, taking into account both .... and ....
- *Possible pitfalls*

  Write down the mistakes you know you should avoid.

DID YOU KNOW? - SOCIAL DIMENSIONS OF INFORMATION

- *Could you fill in the blanks? The answers are in bold. Use this page for revision purposes as you approach the exam.*
- IT is a major contributor to the increasing pace of change in the business environment. It increases the speed at which information is processed and distributed, permitting **faster responses** and **quicker decision making**.
- The **Internet** connects millions of computers worldwide and is having a major impact on ways of communicating and doing business. Companies are setting up their own **intranets** using similar technology.

  TRY QUESTIONS 42, 44 AND 49
- Individuals can be affected by change in a number of areas. The effects can be described as **physiological**, **circumstantial** and **psychological**. Resistance to change can manifest itself in different ways, both active and passive.
- The computer environment should be designed to support employee satisfaction. This can range over a wide area of subjects, from **job design**, for example to eliminate tedium or monotony from what may be essentially repetitive tasks, through to **physical comfort**, for example in design of chairs and other **ergonomic** features of the system.

  TRY QUESTIONS 45 AND 50
- Both 'hard-copy' printouts and the screen display must be well designed, because **they are the media through which the computer communicates with users**. Dialogue design is a related area which addresses not the *appearance* of the output, but the *way* in which it is obtained.
- Input design is concerned with achieving the most efficient input processes, taking into account both **the requirements of the system** and **the capabilities of its users**.
- *Possible pitfalls*
  - **Avoiding questions on the social dimensions of information because you are afraid to express a view**
  - **Failing to take account of people-related issues.**

40 TUTORIAL QUESTION: AUTOMATED OFFICE

(a) Explain what you understand by the term office automation.

(b) Identify in what areas of activity the benefits from office automation are most likely to arise.

Approaching the question

1 Part (a) of this question, being descriptive in nature, is fairly straightforward and is included here purely for revision purposes, as it is certainly not the sort of question which is expected to feature in the IFM paper.

2 In part (b), a possible approach would be to group the benefits into three categories.

(a) changes to the economy of office activity.
(b) changes to the efficiency of office activity.
(c) changes to the effectiveness of office activity.

41 TUTORIAL QUESTION: CENTRALISATION AND OPEN SYSTEMS

Senior management in SGI need to make certain strategic decisions in respect of information technology in the organisation.

They particularly want to know whether the information technology function should be centralised or decentralised. Their main concern regarding decentralisation is that they might lose control over the group's diverse operations.

Required

(a) Analyse the arguments for and against centralisation/decentralisation.

(b) Explain how an open system can help a distributed information system.

Approaching the question

Centralisation offers greater efficiency and control; decentralisation more flexibility to users. It is worth considering the extent to which developments in technology have upset the traditional arguments, for example availability and use of low cost PCs overcomes the 'economies of scale' justification for centralisation.

42 E-MAIL (11/98) *36 mins*

E-mail is becoming one of the most common forms of communication, both for sending messages within organisations, and across the Internet.

Required

(a) Discuss the impact of communication by e-mail on work practices. **12 Marks**

(b) Discuss situations where e-mail would NOT be an appropriate communication medium. **8 Marks**

Total Marks = 20

43 SKO PLC: CENTRAL STORAGE AND DPA (5/96) *36 mins*

SKO plc owns a large number of small retail shops. None of the shops uses Electronic Point Of Sales systems.

Each shop generates a substantial amount of data each week including:

(a) purchase invoices;
(b) copy sales receipts;
(c) details of prices charged;

(d) banking records; and
(e) summaries of prices in competing shops.

In an attempt to manage this volume of information, it is proposed that all documents will be transferred to a central information storage facility located in the middle of the country in which SKO plc operates. The facility will provide not only a secure environment for the data, but also various outputs for use by SKO plc

None of the shops currently shares data, and there are no plans to introduce any direct communication links between the shops. Each shop will continue to produce the daily reports that it requires. A shop will therefore not need to contact the central information storage facility for any information about its own normal operating activities. Information, such as comparative pricing reports between the shops in the SKO plc group, can be transferred back to the shops as required.

Two outputs from the central information storage facility will be:

(a) information on other corporate entities, particularly regarding pricing policy; and

(b) summaries of the information held, including sales by region and estimated market share of each shop which SKO plc owns.

Required

(a) Critically evaluate the proposal to store information in a central location.

14 Marks

(b) Explain what action SKO plc will have to take regarding the Data Protection Act 1984* with respect to the two outputs mentioned. **6 Marks**

> ***BPP Note:** The 1984 Act applied when this question was set. We have added material relevant to the 1998 Act to our answer.

Total Marks = 20

44 PC INC: INTERNET SERVICE PROVIDER (11/97) *36 mins*

PC Inc is an Internet service provider. This means that it allows customers to connect their computers to its own large computer system, normally via the telephone system. Customers then have access to a number of services, as explained below.

The company provides two types of services to its subscribers:

1 *Information services*

The company has recently established its own website which is accessible by anyone using the Internet. The information provided here includes general information on company share prices, dividends declared etc and most specialist information arising from research that PC Inc itself has undertaken. This specialist information is not generally available from other Internet service providers.

2 *Communication services*

The company also acts as an access point to the Internet. For a small monthly fee, customers can maintain their e-mail box on P Inc's computer. Customers can access their mail box or send mail to other people or companies. Access to the full World Wide Web (WWW) is also available. Payment for the WWW is by a combination of monthly fee and on-line access time.

PC Inc competes against other service providers in both of these markets.

Required

(a) Comment on the factors that PC Inc must take into account when setting prices for the information and communication services that it provides. **12 Marks**

(b) Explain the factors that now make information a valuable commodity, which means that a charge can be made for viewing the information. **8 Marks**

Total Marks = 20

45 TUTORIAL QUESTION: WORKING ENVIRONMENTS

(a) 'The design of operating equipment and the layout of working environments are crucial factors in employee recruitment, retention and performance.'

Discuss.

(b) A large company negotiates with suitable members of staff to work from home using a personal computer and modem link to the main computer in order to provide a variety of administrative services.

(i) Describe the typical information technology equipment and resources required by the homeworker.

(ii) Outline the possible advantages and drawbacks for the person working from home.

Approaching the question

1 In (a) you should certainly show some appreciation of the issues involved in working with IT, but your answer might cover other areas too.

2 Part (b) concerns a topic which is becoming increasingly relevant in the UK and one about which you should certainly be reasonably well informed.

46 YK PLC: E-MAIL (11/96) *36 mins*

YK plc operates 20 factories, each of which manufactures and distributes dairy products within its surrounding region. The products are particularly subject to market forces and, as a result, decisions on the pricing and quality of the products are required on a daily basis. Each factory is controlled by a Managing Director and a Finance Director who together take all the operating and managerial decisions for that factory.

Every two weeks, all the Managing Directors and Finance Directors meet in a central location to discuss the results of each factory and to make plans for the coming two weeks. The information exchange is seen to be crucial by the senior executives of YK plc to ensure that the overall corporate strategy is maintained. The Directors also value the meeting because they can discuss various detailed operational problems informally with the Directors of the other factories.

For much of the past year, the senior executives of YK plc had been seeking an alternative to the two-weekly meetings. The reason for this was to avoid the high travelling costs and having all its Directors away from their factories for effectively a whole day, with a consequent lack of decision takers in the factories. As a result of this review, a new e-mail system was implemented with the full approval of the Directors. The result of this is that Directors can share information on a minute-by-minute basis if they want to, and the senior management can communicate strategic information straight to the Directors without waiting for the two-weekly meeting.

Although the implementation of the new systems did have the approval of the Directors, there is now some uncertainty that this was the correct decision. A number of Directors have started meeting Directors from other locations informally even though the e-mail and information-sharing systems should provide all the communication that they require.

Required

Explain the potential problems and benefits of using e-mail in YK plc. Your answer must include an explanation of why the Directors of YK plc are returning to face-to-face meetings on an informal basis.

20 Marks

47 CP LTD: HOMEWORKING (5/97) *36 mins*

CP Ltd is a small but successful company which specialises in selling car and home insurance to individuals. All sales are made over the telephone, and there are no personal callers to the company's offices. The company employs 25 staff, 22 in the telephone sales department and the remaining three running all the accounts and administration functions. As a consequence of its recent success in the market, CP Ltd is planning to expand its operations.

The company has been evaluating its cost structure and has discovered that the cost of providing office space for each worker is £3,500 per annum. New workers would require office space with a cost per worker of £4,000 per annum. This amounts to a significant cost in the company's operating budget. The Management Accountant has calculated that 90% of office costs can be avoided if the telephone sales staff worked from their homes. This idea has, so far, been discussed only at board level.

At present, employees appear to enjoy working in the office, where they spend most of their time using the telephone and computer system to sell insurance. Coffee and lunch breaks are normally spent in the rest area where staff also compare some notes and queries concerning their jobs. All the data that they need to perform their job is otherwise available on the computer system. This data includes:

(a) records on each customer;

(b) access to a value added network (VAN) providing costs of insurance from other companies which sell insurance; and

(c) word-processing and other systems for producing letters and insurance quotes to customers.

The proposal to work from home was put to staff last week and this has met with some initial resistance although the Management Accountant stressed that this proposal was only a possibility.

Required

Write a report to the Managing Director explaining:

(a) from the viewpoint of the staff, the potential benefits that will be gained by homeworking. Explain the concerns that staff may have over homeworking and whether the IT infrastructure can help alleviate these concerns. **12 Marks**

(b) what can be done to encourage staff to accept the proposed change. **8 Marks**

Total Marks = 20

48 PDY LTD: HOW DO YOU DO IT? *36 mins*

You are asked to review the effectiveness of a new product delivery computer system which has been in live operation at PDY Ltd for just three weeks. The system is a new addition to a larger order processing system and its main function is to prepare instructions for scheduling delivery of products from stock. Output, in the form of despatch notes, is printed in the transport office.

Whilst reviewing the operations you meet the stock controller responsible for the despatch notes. He does not appear to know what is happening and does not even know what he is supposed to do. The stationery on the printer runs out and he does not even know how to change it. It transpires that he has not used computers before and that he is aggrieved that his views on the new system, although canvassed, were not actually taken into account when the system was developed.

Required

(a) List the steps you would take to review the performance of the product delivery computer system. **12 Marks**

(b) Explain why the stock controller might not have been suitably prepared for his part in the new system. **8 Marks**

Total Marks = 20

49 WEBSITE DESIGN AND ADVANTAGES (5/99) *36 mins*

SK Products Ltd was established 65 years ago by two entrepreneurs to distribute tools and spare parts to the then small electronics industry. Since that time the company has expanded its product range to just over 100,000 items and supplies electronic and computer components to many major organisations. The components supplied range from small fuses and computer chips to complicated electrical assemblies requiring specialist knowledge to install.

The current directors pride themselves on the organisation's attention to the specific requests of customers and the personal and friendly service that all staff provide. Recent customer surveys show that a significant amount of repeat business is generated by good customer care, even though SK Products Ltd's prices can be higher than those charged by competitors.

The organisation is planned its first website. A review of competitors' sites shows that information provided is little more than an electronic catalogue. Repeat visits to the site are greeted with the same 'home page' whilst most of the information provided appears to be out-of-date.

SK Products Ltd currently supplies a catalogue every four months in paper format.

Required

(a) Explain the advantages and disadvantages of SK Products Ltd providing information on a website rather in a paper-based catalogue. Ensure that your answer shows how a website can provide a more user-friendly presentation system than a paper-based catalogue. **14 Marks**

(b) Explain what information SK Products Ltd can provide on its website to help customers install and use its products. **6 Marks**

Total Marks = 20

50 HUMAN PROBLEMS (5/98) *36 mins*

M O'B is the management accountant of a small company. He is responsible for

- the preparation of the monthly management accounts and annual budgets for the company
- the preparation of the year-end financial statements

- maintenance of the company's Executive Information System (EIS) and transaction processing systems
- the hiring of staff and negotiation of pay and working conditions with each member of staff, and
- preparing and agreeing the company's taxation returns with the relevant authorities (this includes VAT, income and corporation taxes)

The board of directors requires a monthly report from M O'B on all of the above matters. M O'B has a staff of two junior accountants to assist him; they are currently studying for their Stage 2 CIMA examination. Although they work hard, M O'B finds that they do not always have the detailed knowledge to assist him sufficiently in all of his areas of responsibility.

The company's computer system is used to maintain the transaction processing systems which form part of the statutory books of account. The separate computerised EIS does provide some useful information, but it is not always up-to-date. The systems are well maintained with the hardware supplier providing on-site maintenance on a regular basis.

M O'B is now working excessive amounts of overtime and has not taken a holiday in the last 18 months. The board is concerned because recent board reports have contained a number of minor errors, some purely arithmetical, but others where incorrect or out-of-date information has been used. The junior accountants are demotivated because they do not consider they are receiving sufficient responsibility for their level of knowledge or time spent within the company.

Required

Explain the human problems that the management accountant is facing.

Describe what human and IT solutions might help alleviate these problems. **20 Marks**

51 FMF LTD: SHAKE THEM HIPS *108 mins*

FMF Ltd is a specialist furniture manufacturer which uses many woods grown in sustainable growth sources overseas. Central management wish to formalise the way in which they select suppliers, taking into account, besides supplier attitudes, such matters as delivery times, cost, exchange rate movements and substitution of similar woods. At the same time they wish to devolve more operational control to local management in the regional workshops. To achieve these goals, they wish to develop a new computer system.

Currently only the accounts department is computerised. Other departments, including production and sales, operate in a manual environment. There are several stand-alone PCs scattered around these departments, although secretarial staff still use electronic typewriters. The departments provide typed or word-processed reports each week for incorporation into the monthly management reporting pack which is compiled in the accounts department.

The chief accountant has become aware that a number of individual purchasing authorities have been buying PCs and that there has also been ongoing acquisition of popular spreadsheet and word processing packages. It is clear that these recurrent 'one-off' purchases are not economic and it is possible that software licence conditions are not being adhered to.

An initial analysis suggests that the new system must:

(a) provide comprehensive management information and reporting;
(b) run existing accounting software, which is packaged;

(c) run spreadsheets for supplier modelling in purchasing and procurement; and
(d) offer WP to all departments.

Staff concerns

Staff have a number of concerns in relation to the new system.

(a) Some staff in production and sales have not used computers before and are worried that they will lose their jobs, either because they cannot use the new technology or because they fear that the new technology will replace them.

(b) Purchasing staff feel that the core of their roles is to be removed from them. They consider themselves to be experts in a range of subjects from forestry management to the state of third world economies. Having a database of all this information will, they believe, make them into computer operators with no opportunity to use or develop their own knowledge.

(c) Secretarial staff are concerned that other people will be able to access their confidential records.

Required

(a) How can any resentment and opposition towards the new computer system be overcome? **18 Marks**

(b) To what extent will the system be a compromise between prescribed objectives and actual constraints? **16 Marks**

(c) What sort of personnel management issues might the newly appointed information systems manager have to deal with? **10 Marks**

(d) What options are open to the company when purchasing software for its multi-user installation and what points must be clarified in software agreements so that each user has a fully functional and legitimate copy of the appropriate piece of software? **16 Marks**

Total Marks = 60

LONGER CASE STUDIES

This section contains the previous eight 60 mark case studies set in the exam.

The notes below indicate the range of issues covered in each question.

- 52 *Travel Agency*
  Vision and reality
  Implementation
  Human Information Processors
  VANs compared with EISs
  Design of human/computer interface and MIS
- 53 *Chemicals production*
  Information presentation
  Information deficiencies
  Critical success factors
  Business process re-engineering
- 54 *International Airline*
  IT strategy
  Characteristics of information
  Upgrading policy
  The Internet and data security
- 55 *Bread manufacturer*
  Sources of information
  Limitations of a closed loop system
  Using market research information
  Critical Success Factors and performance indicators
  Computerised bulletin board
- 56 *Motor vehicle manufacturer*
  Information characteristics
  Importance of IT
  Data security and data protection
  Human computer interface
- 57 *Theme Park*
  Sources of information
  Analysis and design
  EIS
  Backup alternatives
  Internet and society
- 58 *Office products supplier*
  Comparison of new systems
  Information requirements
  Leasing or purchase
  Human issues
- 59 *International financial services provider*
  Possible reasons for project failure
  SDLC
  Human information processor
  Local information needs
  Data transfer risks and security

52 TRAVEL AGENCY (11/95) *108 mins*

Introduction and old system

Voyager Travel Agency aims to provide customers with:

- a high-quality service
- a friendly, highly-trained and knowledgeable staff; and
- competitive prices.

The shop manager is very proud of the service that his staff provide, and believes that these objectives are being met.

Until this year, the Voyager Travel Agency worked without the assistance of any computerised systems. Customers would visit the travel agency and request details of holidays that were available. The ten staff working in the travel agency would supply the required information after checking various brochures and making telephone calls direct to companies who sell air and rail travel, and also hotel accommodation. Furthermore, because the staff worked in the same room, they would frequently consult each other for information rather than refer to their brochures.

Details of systems changes

On the first day of this working week, 20 November 1995, the staff reported for work to find that a computer system had been installed over the previous two non-working days. The manager stated that he did not tell the staff so that they would have a 'nice surprise'. The manager was convinced that the staff would find the new system much more efficient and easy to use; no training would therefore be required.

The computer system itself was a local area network (LAN) within the office. Access was available to third-party databases showing details of travel and hotels available for holidays (this information was previously obtained only from brochures and via the telephone). Furthermore, the office was linked via a value added network (VAN) to 15 other travel agents operating within the same town so that each agent's specialist holidays could be offered to all customers. All holidays booked using the new system were to be checked by a senior manager before the sale was agreed; this policy had never been adopted before by the company.

Staff reaction to the new system

The reaction of the staff was mixed, although they did attempt to use the new computer system. Problems that were encountered during the first day's operations included:

- staff were expected to work longer hours, with almost constant use of the computer system. Longer hours were required to enable daily backups of the computer system to be taken;
- two VDUs were used constantly, one to access databases of travel and hotel information, and the second to update Voyager's own computer records and details from other travel agents in the VAN. In addition to the VDUs, two keyboards, two mice, brochures and two telephones were also located on each desk. For a typical holiday booking, a member of staff would find himself/herself using both VDUs, at least one brochure, and information from the customer as well as booking the holiday over the telephone with a travel company;
- menu options were not fully explained on screen, whilst each option selected seemed to provide many possible courses of action.

In addition to the above,

- the idea and use of the VAN was not explained to the staff;
- staff were given individual offices to work from.

The problems have now persisted for three days. Shop staff remain very demotivated and shop bookings have fallen considerably. You have been appointed by the shop manager as a consultant to try and assist the manager resolve the shop's present difficulties.

Required

(a) (i) Evaluate the difference between the vision of the shop manager and the reality of the Voyager Travel Agency by the end of Monday, 20 November.

Identify clearly the reasons for any differences that you find.

(ii) Explain the failings of the manager of Voyager Travel Agency in implementing the new computer system, and describe the actions that must now be taken to ensure that staff accept and use the new system. **18 Marks**

(b) Identify the problems that will affect the Human Information Processors (in other words the staff at Voyager Travel Agency) in the use of the new computer system, and propose solutions to these problems. **14 Marks**

(c) Contrast, with examples, the information being provided by a VAN and information that could have been provided by an executive information system (EIS) had this type of system been implemented at Voyager Travel Agency. **13 Marks**

(d) State and explain how a well-designed human/computer interface and management information system (MIS) would help the staff at Voyager Travel Agency to obtain quickly and efficiently the information that they need in their work. **15 Marks**

Total Marks = 60

53 CHEMICALS PRODUCTION (5/96) *108 mins*

Introduction and decision making structure

MQS Ltd produces specialised industrial chemicals to individual customer orders. Each order is treated as a separate project under the control of three distinct management tiers.

(a) The *Production Managers* who are responsible for the making of the product, although they have no control over the input mix or the quality of input used. Each product is made from a large number of chemicals and is very sensitive to any change in the quality of the inputs. To maintain a high quality of output, frequent adjustments are required to the input product mix. These adjustments alleviate any fall in quality caused by changes in the quality of the inputs.

(b) The *Senior Managers* who work in the company's main office. The *Senior Managers* collate and produce weekly management reports on the progress of projects for which they are responsible. The reports recommend actions to the *Chief Accountant* although he must authorise these decisions before they can be implemented.

(c) The *Chief Accountant* who approves changes to the costing of projects, and the quality of inputs and the input mix used.

Order and production process

Each customer order takes four months to complete from the initial receipt of the order at MQS Ltd. The order and production process involves four stages, each stage taking approximately one month. Each stage is followed in sequential order with no time overlap.

(a) *Quotation.* Drafting of a detailed quotation and input requirements listing for agreement with the customer. Only 1% of orders are cancelled during this time, and an initial input requirement can be available in as little as two days, including pricing from standard price lists issued by suppliers.

(b) *Material ordering.* A price enquiry is sent to three suppliers who each return a firm quote including quantity discounts not available on standard price lists. A quote has to be accepted by the *Chief Accountant* before the approved purchase order can be raised, and goods delivered from the supplier. Goods are ordered from one of three competing suppliers. The order is given to the supplier with the lowest quote. Goods are then available ex-stock. MQS Ltd employs a staff of 10 to negotiate prices and saves on average £25,000 per annum in the process, compared to the standard price offered on Trade price lists.

(c) *Production.* Production itself takes about one week. Quality control checks take about three weeks.

(d) *Packaging and shipping.* Specialised containers for the delivery of the goods are ordered. Two weeks later these containers are delivered, and the goods are checked into the container. Another week is taken up in organising a specialist courier firm to collect and deliver the goods.

Information for Senior Manager report production

The main weekly report available to *Senior Managers* from the computer system includes the following information.

MQS Ltd					
Production report Week to 30 April 1996				Report date: 19 May 1996	
Project	*Production cost per batch*	*Profit for week*	*Manufacturing cost*	*Cost to date*	*Sales value*
A	453.98	2,563.98	10,002.43	777,734.9	1,000,000
B	664.23	655.83	8,444.93	76,339	500,000
C	76.34	27,736.9	57,223.94	299,433.93	750,000
D	266.87	17,117.28	38,339	89,222.9	350,000
Project A - input mix		*Cost*	*Stock at 30 April*		
Material X	453 tonnes	4.53	34		
Material Y	65 tonnes	877.30	233		
Material Z	477 tonnes	500.00	78		

Each report has a separate line for each project that the *Senior Manager* controls. The input mix information is repeated for each product.

Additional information concerning the printout above.

(a) Information on the reports is manually transferred by *Senior Managers* onto their own summary reports

(b) Reports are regularly sent by the company's electronic mail (e-mail) system. Many *Senior Managers* see e-mail as a hindrance, forcing them to review reports on-screen and waste time as the reports are printed out. As a result, their e-mail is not regularly reviewed. When they do review reports on e-mail, the *Senior Managers* tend to be in a hostile frame of mind, resulting from their dissatisfaction with the system.

Senior Managers must produce a report to the *Chief Accountant* on a weekly basis which shows the progress on each of their projects to a high level of detail. The reports recommend actions to the *Chief Accountant*, including those relating to input mix and quality of inputs. The *Chief Accountant* then approves changes to the costing of projects and authorises decisions on input mix and quality before they are implemented.

Additional information on Senior managers' reports

To assist them in their report writing, *Senior Managers* also collect information from the following sources.

(a) Verbal reports from *Production Managers* who produce the chemicals.

(b) Technical journals providing details of chemical formulae and tolerances for manufacture of those chemicals (*Senior Managers* normally purchase these journals themselves).

(c) A weekly production meeting.

The company's own technical database is used infrequently due to poor access for *Senior Managers* and the confusing presentation of information.

Office environment

All the *Senior Managers* work in a large open-plan office of 50 people. Printers are not sound-proof, and the main form of communication is by telephone. Each *Senior Manager* is involved with a large number of projects requiring daily managerial input.

MQS Ltd is considering whether to implement a business change (Business Process Re-engineering project) for its ordering and production process.

Required

(a) Assess how effective the production report is in assisting *Senior Managers* with their decision making. Explain the weaknesses you identify in the format and method of transmission of the report, AND propose amendments to overcome these weaknesses.

You are NOT required to re-draft the report. **12 Marks**

(b) Identify the weaknesses in the company's current provision of information to *Senior Managers* explaining how these weaknesses affect their decision making ability.

Suggest how these weaknesses may be overcome. **20 Marks**

(c) Assume that MQS Ltd will change its ordering and production process.

(i) Describe two critical success factors that can be used to judge the success of the change **6 Marks**

(ii) Explain the potential benefits of the change to MQS Ltd as a company, and to the staff employed by MQS Ltd. **14 Marks**

(iii) Explain how time could be saved within the order and production process. Provide a detailed estimate of the new production time from the receipt of order from the customer to the delivery of the finished goods. **8 Marks**

Total Marks = 60

54 ARG INTERNATIONAL AIRLINES (11/96) *108 mins*

Background

ARG is an international airline operator, based in a central European country. It maintains a fleet of approximately 350 aircraft, and its core activity is to provide passenger and freight services to over 200 destinations worldwide.

ARG maintains offices in each country to which its aircraft fly. Each office provides the following services:

(a) information provision on the airline services offered by ARG, including flight times and destinations serviced by ARG; and

(b) access to ARG's passenger and freight booking system for customers who wish to book either passenger or freight carriage services with ARG.

Each office also has access to ARG's confidential internal data systems which provide information on aircraft location, servicing history and the company's personnel. The latter includes salary details as well as staff locations.

Systems specification

To support its core business activity, ARG recently invested in a high-speed international WAN. This system enabled ARG to transfer large volumes of data relating to its operations between its 200 offices worldwide with a minimum of delay. The systems specification for the new ARG system was quite rigorous. The specification included the following requirements:

(a) the basic infrastructure of the WAN, including such items as the cabling and communication hardware, had to have an expected life of 10 years;

(b) computer chips and other similar system elements had to be upgradable as technology improved; and

(c) the entire system had to be easily upgradable with a fixed capital amount being allocated for this upgrade each year. System upgrades were not to exceed this capital amount under any circumstances.

ARG also assumed that its WAN infrastructure and its core business as an international airline operator would remain unchanged for the next 10 years.

Very few equipment suppliers were willing to provide this level of commitment to the system. Finally, a small but financially stable company called AP Ltd successfully tendered for the contract, even though some of AP Ltd's systems were not industry standard.

Systems implementation

The actual systems changeover and implementation were performed with few problems. The staff at ARG were using the new system efficiently within one week of implementation.

It should be noted that the Board of ARG made the decision to invest in the WAN on the basis that the company must be at the forefront of the use of technology to support its core business activities. This strategy is seen as being essential to produce a sustainable competitive advantage in the airline industry.

Post-implementation review

In the three months since the system was installed, ARG has seen significant increases in productivity and levels of customer service. The investment has therefore been judged to be a success.

During the post-implementation review of the system, it was found that the WAN had considerable excess capacity to take additional network traffic. ARG's initial forecast showed that it would use only one third of the capacity of the network in its first two years of operation. Even optimistic forecasts of network traffic growth indicate that this excess capacity would not be used by ARG for at least another 7 years. The Board of ARG therefore asked the IT Director to consider ways of providing additional revenue to the company from this excess capacity.

After detailed consideration of the problem, the IT Director reported back to the Board. The main proposal was to make this excess capacity available to other companies which required a WAN but either did not have the money, or the strategy to build a WAN for themselves. Should the proposal be accepted, then it is expected that these other companies would require:

(a) a guarantee of the level of service that they can expect from ARG, including access rights to the WAN and delivery times of information across the network;

(b) Internet access to transfer data to customers and receive information back from customers;

(c) guarantee of security of data both from non-ARG WAN users and from the staff of ARG itself.

The IT Director considers that ARG could provide this service whilst at the same time giving a positive contribution to profits. The Board has therefore decided to accept the IT Director's proposal and make the required additional investment to provide the additional services noted above. This decision was made against the advice of a minority of Board members who saw potential conflicts between the core business strategy and the IT strategy of ARG.

Required

(a) (i) Explain why large companies should have an IT strategy. You should make reference to ARG's situation in your explanation. **8 Marks**

(ii) Comment on the decision of ARG to diversify away from its core business by making the WAN services available to other users. Explain the potential advantages and disadvantages this will provide for the company. **14 Marks**

(b) Explain the characteristics that information provided across the ARG WAN, to ARG offices, must have. Show why these characteristics are relevant to ARG. **10 Marks**

(c) Comment on any problems that will arise in ARG's IT systems from the decision not to upgrade ARG's basic IT infrastructure for the next ten years. Explain any impacts this will have on the core business of ARG. **8 Marks**

(d) (i) Evaluate the potential dangers and benefits, both to ARG and to its potential WAN users, of providing Internet access. **8 Marks**

(ii) Explain how ARG can provide adequate data security to the companies which are paying to use its WAN.

You should consider the potential security problems posed by other WAN customers, by ARG's airline customers and by the employees of ARG itself. **12 Marks**

Total Marks = 60

55 JTK LTD: DAILY BREAD (5/97) *108 mins*

Company background

The SF group is in the food processing and production business. The group comprises 42 companies, each of which specialises in a particular food. For example, some companies manufacture sweets and confectionery whilst others produce bread, drinks or other basic consumer foods.

One of the companies in the group, JTK Ltd, produces bread, cakes and similar products. It produces 3 million loaves of bread each day and supplies 15% of the total bread demand for the country in which it operates. JTK Ltd's strategy is to sell as much bread as possible, making only a small margin on each loaf sold. This strategy has worked well in the past because most customers base their decision to purchase bread more on the price than the quality of the product.

Over the past 20 years, JTK Ltd has had two instances of adverse publicity about the quality of its bread. As a result of these, JTK Ltd ensured that the quality of the product was improved and quickly regained its market share.

Production process

The bread manufacturing system is based on the feedback model. This is shown on the diagram below.

JTK Ltd - Overview of production quality control system

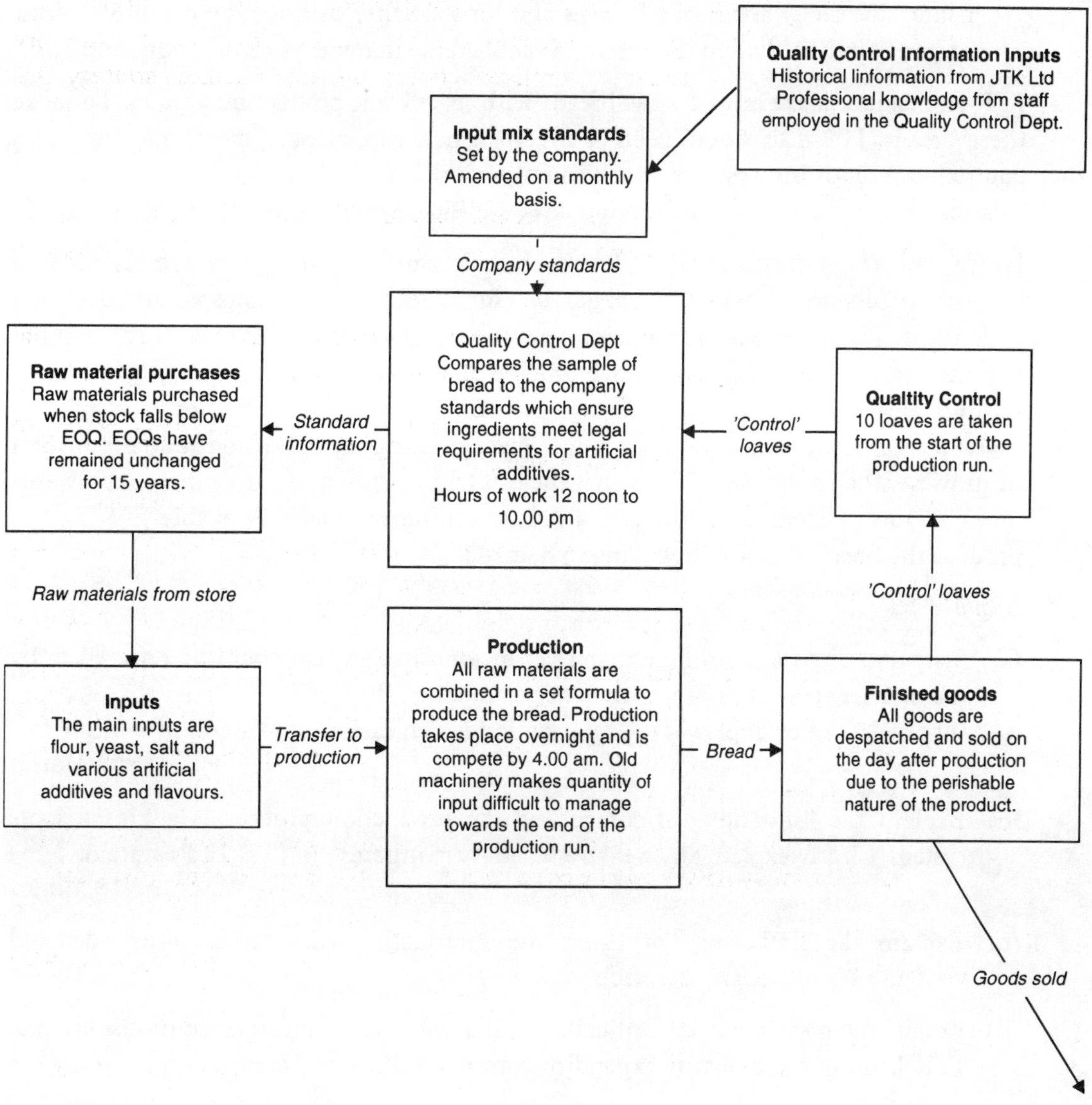

Average raw material stocks have shown a small but marked increase over the last five years although suppliers have improved the efficiency of their delivery systems.

The production process is operating at full capacity.

Different staff work in the quality control department each day, on a rotation basis. Results from the day's quality control checks are pinned to a notice board along with summaries of changes to input mixes and any problems. This attempts to ensure that information concerning each day's quality control checks reaches the staff working on the next day.

Board opinions and market trends

Janice, a recently qualified and newly appointed Management Accountant, has obtained a copy of a market survey into the bread market. The survey predicts that:

(a) the demand for basic cheap bread will change in the next three years in line with the following information:

Probability	*Demand*	
0.1	Increase by	10%
0.3	Decrease by	10%
0.3	Decrease by	15%
0.2	Decrease by	25%
0.1	Decrease by	35%

(b) over the same timescale, it is certain that demand will increase for breads containing fewer artificial additives and for speciality breads (like bread with fruit or honey in it) although the extent of the increase in demand cannot be quantified.

JTK Ltd cannot make any of these breads with its current production system. To make these breads, JTK Ltd would need to invest in new capital equipment and computer-controlled monitoring systems for this equipment. This investment would replace the existing capital equipment and provide some additional production capacity.

Janice took this information to a board meeting and presented it in a fairly forceful manner in support of her recommendation for investment in new specialised capital equipment. The other board members were very sceptical of it. They are of the opinion that the company has made profits over the last 20 years and will continue to do so in the future. They consider that the market research information is incorrect and plan to invest a significant amount of money in new capital equipment to continue production in its present form. Janice believes that the capital investment must be directed towards new computer systems and specialised capital equipment that will enable JTK Ltd to produce the breads that are increasing in demand.

Required

(a) State and discuss the different sources of information that could be referred to by the management of JTK Ltd in order to monitor the quality of bread that is being supplied. Give examples of the information which each source might provide.
14 Marks

(b) Explain the limitations of controlling the production process as a 'closed loop' system. Clearly explain any weaknesses that are inherent in JTK Ltd's system.
18 Marks

(c) Explain the limitations of using the information concerning future demand contained in the market research survey. **8 Marks**

(d) Comment on the financial Critical Success Factors and Performance Indicators that JTK Ltd can use to justify expenditure on its capital equipment as proposed by the new Management Accountant. Comment on any problems that might arise with using these CSFs and PIs. **12 Marks**

(e) Comment on the problems that quality control staff may find with using a notice board to display quality control information, and explain how a computerised bulletin board system could help to alleviate these problems. **8 Marks**

Note. No knowledge of actual bread production processes is required to answer these questions.

Total Marks = 60

56 SPK PLC: MOTOR VEHICLES (11/97) *108 mins*

Company background

SPK plc manufactures motor vehicles, with annual sales of £560 million. This represents about 50,000 cars sold per annum.

Five years ago, the company formed a strategic planning unit to review the market for motor vehicles. Its remit was to report back to the Board on a regular basis concerning potential changes to the market, and make recommendations concerning the future production of motor vehicles within the company.

The most recent report from the unit identified a growing customer preference for motor vehicles which are highly tailored to customers' individual requirements. Customers are starting to express preferences, not only for the colour of the vehicle being purchased, but also more fundamental features like the size of doors and the ability to add, on demand, extras like air conditioning. The unit has recommended that SPK plc should establish a new production line which can produce motor vehicles to individual customer orders. In the past, catering to customer requirements to this extent has been possible only in expensive, non-automated, factories.

If the unit's proposal is accepted, the new production line will provide a similar product, but at a reduced cost because of increased use of industrial robots. The customer will, in effect, be able to design the motor vehicle that they require, using a computer terminal in the car showroom, and then have this built by the new production line. It is recognised that many customers in the showroom will not be computer-literate. While customers might therefore expect that the designing of their own car will be fun, it is also likely that they will require some guidance from the system to explain how it should be used.

Decision on new production line

On 14 November, the Board agreed in principle to the proposal to establish a new production line, although more information was requested. Three separate requests for information were sent on behalf of the Board to different sections of the company: to the chief executive office, the production manager and the operational manager. Extracts from the responses to these requests are shown below.

MEMORANDUM

From: Chief Executive of SPK plc — To: The Board of SPK plc

Private and confidential — 14 November 1997

Proposal to build new production line

The proposal to build a new production line will involve the following:

- Increase in factory space. This will cost between £5 million and £20 million.
- Use of CAD/CAM production processes.
- The assumption is that the market will expand by 20% per annum over the next five years.

Board authority will be required for:

- the total cost of new proposal including factory, investment in automation and additional annual costs of employees, and
- the design and build of CAD/CAM system including customer interfaces at car showrooms.

The critical success factor for the investment will be the raw material cost per tonne of steel used in the production process.

MEMORANDUM

To: Chief Executive of SPK plc — From: Production Manager

Private and confidential — 20 November 1997

Proposal to build new production line

Information requested in your memo of 14 November:

Budget for production line - assumption 15,000 units produced per annum:

	£'000
Materials	51,326.94
Labour	32,223.90
Automation expenditure	19,294.96
Sales forecast (at average selling price)	180,008.08
Additional staff required	1,702

Detailed budgets are on the enclosed disk because it would take too long to print out all the information. The budgets should be reviewed to ensure that a complete picture of the proposal is obtained. The program used is the new spreadsheet purchased by the department last month.

MEMORANDUM

To: Chief Executive of SPK plc

From: Operations manager's assistant:
Personnel and Requisitioning Dept

Private and confidential

16 November 1997

Proposal to build new production line

Information requested by your memo of 14 November. Unfortunately, the operations manager is on long-term sick leave. I have therefore produced this information to show my best guess of the future figures. A more detailed report will be available when the manager returns.

Personnel

Additional staff can be hired at £325 per week. The labour market is generally buoyant at present and it is unlikely that more than 1,200 workers can be found in the local area. Increasing wages to £350 per week should provide up to 1,500 workers. A recruitment company can help find the required staff at a fee of 15% of wages, although there is a 20% chance that 35% of these workers will still need £365 per week. This means that 20% of them will leave in the first six months with a probability of 0.1.

Absenteeism rates are currently at industry standard of five days per annum. In fact we are doing about the same here compared to other similar industries as well.

Materials

The average material costs are:

	£
Body	1,252.89
Car interior	483.32
Engine and accessories	739.16
'Extras' requested by customers	328.24

Each car produced could vary by a further £387 from the above depending on the complexity of the specification received from the customer.

Factory cost

The factory cost will be in the region of £5 million to £20 million.

Required

(a) (i) Explain briefly the characteristics of information that will be used at each of the strategic, tactical and operational levels of management in SPK plc. **6 Marks**

(ii) Critically assess the information provided in the three reports. Your answer should show whether or not this information meets the required characteristics for information at that management level. **18 Marks**

(b) Appraise the importance of information technology in SPK plc's new system. In particular, suggest which parts of the new system could not work without the use of information technology. **10 Marks**

(c) Explain the responsibilities for, and action that should be taken in respect of, data security for each of the strategic, tactical and operational levels of management in SPK plc.

You may refer to appropriate data protection legislation when answering this question. **12 Marks**

(d) Explain the different hardware and software elements of the human computer interface which will be used in the showroom where the customers design their own cars. Show how these elements can be made to help the customer make a complete and accurate input into the computer system. **14 Marks**

Total Marks = 60

Note: No knowledge of the car manufacturing process is required to answer this question.

57 TEP PLC: THEME PARK (5/98) *108 mins*

Scenario

Background

TEP plc runs a theme park offering a wide range of activities including rides, shows and parades. The rides vary from 'thrill' rides, where visitors sit in vehicles which travel around a hilly track at high speed, to slow electric-powered cars in which children can drive around. Visitors pay an entrance fee which gives them unlimited access for one day to the park's activities. The average entry price is £16 and the park received 2.6 million visitors in 1997. It employs about 6,000 staff for about 9 months of the year: the park closes during a season of poor weather.

It is considered to be the most popular park in the country in which it operates, although in recent years it has tended to attract more young adults and fewer families with younger children. Market research undertaken by TEP plc indicates that families tend to avoid the park because there are very few attractions for children below the age of 10. Many of the technologically advanced rides built by TEP plc have age and height restrictions, making them unsuitable for young children.

The objectives of TEP plc are to

- maintain net profit margins at 10%, and
- offer the most technologically up-to-date rides.

The company has met these objectives during its last seven years of operation. However, a number of other parks have opened in recent years, offering similar state-of-the-art attractions and rides. These parks have placed considerable competitive pressure on TEP plc. The main area of competition between the parks is in providing the most technologically advanced ride possible, whilst at the same time making the ride sufficiently attractive for customers to want to return to the park to go on the ride again. As a result of this competition, the average cost of providing a new ride is £6 million with annual maintenance costs running at 10% of this amount.

Current information systems

The theme park's information system was installed seven years ago and has received only minor modifications since then. It concentrates on collecting information concerning:

- customers entering the park, including cash collection and banking (payment is accepted by cash and credit cards),
- stock and sales control of the retail outlets, and

- the number of customers using each ride.

The Directors' Executive Information System was also installed seven years ago. The EIS is linked to the park's information system, providing the ability to view the daily totals from this system. In the early 1990s, this was considered to be the only data that the Directors required from the computer systems. The Directors now hardly ever use the EIS.

Both the EIS and the park information system are backed up daily with the backup disks being kept in a fire-proof safe in the ticket office on site.

Although there are plans to advertise the park on the World Wide Web, the project has been delayed.

Investment decision in 1998

After a substantial review of the theme park market, TEP plc has identified what it considers to be a new area where competitive advantage can be obtained. At present, all the theme parks in the country only offer facilities at the park itself. The board of TEP plc believes that the company should

- build a modern hotel within the park offering accommodation for families with children
- offer a complete holiday package to customers including travel arrangements, accommodation at the hotel, special offers like early entry to the park and souvenirs such as special mugs
- provide more shows and rides suitable for younger children to encourage more families to visit the park and
- purchase a specialist travel agency to provide the holiday package service

The cost of this investment would be in the region of £6 million, although the hotel would not be operational until the 1999 season.

If the investment is undertaken, it is expected that the travel agency will be able to

- access the hotel's computer system to book accommodation via an Internet connection
- provide details of special events directly from TEP plc's theme park Web Site and
- provide an on-line booking and payments system through its own Web Site for customers who prefer using the Internet to book their holiday

If the hotel investment is made, then no new ride would be produced in 1998. The policy of building one new ride per year would be re-introduced in 1999.

As an *alternative*, TEP plc could continue its present policy of investing in one major new ride each year. This would help it maintain its position of being the most technologically advanced park in the country. The ride under consideration is a virtual reality simulator of a spaceship crashing into one of Saturn's moons. It will cost £6.2 million to develop and build. So far, no other theme park has considered using virtual reality on such a large scale.

The Board must choose between these two investment decisions by the end of June this year.

Required

(a) Identify possible sources of internal and external information that could be used to assist the directors of TEP plc in choosing between the two investment decisions.

Explain why each source of information is relevant to the decision-making process. **14 Marks**

(b) For this part of this question, assume that the first investment alternative is taken up, ie including the building of the hotel and the purchase of the travel agency. In this part, you must concentrate on the amalgamation of the computer systems in TEP plc and the travel agency.

Required

Explain the key areas that the systems analyst will have to investigate during the analysis and design phase of the Systems Development Life Cycle in respect of the above. **16 Marks**

(c) For this part of the question also, assume that the first investment alternative is taken up, ie including the building of the hotel and the purchase of the travel agency.

Required

Explain the changes that need to be made to the EIS and the information it provides, to enable the Directors of TEP plc to receive the information needed to evaluate the success of this investment. **10 Marks**

(d) Comment on the backup alternatives available to TEP plc and provide a recommendation for the secure backup of its computer systems. **8 Marks**

(e) Comment on the effect on society and on working practices within the organisation of the decision of many companies to concentrate their advertising and booking systems on the Internet. 'Booking' in this context means customers being able to access TEP plc's computer system via an Internet connection, and then choosing and paying for their park visit using only the computer system. **12 Marks**

Total Marks = 60

58 KJ PLC: OFFICE SUPPLIES (11/98) *108 mins*

Introduction to KJ plc

KJ plc supplies office and stationery products by mail order to a wide range of companies and individuals. Customers telephone or fax their orders to KJ plc's sales department which takes the order details, checks the stock in real-time to ensure that the order can be fulfilled and then transfers the order to a central warehouse for packing the stock ready to deliver to the customer. All orders received before 5.00pm are delivered on the next working day.

Because KJ plc is in a service industry, it has always tried to maintain a good standard of customer service. On the whole, this objective has been met. A recent survey of 100 customers, which asked them to rank the importance of various aspects of the business, produced the information shown in *Table 2* on page 65.

Existing computer systems

KJ plc's transaction processing system provides a vast amount of information, which is used by managers at all levels in the organisation. Very few complaints have been received concerning the information that is normally supplied. The DP department has therefore concentrated on maintaining the system and fine-tuning this to requests of employees, where the managing director would allow this. Significant change was not allowed because of the authoritarian approach of the MD.

IT strategy

The main objectives of the IT strategy have been to

- ensure goal congruence between the different sections of the company (such as sales, warehouse despatch and stock control) so that they are all working together to provide good customer service,
- ensure that good service has been provided to customers, *from the point of view of the customer*, and
- maintain an acceptable transaction processing system.

This strategy has been successfully implemented in recent years. However, there is now evidence of potential problems: a meeting of managers has revealed that some managers are uncomfortable with the MD's authoritarian style of management, and the latest customer survey indicates revised customer priorities.

Management structure

The MD takes most tactical and strategic decisions. This limits the decision-making ability of managers and has resulted in a fairly high staff turnover in middle management positions.

Middle management now consists of two distinct groups: a minority of long-serving managers who are satisfied that the MD should continue to make most of the strategic/tactical decisions, and a majority who have been recently appointed and would like to take a more active role in decision-making. The concerns of the majority were expressed to the MD in a recent meeting. One manager from this group resigned following the lack of any definite action plan from the MD. Also, as a result of this meeting, some long-serving managers have been expressing dissatisfaction with the amount of control exercised by the MD.

The MD has finally recognised the need to enhance the decision-making opportunities of his managers, although he does not know how to implement an acceptable solution.

Systems change information

Because the computer systems are now approximately 5 years old and maintenance and other costs are increasing, the board of KJ plc has decided to replace the Transaction Processing System. Two alternative systems are currently under review, details of which are given in *Table 1* over the page. The company could pay for either alternative by outright cash purchase or an operating lease agreement.

Table 1

	Alternative One	Alternative Two
Supplier	KJ plc's current supplier (well-established but not industry-standard).	Y plc, an established supplier specialising in IBM-compatible equipment.
System structure	Centralised, with one large main-frame computer being maintained by a specialist department. All staff would have access to a common database, which would keep information concerning all of the company's activities. The MD would retain control of major decisions regarding the computer system.	De-centralised, with each department maintaining its own computer systems and making its own decisions regarding the use of those systems. Managers would be given responsi-bility to make the tactical and opera-tional decisions necessary to run their own departments and computer systems. Essential information, like store transactions, would still be shared, but via an internal Intranet system, not by all individuals having access to a shared database.
New features	Delivery times decreased to allow same-day deliveries in major cities for orders placed before 11.00 am. A fully integrated system will mean that stock-outs can be rectified within 24 hours, not 72 which is the fastest time under the existing system.	E-mail for all employees and Internet access for some employees. Ease of upgrade due to purchase of industry-standard equipment. Customer orders will be taken by telephone, fax, e-mail or Internet, with the company's own branded products being offered as a first choice in all ordering methods. Speed of delivery is likely to be adversely affected be-cause of the increased time required to transfer information between the company's new computer systems.
Information to be provided	The same as KJ plc's existing system with the addition of a strategic planning module for use by the MD. Historical data from the old system would not be transferred, although access to this would continue to be available up to six months after the system changeover.	A full range of strategic to operational information to meet all managers' information needs, including some powerful database query tools designed for analysis of old data-bases. Key historical information would be available on the new system if managers can afford to make the transfer from their own department budgets.

Table 2

Customer survey information

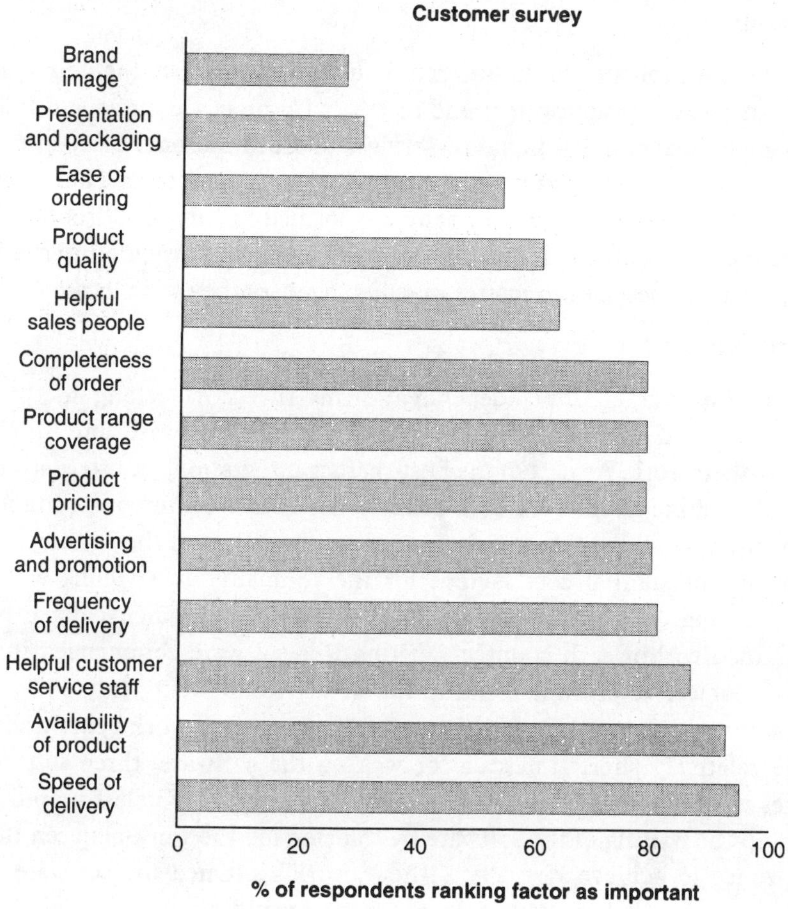

Required

(a) Compare the two new systems to show whether either of them would provide an acceptable basis for the three key areas of IT strategy for KJ plc. **22 Marks**

(b) Explain to what extent KJ plc's current system meets the information requirements of managers in the company, and whether you consider Alternatives One and Two would provide any improvement in the information provided. **14 Marks**

(c) KJ plc is considering obtaining new computer equipment either by outright cash purchase or by an operating lease.

Required

Contrast the strategic and operational advantages to KJ plc of these two alternatives. **8 Marks**

(d) Assume that Alternative Two is adopted by the company.

(i) Discuss how the motivation of all managers can be improved by implementing this system. **10 Marks**

(ii) Comment on the actions that can be taken with the introduction of Alternative Two that might lead managers to accept more responsibility. **6 Marks**

Total Marks = 60

59 JHG PLC: FINANCIAL SERVICES (5/99) *108 mins*

Scenario

Background

JHG has 256 branches in 26 different countries worldwide including the USA and the UK; in most European capitals, and in Kuala Lumpur, Colombo and Johannesburg. The company offers specialist financial services to multi-national companies including audit and assurance advice, systems analysis and systems assurance. The company employs in excess of 21,000 people. The company was formed in July 1998 from the merger of firms within the 26 countries. The aim of the merger was to provide international companies with a standard service, no matter in which country they were located.

Use of software

Prior to the merger, the independent firms that now belong to the JHG Company established and maintained their own computer hardware and software systems to support their work. As part of the post-merger integration, an international committee of senior Board members from each country has been working on producing software that can be used by all branches of the company, regardless of the country in which they are operating. Substantial cost savings for the company, as a whole, will be achieved by amalgamating and rationalising the system development departments currently maintained within each country. Writing this software commenced in December 1998 with the objective of implementing the new system during July 1999, just prior to the busiest months from the point-of-view of the amount of work being undertaken. Because of the relatively short timescale for writing the software, three software development centres were established in London, San Francisco and Kuala Lumpur. The aim was to speed up the writing of the software by transferring the work between the three different time zones to achieve virtually 24-hour working. Once the software is implemented, employees will easily be able to share work, including confidential client information, because they will be using the same system. This will help to provide an enhanced service to JHG's international clients. The client data refers to individual client companies and some of their employees by name.

Additional project information

Reports produced in early March 1999 indicated that the development was proceeding well. Development deadlines were being achieved and the software writers in the three locations had adapted well to the working arrangements.

Key milestones still to be achieved included:

- July 1999 — Confirmation of hardware and software requirements to run the new software
- August 1999 — User input regarding the acceptability of the system
- September 1999 — Release of software and implementation in each country
- January 2000 — Full training material and user guides available

Where the particular laws of any country are not fully accommodated by the software, minor amendments will be required on a national level. This local tailoring will take place towards the end of August 1999.

Current situation - 27 May 1999

The international team of software writers, being quite pleased with the software written to date, decided to release an example of one of the main information screens to be displayed in the system. The team is particularly proud of the innovative use of navigation icons and the inclusion of flower pictures on-screen to provide a more relaxed working environment. An example of the screen to be used is shown below.

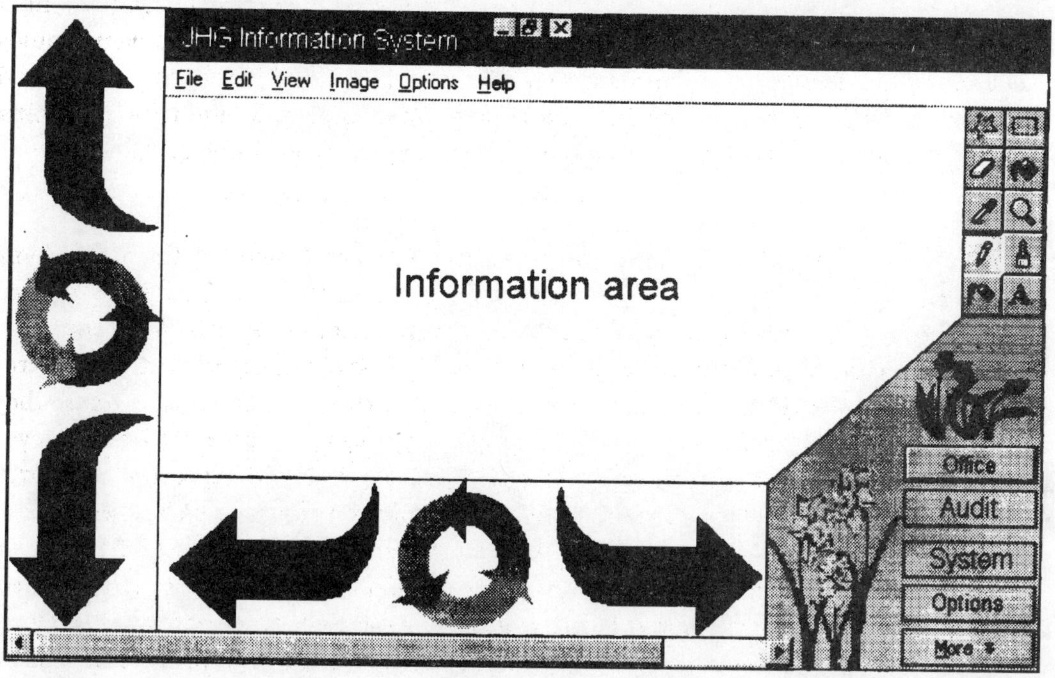

However, the project is failing considerably behind schedule. The international Board is considering two alternatives:

- cancelling the implementation in 1999; or
- asking all branches to use the international version of the software this year, which will mean postponing any local tailoring of the software until the year 2000.

Neither option is particularly acceptable and the Board has yet to make its final decision on this matter.

Required

(a) Explain the reasons why the project as a whole may fail, referring to the stages of the Systems Development Life Cycle as an outline for your answer. **20 Marks**

(b) Explain, from the point-of-view of a Human Information Processor, why the proposed screen layout will make the system difficult to use efficiently. **14 Marks**

For part (c) only, assume that the software system will be implemented this year (1999) without local tailoring

(c) Discuss whether the information needs of local managers will be met by the use of internationally- written software. **14 Marks**

(d) Comment on the risks to JHG of transferring client information between its branches worldwide, and explain the controls that could be implemented to decrease these risks. **12 Marks**

Total Marks = 60

Answer bank

1 TUTORIAL QUESTION: LEVELS OF INFORMATION

(a) **Levels and examples**

Information used **within** an organisation is distinct from information provided by an organisation to **external** users, such as shareholders, the general public, pressure groups, competitors, suppliers and customers.

Internal information can be analysed into three levels: strategic, tactical and operational.

(i) **Strategic information** is used by **senior** managers to plan the **objectives** of their organisation and to assess whether the objectives are being met in practice. In a manufacturing company such information includes overall **profitability**, the profitability of different **segments** of the business, future **market prospects**, the availability and cost of raising **new funds**, total **cash needs**, total **manning levels** and **capital equipment** needs.

Much of this information must come from **environmental sources**, although internally-generated information will always be used. Strategic information will be used for management decision making in **strategic planning** and will be communicated on an **ad hoc** basis rather than as a regular event. Strategic planning may use information gathered **several years ago** and associate it with **current** information both internal and external, so as to analyse **past trends** and predict the **future**.

(ii) **Tactical information** is used by **middle management** to ensure that the **resources** of the business are employed (and the efficiency and effectiveness of their use monitored) to achieve the strategic objectives of the organisation. Such information includes **productivity measurements** (output per man or per machine hour), **budgetary control** or variance analysis reports, **cash flow** forecasts, **manning** levels and **profit** results within a particular department of the organisation, **labour turnover** statistics within a department, **short-term purchasing requirements** etc.

A large proportion of this information will be generated from **within** the organisation (ie as feedback) and is likely to have an **accounting** emphasis. Tactical information is usually prepared **regularly**, perhaps weekly or monthly, and is used for the decision making process usually referred to as **management control**. Management control may also use information several years old (to compare past and current performance) but **historical information** is more likely to have a **limited useful life**.

(iii) **Operational information** is used by **front-line managers** such as foremen or head clerks to ensure that **specific tasks** are planned and carried out properly within a factory or office. Information such as the amount of **raw materials** being put into a production process may be required **daily, hourly** or, in the case of automated production, **second by second**.

Operational information relates to the level of decision making usually referred to as **operational control**. Operational control information has a **short life span**.

Destination and presentation

The destination level of the information is very important as the information must be **material to the user** but without going into **unnecessary** and **time consuming** detail (for a particular user) in order to achieve pointless accuracy.

(i) **Operational control** may need information to be accurate to the nearest penny, minute or kilogram (eg for job costing).

(ii) **Management control** may be satisfied with costs rounded to the nearest £100 or £1,000. Greater detail would serve no purpose.

(iii) **Strategic planning** may be satisfied with figures to the nearest ten thousand, hundred thousand or even million pounds. Estimates to the nearest penny at this level of decision-making could be so inappropriate as to undermine the receivers' confidence in it.

The destination level may also affect the **language** used (for instance technical jargon) and the **medium** (e-mail, confidential report, noticeboard, video, mass meeting and so on).

(b) **Deterministic systems**

A **deterministic** system is one in which various states or activities follow from each other in a completely **predictable** way, ie A will happen, then B, then C. A fully-automated production process is a typical example. A computer program is another.

Probabilistic systems

A **probabilistic** or stochastic system is one in which, although some states or activities can be predicted with certainty, others will occur with **varying degrees of probability**. In business, many systems can be regarded as stochastic systems.

(i) A company's **credit control** department can analyse customer's payment schedule as 10% cash with order, 50% within 1 month of invoice and 40% within 2 months of invoice.

(ii) A purchasing department might assess a **supplier's delivery times** as 0.75 on schedule, 0.20 one week late and 0.05 two weeks late.

These systems are common in advanced technological processes and man/machine relationships. Controlling them involves **quantification** of probability and risk.

Adaptive systems

An **adaptive** system is one which adapts and reacts to a stimulus. The way in which it adapts is uncertain and the same input (stimulus) to the system will not always produce the same output (response). **Social and psychological systems** come within this category. Examples might be as follows.

(i) A **bank** which pays a rate of interest to depositors **depending on the amount of money** in the deposit account. Interest calculations (the output of the system is the calculated interest) will vary as the money in each depositor's account goes up or down.

(ii) A **stock re-ordering system** where the quantity of a stock item that is ordered from a supplier **varies according to changes in the usage** of the item. For example, if consumption of stock item 12345 goes up by 20% in a week, the reorder quantity of the item will be increased.

2 TUTORIAL QUESTION: INFORMATION THEORY

(a) **Control systems**

Control is required because **unpredictable disturbances** arise and enter a system so that **actual** results (output of the system) deviate from the **expected** results or goals.

Examples of disturbances in a business system like that represented by FBK Ltd would be the entry of a **competitor** into the market, an unexpected **rise in payroll costs**, the **failure of a supplier** to deliver promised raw materials, or the tendency of **employees** to stop working in order to chatter. A control system must ensure that FBK's business is capable of **surviving** these disturbances by dealing with them in an appropriate manner. A control system needs to receive and process **information,** and then **act on it** in the appropriate way.

(i) A **sensor** is used to **collect** information about the system, usually recorded on paper or in computer files. Some sensors are **more efficient than others**. A computer turnround document, for example, is better than a manually prepared computer input form because it saves data collection time, and reduces both clerical errors and also data preparation time and effort.

(ii) A **comparator** is the means by which the **actual** results of the system are **measured** against the pre-determined **plans** or system **objectives**. In FBK, the arithmetic of comparison (eg the calculation of variances, or productivity ratios) will be done by computer. Managers, however, will be expected to make some **judgement** on the results of the comparison, to decide whether investigation of the variance is advisable, and then (after investigation) whether control action is required.

(iii) An **effector** is the device or means by which control **action is initiated**, for example a manager's instruction and a subordinate's action, or an automatic adjustment to the input to an advanced technology production process (eg the contents of the adhesive gum on the flap of an envelope).

(iv) **Feedback** is the **return** of part of the **output** of a system to the **input** as a means towards **improved quality** or **correction of error**. A feedback system or a feedback loop is known as a closed loop system while an open loop system is a system with no feedback. A business organisation uses feedback for control, and therefore has a closed loop control system.

(v) **Entropy** is the amount of **disorder or randomness** present in any system. Entropy arises because of the natural tendency of objects and systems to fall into a state of disorder. All inanimate systems display this tendency to degenerate. The term entropy is therefore used as a measure of **disorganisation**. A system will increase its entropy unless it receives **negative entropy** in the form of **information** from its **environment**.

The existence of FBK, for instance, might be threatened by changes in its environment: **changes** in raw material costs set by suppliers or in selling prices set by competitors might cause a company's products to become **unprofitable** and lead to the company's insolvency.

(vi) A **closed system** is a system which is **isolated from its environment** and **independent** of it, so that no environmental influences affect the behaviour of the system, nor does the system exert any influence on its environment. An example of a closed system is a chemical reaction in a sealed, insulated container.

(vii) An **open system** is a system **connected to and interacting with its environment**. It takes in influences (or 'energy') from its environment and also influences this environment by its behaviour (it exports energy). An open system is a stable system which is nevertheless continually changing or evolving. **All social systems**, including **business organisations** such as FBK, are **open systems**.

(viii) The **law of requisite variety** applies to self-regulating systems, such as social systems, including business organisations. The law states that the **variety within a system** must be at least **as great** as the **environmental variety** against which it is attempting to regulate itself. In other words, if there is variety in the environmental influences in the system, then the system itself must be suitably varied and variable to **adapt itself** successfully to its environment. For example, if FBK Ltd's **controls are too rigid** it will eventually find that they are **not appropriate** to deal with **changed conditions.**

(b) **Feedback control**

In a financial systems environment, feedback controls take place where the **results of transaction processes** are used as **input to subsequent processes** to improve quality or correct errors. The feedback data is generated by comparing **actual** results with **pre-set standards** and producing appropriate **exception** information.

Feedback controls in standard costing, credit control and stock control systems are described below.

(i) **Standard costing**

Standards will be pre-set for all the **cost** elements of a product, such as paper, glue, printing costs and packaging, and the system will produce an analysis of **actual costs against these standards.** Exception reporting is a key ingredient of such a system, with 'normal' feedback being ignored. Adverse variances are investigated and appropriate actions taken.

The feedback in a standard costing system will often result in decisions and actions being taken by **people** rather than automatic actions being taken by computers or machines. Action may be taken to **change the standard** rather than attempt to change actual performance, for instance if the costs of a certain weight of paper make the product uneconomic to produce.

(ii) **Credit control**

Feedback from FBK's credit control system will revolve around the trading relationship with customers. The setting of **credit limits** will depend on information supplied by potential customers (actual) achieving the criteria set by the company (plan). A form of **automated control** will be the rejection of sales orders (actual) by the system if existing credit limits (plan) would be exceeded by executing a further order. However, this will often take the form of an **exception report** so that **management** can take the final decision rather than the machine.

Regular **aged debt analyses** are an important form of feedback in a credit control system, resulting in action being taken to collect outstanding debts, and in extreme cases legal action being initiated.

(iii) **Stock control**

Feedback control routines in FBK's stock systems are likely to be **more automated** than in the other areas described. For instance, setting minimum, maximum and **re-order levels** enables the stock system to make **automatic decisions** about re-ordering stock, with the production of a purchase order being the action taken. If just-in-time links with suppliers are in place the system may even decide which supplier to order from.

Another common example of feedback in a stock system is the preparation of **slow-moving stock listings** which may lead to increases in obsolescence provisions or bulk sales of slow moving parts. In FBK, stationery pre-printed with an old date or an old format phone number might be prime candidates.

3 TUTORIAL QUESTION: LOGICAL DATABASE MODELS

Once Traders plc has completed its data analysis it will have built up a picture of **entity and attribute types** in the system and of the **relationships** between them. This picture will be in the form of a **conceptual model.**

(a) A model which consists entirely of '**one to many**' or '**many to one**' relationships can be expressed in a **hierarchical** structure. Traders plc may maintain a database of its raw materials stock in this manner.

Each data item is related to **one item above** it, but to **any number of items below** it. The search for data is split into levels, reducing the search time required and speeding up access times. The main drawback is that users are **limited in the number of ways** that they can **search** for records, which can create inefficiencies where there is not a true hierarchical relationship between the data items.

(b) Relationships can also be expressed in a **network** structure. Traders plc may use a network model to represent the above relationship.

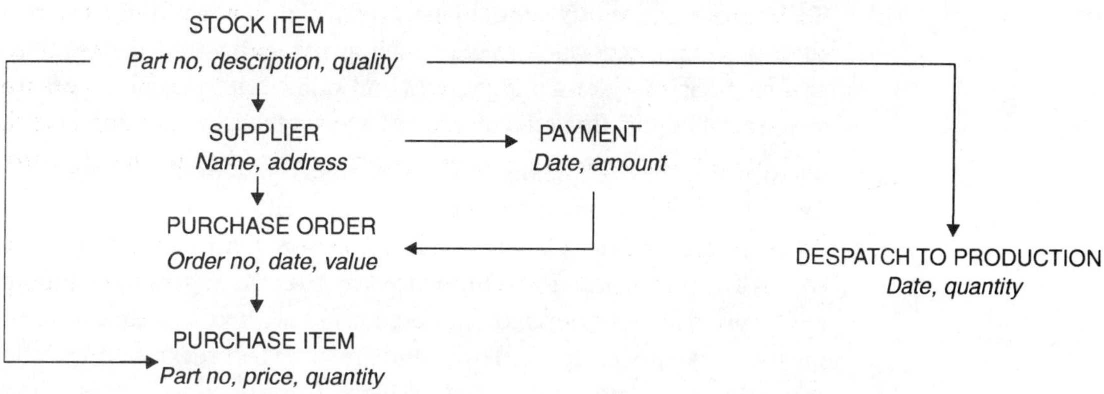

Here, the hierarchical structure does not exist. The network data structure also allows **many to many** relationships to be expressed, as where a record has **more than one parent**. In this model a **search** can be made **in any direction,** not just downwards through the levels. The disadvantage is that there may still be some **duplication** of data.

(c) The **relational** model is the **most commonly used** model in current database design. A relational model organises data elements in a **two dimensional table**. Each **row** represents an **entity** and each **column** shows the **attributes** of that entity.

STOCK ITEM	*Part number, description, quantity*
SUPPLIER	*Name, address*
PURCHASE ORDER	*Order number, date, value*
PAYMENT	*Date, amount*

The relational model does **not** represent **all** connections within a set of information. Instead it shows an **association** between **certain data items**. In the relation **STOCK ITEM**, there is an association between the part number, the part description and the quantity in stock.

Associations can be established outside an individual relation where two rows have the **same value for a shared attribute**, eg if **value** for **PURCHASE ORDER** is the same as **amount** for **PAYMENT**, then the two may be **linked**.

The key to successful relational models is that **no information about the associations between items must be omitted** from the model. The process of reducing complex relationships to a two-dimensional tabular form is **normalisation**. In this process each set of relations is broken down into new sets, each of which has a progressively more regular structure.

4 TUTORIAL QUESTION: CRITICAL SUCCESS FACTORS

(a) **Critical Success Factors**

The critical success factors which apply to SEC may include the following.

(i) **To provide a quality education**. This will be difficult to measure, because its achievement can only really be assessed by comparison with other local education authorities. Nationally-based standards might be used in this regard.

(ii) **To improve secondary school pass rates**. This is one of the most important success factors and would need to be analysed by subject or subject area against a backdrop of demographics and other criteria such as geographical area, age of pupils, first/second attempt and actual grades received.

(iii) **To provide further education for secondary school leavers**. This will depend to a large extent on the outcome of (ii) above. There will be little point in many of the less successful candidates continuing in education and so this factor is bound to be influenced by pass rates, as well as by the range and type of courses offered (for example does 'tertiary education' include modern apprenticeships?). Better students may be prepared to travel outside the authority's region and study elsewhere. It is not clear if this is allowed for in the current calculation of figures.

(iv) **To increase public confidence**. SEC has set itself an objective of increasing public confidence by 1% per annum. This is a long-term CSF which, as the current situation shows, is difficult to measure as well as difficult to achieve. Again this will be largely dependent on exam pass rates. Another factor to consider is the percentage of school/college leavers actually in full-time employment, say, 6 and 12 months later.

There may be other factors such as, for example, class sizes, teacher-pupil ratios, primary school pupil ability/testing and truancy which are crucial to success: those listed above are derived directly from the mission statement and stated objectives.

Data sources

These critical success factors can be reviewed and the company's ability to meet them checked by reference to the following data sources.

(i) **External examination results.** These will be issued by the various examination boards following each exam sitting. They will provide information for the authority's region and also nationally, providing a useful measure of how well the authority is performing.

(ii) **Enrolments at further education establishments.** This will provide information for establishing the proportions of pupils going into tertiary education. As noted earlier, 'imports' and 'exports' will need to be considered. This information will be available from individual colleges.

(iii) **Internal examination results.** These will be useful for forecasting how well future generations of exam candidates can be expected to perform. They will be available from each school.

(iv) **Numbers of leavers in employment.** This can only really be done by staying in touch with leavers and finding out what they are doing. This will need to be handled at individual establishment level, as this is where lines of contact exist already. Reference to national figures may provide scope for limited comparison, but local factors will influence these figures considerably.

(v) **Public satisfaction.** This will be hard to measure as a separate factor. Parents of children at primary and secondary school can be canvassed, perhaps by means of questionnaires. Students can also be asked to provide feedback on their courses. Records should be kept of complaints made and how they were dealt with.

(vi) **Reports by school inspectors** will give an objective view of aspects of performance.

(vii) **Performance figures for other education establishments,** such as private sector ('independent') schools.

(b) **Limitations of performance indicators**

Whatever performance measurements are used by SEC, it is inevitable that they will suffer from the standard statistical weakness of **comparing 'like with like'**. In the case of the comparisons between authorities and between establishments described above, there are naturally areas where different social classes tend to gather, and dwell, which means that unfair comparisons will be made when looking at **pass rates** for example.

Individual indicators can also be **misleading**, eg a school with few teachers could be showing very high exam successes per member of staff ratio compared with a better funded school with more staff. It is, therefore, important to use **several indicators** to obtain the **full picture**.

The **collection and interpretation** of data also represents a limitation of the performance indicators. In the case of public confidence, questionnaires with **ambiguous questions and/or answers** can distort the measure.

5 WR RAILWAY CO: INFORMATION EXCHANGES

> **Pass marks**. This question requires knowledge of the different types of information required at different levels of an organisation. This does not mean that you should churn out lots of theory on the Anthony hierarchy, but you should think carefully about how the theory applies to specific situations.
>
> **Examiner's comment.** In (a), many answers jumped straight to providing a solution to any perceived problems, instead of providing an analysis of those problems first. A minority of answers simply listed the attributes of information and therefore failed to obtain many marks. A number of candidates commented that there was little difference between part (a) and part (b), but it is quite clear that part (a) is about accuracy and (b) about presentation.

(a) **Information exchanges and proposed changes**

The exchange of information within WR has some **serious defects**, which can be summarised as follows.

(i) The origin of all the information is the summary of the transactions produced at the end of each day by the **ticket office clerks**. It is known that this information 'is collated in a hurry and **mistakes** are common'. The exchange of this information to the Analyst is therefore lacking in the most important feature of information - **accuracy**. Decisions based on this information may therefore be flawed.

The information would be **improved** by allowing a **delay** in collating it. If the collation were done during the course of the following day, perhaps outside rush hours and other peak travel periods, when there is an **absence of time pressure**, the results could be made more accurate, and there may be opportunities for **checking**. Thus in the exchange of information **speed** will be sacrificed for **accuracy**.

Currently, it is unlikely that income will be correctly allocated to trains. If this income per train could be reconciled to ticket sales, **greater confidence** in the figures would be possible.

(ii) The **Analyst** uses the information to produce information on the profitability of each train and passes this to the planner and the senior manager. However, there is **no summarisation** of this information, and therefore **no analysis of trends** or **identification of patterns**, no correlation of profitability and the classification of data. The analyst has simply added more information, **not analysed** it. There is far too much detail, especially considering that there are 189 stations and 75,000 kilometres of track. The exchange of this information to the senior manager and planner **lacks clarity**. The senior manager and planner will both have to analyse the data received. Some form of **exception reporting** is essential.

(iii) The **planner** receives the information from the analyst, so the actual analysis will need to be repeated. The information **exchange** is therefore **occurring at the wrong point** in the information chain. The process would be improved by the analyst producing summaries of the daily data: highlights should then be passed to the planner.

Given the key nature of the **planner's role** and his impact on major decisions, the **information** he receives is **totally inadequate**. Decisions on changing timetables or opening new services **cannot be justified** on the basis of the information received currently. Nor should they be made after only two weeks (maximum) investigation and analysis. A fifty report prepared in this way is certain to compound earlier inaccuracies and introduce new ones.

A standard **feasibility report format** should be agreed and a **longer time period** provided for **proper analysis** of base data, which as noted above, should itself be more accurate.

(iv) The **senior manager** will make decisions concerning the number and frequency of trains being run, but the planner is using the same information to give recommendations for these decisions, so the **summarised information** should go to the **senior manager** together with the recommendations from the planner, not separately. In turn, the **senior manager** needs to communicate with the planner to **provide feasibility study briefs**.

The whole system could benefit from **automatic data collection** and **computerised analysis** tools. The railway already has its own communication links which could be used to facilitate **networking**. Any **cost/benefit** analysis of using information technology this way would have to include the cost of making decisions on the inaccurate data presently available.

(b) **Effective presentation and use of information**

The information required by the **ticket office clerk** is the **timetable** itself. The written page will be familiar to the clerk who doubtless will be able to use the information well. However, for passengers requesting complex journeys that require connections between trains on different routes, with the possibility of alternative choices, the process of referring to different timetables and **cross referencing** them can be **very time consuming**, even for an experienced clerk.

The most effective way of presenting this information would be via a **computer program** that would allow the entry of **start** and **destination** points with desired **time of arrival**, and would print out and display the times and connections of the optimum route. The clerk's prime task is to provide a service to the customer, and the **rapid supply of answers** to the customer needs is a key element of this service. Such a service could include **ancillary details** such as location of guards van (for bicycles and other bulky goods), availability of dining car or through-train buffet service, location of first class carriages etc.

The **analyst** would be best served by data presented as formatted **computer files**, which could be **manipulated by statistical programs**, possibly using spreadsheets. This would allow the analyst to summarise the data consistently, and introduce statistical monitoring for unusual occurrences. Manipulating data is the analyst's job.

The **senior manager** would be best served by a combination of **written report** and **verbal presentation** by the planner. Key strategic decisions rest on the quality of understanding of the senior manager, so the planner should be given the opportunity to **explain** his or her recommendations, **answer questions** and **investigate further** as required.

The role of the **senior manager** is to **maximise return** on capital, whilst satisfying **social criteria**. Deciding to change timetables, and extend the rail network, involves considerable commercial risk. The information the senior manager uses is designed to enable him or her to maximise return while minimising that risk.

The **planner** is using **external** data as well as **internal**.

(i) The **internal** data is best presented in summary form, using **graphics** to highlight **exceptions**, and ideally with a **visual model** that will represent the **volumes of traffic** at different times on the various routes. The model should also be able to show the effect of through journeys, so that the dependence of different lines upon each other is considered when making recommendations.

(ii) **External data** should include **population** densities within a given radius of each station, **geodemographic** data, data on **socio-economic trends** (commuting, private motor vehicles etc) and alternative means of transport.

Only when all this information is available can the planner do his/her job properly.

6 RG LTD: INFORMATION NEEDS

Pass marks. Part (b) is typical of Stage 4 in that it takes standard information that candidates are likely to have learned from textbooks and asks for the **opposite** of that information. In other words it forces you to **think**. You can practise this technique whenever you are studying. For instance if you are learning a list of the qualities of good information, write out a list of qualities that you would expect **bad information** to possess, and try to think of an example.

Examiner's comment. In part (a)(i) it was not enough just to identify weaknesses (for example the business plan is prepared by someone new). More marks were earned by candidates who gave some further explanation of the weakness (for example a new person is unlikely to have a sufficiently deep understanding of the company). In (a)(ii) poorer answers simply listed the general features of a MIS without reference back to the case study material. In (b) candidates who merely provided a list of the outputs that a MIS or EIS **can** provide missed the point of the question and scored few marks.

(a) Overall (parts (i) and (ii)) the information currently provided is of an **operational** level and **not suitable** for **senior** managers. The strategic information that the MIS will be able to generate is only one part of the information required by directors, and for their use it should be **summarised** and targeted specifically at the **critical success factors** of the company so that information overload is avoided.

(i) **Weaknesses in the current information**

Business plan

The summary business plan does not take into account the **past data** and therefore it does not take account of past **trends**. Past trends are not necessarily relevant to what will happen in the future (their relevance will vary from organisation to organisation, industry to industry and year to year), but they do give an indication of the RG's **current** ability to respond to changes and may suggest what problems brought the company to a position where it was only just breaking even.

The plan was prepared by a **new** (and perhaps fairly junior) member of staff who is **unlikely to have a full understanding** of the company or the industry.

Although the plan includes estimates of the future incomes and expenditure on **existing** product lines, it does not include any **potential** development such as **new** products. In any case, it is not clear whether this information was derived from a **reliable** source.

Arguably, the plan **does not look far enough ahead** (only two years). Uncertainty invariably increases the further one looks into the future but two years is probably not long enough to give the company a real sense of long-term direction. (It could be argued, though, that **short-term survival** is so crucial that this emphasis is correct.)

Stock balances

The stock balances are **much too detailed** for directors. They would not be able to spot trends or even identify quickly the areas that needed special attention. The data here is **operational** information for stock controllers or purchasing staff.

In any case, with 400 inputs going into only 35 outputs, **individual balances do not give the complete picture**. For example, how could management assess whether raw materials stock levels were too low to make a particular product, or much higher than necessary, even taking into account each different product's raw materials needs?

Summary of changes in demand

The summary of changes in demand appears to be **difficult to view** on screen and therefore the **impact of the information will be lost**, however useful it may be in theory.

Apparently the information is all numerical and it is segregated into sections so it is **difficult to make any meaningful comparisons** or identify trends. The **summary is not at a high enough level** for senior managers, and the **lack of narrative** also detracts from the usefulness of the report.

The information looks only at **past data** which, as noted above, is not necessarily a good guide to what will happen in the **future**.

(ii) **Suggested improvements**

Business plan

The business plan should include **past data** as a reference point for future projections and should include any **planned developments**, such as new products. The MIS will be able to provide past data and may also already incorporate plans and budgets for new products.

Ideally the plan should be **extended further into the future** to give the company a clear sense of mission, and something against which to measure progress. Companies often incorporate elements of **probability** within projections so that the required response to **different future scenarios** can be assessed. This technique may be incorporated within the MIS if facilities are available for holding more than one budget or project. Any modern spreadsheet package would be able to do this.

The plan would also need **external** data which is not typically provided by a MIS. See the answer to part (b).

Stock report

The stock report should be **summarised** and presented together with relevant **ratios** such as percentage of sales held in stock (for example two weeks sales of finished goods or two weeks production worth of raw materials. This will enable the directors to assess the **level of capital tied up in stock**.

The report might also include **exception reporting**, where only those items that are worthy of note - and the **control actions taken** by more junior managers to deal with them - are reported. An example might be excessively high usage of a particular material together with a recommendation to invest in a replacement for the machinery that had been found to be causing the wastage.

Summary of changes in demand

The summary of changes in demand would benefit from **summarisation at a higher level** and from **graphical** presentation, allowing **trends** to be quickly assimilated and relevant action decided upon.

Information about **future demand** would be more useful than information about past demand. Again, the summary would also need **external** data which is not typically provided by a MIS. See the answer to part (b).

(b) **Strategic information that the MIS is unlikely to be able to provide**

Senior managers' need for information incorporates **external** as well as internal data. Conventionally a MIS is able to provide a wealth of internal data, but external data has been collected by less formal methods.

With the growth of **information services via telecommunications** links (for example Internet 'push' technology, which can automatically deliver information of relevance from selected sources on the Internet), it is likely that MISs will become less internally focused, and **environmental scanning** will become a more regular and formal process.

As it stands however, RG Ltd's MIS is unlikely to be set up to provide information such as the following.

(i) Information on **competitors** is required to asses the competitive position and develop the strategy in the market place. Industry benchmarks and competitor performance can ensure the company remains on a par with or ahead of the field. Market share and potential market share are also important pieces of information.

(ii) **Industry trends** can be obtained from industries bodies as well as general trends gleaned from the press about aircraft manufacturers and construction companies.

(iii) Information about **technological development** in solvents would be needed as well as **other potential markets / customers**.

(iv) An analysis of the **wider environmental influences** generated through frameworks such as **PEST** are required to identify opportunities and threats that may have an impact of the company. **Ecological and legislative factors** may be of particular relevance to the industry including such things as pollution and health and safety regulations.

7 KN COMPANY: CENTRAL DATABASE

Pass marks. Conventional IT wisdom would say that central databases are 'a good thing' because they avoid duplication of work and inconsistencies between different sets of data. This question is typical of Stage 4 in that it asks you to **question** conventional textbook knowledge: is it true **in this case** that a central database is the best answer? Are there any merits in **not** taking this approach. Even if not, what are the practical difficulties involved in changing the system? Note in part (b) that the requirement is to **evaluate,** not just 'make a list'. How **important** are the problems? What measures or resources will be needed to overcome them?

Examiner's comment In (a) whilst most candidates produced a wide ranging list of potential advantages and disadvantages, many answers failed to provide the explanation to show why the points were relevant to this particular question. A small minority of answers tended to concentrate on the amalgamation of the different databases mentioned in the scenario to the exclusion of providing the advantages and disadvantages of each type of database. In (b) some candidates discussed hardware problems (specifically excluded by the question), and others spent too much time on the topics of normalisation and relational databases. Read the question!

(a) **Concentrating data and information on individual departments**

At present the KN company has six different sales departments, reflecting the **diversity of its range of customers**. Its sales systems were originally computerised in a way that reflected this business structure, probably solely with a view to **automating existing clerical procedures** to gain typical computer advantages such as speed of processing, greater accuracy, better presented reports and so on.

The **present system** has other **advantages** that should not be overlooked when considering change.

(i) Both sales staff and IT **staff are familiar** with the present system and it appears to **meet current requirements**. There may be some **opposition** from staff to attempts to change the system: they may very reasonably argue 'if it ain't broke, don't fix it'.

(ii) The division into six **separate departments** is likely to have occurred for **sound organisational reasons**, and these are now likely to be supported by the systems operating in separate departments.

   (1) Perhaps the division allows sales staff to **specialise** in dealing with a certain type of customer and give a better service.

   (2) Perhaps it is a way of coping with **large volumes of processing**, keeping the work within a manageable span of control.

   (3) Perhaps systems in some departments are set up to process **small volumes of high value** transactions while others are designed to process **large numbers of small** transactions.

   Changing the system may **undermine the benefits** that accrue from current arrangements.

(iii) **Amalgamating** the systems is likely to be **problematic**. This is discussed further in part (b).

Centralising the database

Conventionally the central database approach is felt to have advantages for the following reasons.

(i) It **avoids duplication** of data. For instance (assuming that a plastic moulding may serve a number of different purposes), KN may have customers that buy components through separate departments, so that a single customer will have several different accounts with KN, and their personal details will be held on several different parts of the system. This is a waste of storage space, and a waste of inputting time, because any changes have to be re-input several times to each different system.

(ii) It **ensures consistency** of data. Continuing with the example, Department A may receive notification of a change in a customer's personal details and amend its records accordingly. If Department B does not receive notification of the change it may, say, send out marketing mailshots to the wrong address. KN as a whole may not know which set of details is the most up-to-date.

(iii) **Analysis** of sales information at a management level above that of the six divisions is much easier, and understanding of customers' needs should improve. A customer's buying patterns with one department may suggest useful marketing initiatives in other departments, and a centralised database will make this analysis and action possible. **New patterns** may be revealed by a comparison between different sets of sales data that had not been realised in the past, facilitating **forecasting** and giving rise to **new ideas** to improve the level of service given to customers.

(iv) Systems development in the future is forced to take account of the **compatibility** of systems and standards. Compatibility between systems will simplify the support work of the IT department, offer **more flexibility for staff** (who can more easily move between departments), and **avoid being tied** to specific IT suppliers. Upgrades can be global rather than piecemeal, and this should **enhance control of expenditure** on IT and probably save money, thanks to bulk discounts and the like.

Relative merits

The database approach has clear advantages if there genuinely is **duplication** of data and processing effort. Opposition from staff can probably be overcome if they can be convinced that the new system has strong **business benefits**, will help them to do their present jobs more effectively, and perhaps offer them **new opportunities** within the company.

However, it is not at all clear from the scenario that there **is** duplication of data: perhaps it is unlikely that motor vehicles use many of the same components as pieces of garden furniture or children's toys. **Further investigation** of the business benefits is desirable, to ensure that there are likely to be **new revenue-earning opportunities** and that processing **costs will be reduced**. Problems such as those detailed in part (b) must be identified and solutions must be found before the changeover goes ahead.

(b) **Problems in amalgamating the company's data**

Problems are likely to be numerous.

(i) The **compatibility** between systems has already been mentioned. This is not just a matter of whether one system's files are **computer-sensible** to another system. It may extend to matters such as different systems of **coding**, different **formats** for personal data (with/without a contact name? with/without phone or fax number, and so on), different **field sizes**.

New standards that apply across the board can be developed, but implementing them is likely to require a great deal of **collection** of data and **inputting**. KN must acquire and test **conversion software** and ensure that they have **sufficient staff** to perform and check the conversion.

(ii) There is great potential for **loss or corruption of data** during the conversion process. Depending on the extent of the loss this could mean a small amount of rekeying or it could be a disastrous, permanent loss of valuable information needed for sales management.

Full **back-ups** should be taken at the start of the process, and back-ups of information on the old system should continue during any period of parallel running.

(iii) It is unlikely that current individual systems have sufficient **storage** space to accommodate the combined data. This can easily be resolved, but it must be resolved with an eye to the **future growth** of the combined business and future use of the database to store both **existing information** and **new information** that has not been available in the past.

(iv) **Access** to data must not suffer. Operational users will be attempting to **extract information from a much larger pool**, and the system must be designed in such a way that they do not have to wade through large amounts of data that is **irrelevant** to them to find what they need. If this aspect is neglected the new system could seriously undermine users' ability to respond to queries.

Those developing the system therefore need to **consult widely with users** at the sharp end of processing to ensure that their current **information needs are understood** and can be **met** by the new data architecture.

(v) As well as offering the potential for **new kinds of report** the system must **continue** to support **present requirements** for management reports that are essential to the smooth running of the business. Amalgamation could inadvertently **break down links** between data items and make it impossible to run a much needed daily report.

Once more, extensive **consultation with users** is essential.

(vi) Once the data has been amalgamated the business faces the task of ensuring that it is **secure**. A systems failure will now mean that no part of the sales function can operate, rather than at most just one part.

Dealing with this is likely to mean changes in the role and structure of the IT department. New, **centrally administered back-up procedures** will be needed, and **contingency arrangements** must be worked out and put in place to ensure that the risks to the business of systems disasters are minimised.

8 JBCC: DECISION SUPPORT SYSTEM

Pass marks. This is a straightforward question. There is plenty in the scenario to get your teeth into. In questions like this you will probably find it easier to do the **software** requirements first, and this is more logical because, as we say in our answer, the hardware needed is the hardware that is capable of handling all the things the user wants to do with the software. The hardware specifications we give are probably about right at the time of preparation of this Kit, but **do not worry unduly** about how many MHz to suggest. The key words to use to show your understanding of the situation in this case are words like **'powerful', 'fast'**, and **'reasonable quality'**.

Examiner's comment. The main problems were providing detailed explanations of the hardware and software that the company could implement without explaining why these items were necessary, and failing to provide complete systems in the answers (eg not mentioning communications equipment). Common misunderstandings were suggesting that the company had to establish a WAN to enable the travelling staff to access the central computer, and inputting to a database via a spreadsheet program (a good database program like Access provides much better data entry tools than a spreadsheet like Excel). Many answers to part (b) tended merely to repeat one or two points throughout: a broader answer including a wider range of ideas would have gained more marks.

(a) **Hardware and software requirements**

The **current situation** is that a staff of 30 use and maintain a database from ten terminals linked to a mainframe computer. The database contains information about individuals and information about benefits available. However, users spend much of their time away from the office and without manual input the current system does not appear to be capable of matching **changed personal circumstances** to **existing rules** or **changed rules** to **existing circumstances**.

This being the case, the new DSS will have the following requirements.

(i) **Software**

The present database of information about people and information about benefits must be supplemented by a **further database** containing the 6,500 or so **rules** that determine who is entitled to what.

All of the information is subject to frequent change and so it must be **easy to update**.

(1) The **rules** are likely to updated by means of **update programmes** that automatically delete out-of-date rules and add in changed or new rules. These should be issued by central government, or whoever the policy-

makers are. A facility should be available that enables staff to see at a glance **'what's new'** in the latest update.

(2) **Personal details** about individuals will be **updated on site**, probably in front of the client during visits, and the **language subsystem** of the DSS must therefore be **easy to use**. A **menu-driven** system, with a **GUI** and **on-screen forms** to fill out, and clear choices of options is desirable. Since the number of combinations of personal details will be practically unlimited, care needs to be taken, in designing the software, that choosing option X does not prevent the user from choosing option Y, and that it is not necessary to click though many levels of screens to get between different options.

Once personal details are entered the **decision support** software should take over, apply the rules, and output benefit entitlements. This entails software with a **knowledge subsystem**, capable of making the required links. The DSS should also have **problem processing** capabilities so that it can handle **'what if'** type enquiries ('what if I give up my job and become a carer', 'how will my benefits be affected if X happens', and so on).

Other software requirements are (of course) an **operating system**, and **communications software** to enable handling of fax, e-mail and data transmissions. To avoid the possibility of fraud, **dial-back security** software may be operated at the central office, using **password matching** to ensure that requests to send information in or to receive new information are legitimate.

Common office software such as a **word processing** package and a **spreadsheet** package may well be necessary to produce letters, reports, and analyses. A **presentation** package may also be useful for 'slide show' type presentations of new information that staff would otherwise have to repeat over and over again to all claimants. Windows and the basic Microsoft Office package (without Microsoft Access) would fulfil all of these needs.

(ii) **Hardware**

The hardware required to perform the above tasks is likely to be as follows.

(1) A **powerful portable computer**, probably a Pentium processor with a fast clock speed of at least 300MHz

(2) Substantial **hard disk space** (perhaps 4 Gb or more) to store the large amounts of data required in the system

(3) At least 32Mb **RAM,** otherwise the system will be frustratingly slow at processing claims, to the annoyance both of the staff using it and their clients

(4) An internal **fax modem**, fast enough to **avoid unnecessary delays** in transferring data into the main system in the office or downloading new rules and other messages from the central office

(5) The appropriate **telecommunications infrastructure** will also have to be installed at the central office

(6) Possibly, a **mobile telephone** for urgent messages from central office and to discuss problems in depth where necessary.

(7) **Portable printing facilities** giving reasonable quality output, particularly because clients are likely to want to check over the details that have been entered into the system and keep a hard copy for their own reference

(b) **The DSS and staff retention**

Morale is low at JBCC. This could be due to low pay or poor conditions in general, but the implication of the question is that **frustrating working methods**, leading to the inability to apply the rules consistently, are a significant cause or staff turnover.

The DSS may **improve** this situation in the following ways.

(i) Staff will **no longer feel overloaded** with new rules to learn and old rules to unlearn.

(ii) Staff are likely to do a **better job** and find it **more satisfying**, because they do not have to keep all the rules in their heads. They can concentrate on **understanding and explaining the consequences** of rules to clients, instead of simply hoping that they have remembered to take everything into account, only to be undermined by subsequent checking of claims.

(iii) Staff will no longer have to face the frustration of making promises to clients only to find later that they cannot **keep those promises** because the rules have **changed** in their absence from the office. Again this helps them to do a better, more satisfying job.

(iv) A common problem with staff who work out of the office for much of the time is a sense of **isolation** from the organisation as a whole. JBCC is a large organisation with 2,450 staff, and it will be very difficult for on-the-road staff to feel as if they belong and are part of the culture of the organisation. The new DSS has, as a side benefit, **improved communication** with the central office, including informal communication. There may also be improved communication between welfare staff so that they feel more of a team.

(v) At present it is likely that the welfare staff's inconsistency gives rise to **complaints** that have to be dealt with centrally, and extra work rectifying mistakes that were made. Welfare staff will be blamed and resented. Thanks to the DSS, however, **errors and delays should be far less frequent** and the **reputation** of the welfare team within JBCC as a whole is likely to **improve**. This will **improve relations and morale**.

9 EF LTD: KEY INDICATORS

> **Pass marks**. The suggestions given here are not the only 'right answers'. (Of course, there is usually no such thing as a right answer at stage 4 anyway.) If you have suggested other key indicators, and it is almost inevitable that you have, test them by re-reading critically your justification for selecting each one.
>
> **Examiner's comment.** A minority of candidates concentrated on financial indicators, omitting reference to the other two changes mentioned in the question. Nearly all candidates found it difficult to explain why the indicators given were relevant.

REPORT

To: The Managing Director, EF Ltd

From: Accountant

Date: 23 November 1995

Subject: Recommendations for key indicators

In evaluating the effect of the recent changes within EF Ltd the following indicators can be recommended.

(a) **Added value per employee** is useful as a possible measure of **productivity.** This could, for example, be defined as sales income less bought in services (including finance charges) and material, divided by the number of employees.

The company has proceeded down the route of replacing personnel with capital equipment. The productivity of the remaining workforce should therefore be significantly greater than before.

The **information** for this indicator is readily available from the **usual management accounting sources**. Knowing the cost of capital, the savings in payroll costs, and the budgeted throughput, a target added value per employee can be calculated that represents breakeven on the financial effect of the changes.

A **weakness** with this indicator is that certain elements are susceptible to **changes in economic conditions** as well as to internal changes.

Any business process re-engineering of this nature should bring about significant gains in productivity by **eliminating inefficient and outdated processes** altogether. New procedures should reflect **best practice** in the industry, and, for this reason, some use of **benchmarking against competitors** in the industry is also recommended.

(b) **Responsiveness** to customers and the marketplace is vital.

The purpose of the changes is not simply to save money, but to enable the company to **react speedily to consumer needs**. The information technology industry is becoming a prime example of 'relationship marketing', wherein the supplier is attempting to become closer to each customer. This is a means of seeking competitive advantage. Thus the organisation will be trying to behave as if it were 'lean and mean' and provide fast response to each customer, not simply manufacturing 'boxes'. Hence the introduction of CAD/CAM.

An **important indicator** therefore, as an example of speed of reaction, is the **speed at which bespoke customer needs are met**. To make this indicator consistent, project times from agreement of customer specification to delivery need to be measured.

A **problem** with this is that the size of the project will affect the speed of delivery. Perhaps project times could be divided by the sales margin for comparability and consistency. The lower the ratio the better. A company target figure should be established as a yardstick.

(c) **Financial** indicators, such as **management accounting ratios** (credit risk, debtor days, WIP turnround etc) should also be used. Although **care** is needed in **interpretation**, because of distortions caused by accounting policies and the need for consistency from period to period, the **traditional measures** of working capital efficiency (summarised perhaps as 'working capital days' being debtor days plus stock days less supplier days) are **as relevant as ever** to modern industry.

The improvement in the **manufacturing systems** will have included measures designed to improve **stock management** and **financial control**, probably one of the variants of JIT and perhaps ABM (activity based management) or other relevant costing/management systems. The effect on cash flow should be dramatic once the new systems are in place.

These cost savings can be set against the capital costs incurred in developing new systems. Standard **investment appraisal** techniques can be used here: current thinking suggests that a balanced measure, incorporating NPV, payback and IRR gives the most rounded view. In addition **project management measures** relating to budget, timetables and quality (availability, response etc) can be used.

(d) **Strategic direction** is extremely difficult to assess as it involves such long-term factors. Major systems change of the type undertaken is certainly part of a strategic process and its success can only be seen by reference to the **overall market position** of the company and its **reputation**. The value of the **brand name** may be measured, but such measures are **subjective**. Better is a **long-term tracking of share price** and **market share**.

Although **strategic planning is long-term**, IT can sit awkwardly with this, as so much **technology is short-term** in nature, with manufacturers reducing product life cycles in their quest for competitive advantage. This means that IT-based decisions may need to be changed within the life of a particular strategy. This problem can to some extent be addressed by a formal **Information Systems Planning** exercise, which creates a framework for development, providing guidelines over a period of time to ensure that activities fit into strategic criteria.

(e) **Critical success factors** can be used. Each CSF will already have been ascribed one or more performance indicators. CSFs are fundamental to the strategic direction of the company. Here, the changes to be evaluated are more than just small improvements to individual parts of the company, they are a fundamental change to the very nature and shape of the organisation.

The ultimate measure of their effectiveness could be said to be in the **bottom line results** of EF Ltd; however, other factors will also be relevant, for example, **reliability indicators**. This might take the form of warranty claims/sales, or claims/number of products supplied, or may be based on customer surveys measuring the elusive characteristic of 'customer satisfaction'. The reputation of the company, and thus its potential to generate future cash flows - the definition of the value of the enterprise - depends on the quality of its service. It is important to know that the reduction in personnel numbers, and the introduction of automation has not compromised quality.

The above should be read in the light of the assumption that **systems development** is undertaken in general to **meet business needs** and **fulfil organisational objectives**. These might be categorised as:

(a) **reductions in cost** base;
(b) **investment** in **IT infrastructure**;
(c) responding to, or anticipating, **changing market conditions**;
(d) ensuring that **IT supports strategic plans.**

It is only by setting **appropriate performance indicators**, such as the above, that the success of systems development can be **measured**.

In conclusion, the measurement of the key components of the strategy of the company are vital to the **control and updating** of that strategy as it links '**hard**' cost/benefit analysis with '**softer**' areas which are difficult to quantify and often subjective.

Signed: Accountant

10 GOOD QUALITY INFORMATION

> **Pass marks**. This question should have provided the well-prepared candidate with the opportunity to score heavily. Remember that theory **must be applied** to the question asked, and that if **examples** are asked for you must provide them!
>
> **Examiner's comment.** Areas of weakness included not providing examples of poor quality information and limiting the explanation to comments such as 'Information must be timely; if information is not timely then it is of poor quality'. Re-stating the characteristic with a negative does not provide an explanation. To gain more marks, candidates should show why a lack of timeliness was a problem, for example because operational decisions are frequent by their nature. A minority of candidates provided a detailed answer on the particular systems they had been working on. While the information in the answer was no doubt correct, there was no attempt to focus the answer onto the characteristics of information. Areas where scripts showed a particularly good standard or format included use of the ACCURATE mnemonic to structure an answer. This also helped ensure the answer was complete.

There are a numbers of reasons why information provided to operational decision-makers (ODMs) may not be of good quality.

(a) **Accurate information may not be cost-beneficial**

The **cost** of providing any information should always be **less than the benefit** obtained from using it. 100% accurate information may be available, but may be very expensive to obtain. Therefore, in many situations ODMs have to **rely on estimates and forecasts.** For example product costings often include an element of overhead that is allocated on a fairly arbitrary basis (such as machine hours), as it is uneconomic to allocate the overhead with complete accuracy.

(b) **Timeliness**

Operational information is often acted on soon after it was provided. The more **up to date** the information the greater its relevance to operational decision-making. This often leads to **accuracy being sacrificed for speed**. For example, in order to produce a monthly sales report to a tight deadline, sales for the final day(s) of the month may be estimated. If the estimate is significantly inaccurate, inappropriate decisions may result. Delaying a decision until completely accurate information is available is often impractical.

(c) **Completeness**

Information passed to an ODM may seem to be of good quality in isolation, but in fact **excludes** a vital piece of information. For example a manager may request and receive a comprehensive report detailing three employees recent performance, in order to decide who should be promoted to foreperson. If one of the employees has recently resigned, and the report fails to mention this, then the information is incomplete and of poor quality.

(d) **Relevance**

Information must be **relevant to the purpose** for which a manager wants to use it. If an ODM asks for a breakdown of last month's sales by customer they should not also (or instead) be given a breakdown of sales by product (unless they later request this information too). Irrelevant information **wastes time.**

(e) **Communication channel**

The method of communication used will affect **who** is able to use the information and **how** the information can be used. Some information may be best sent by e-mail, perhaps as an attachment allowing editing by the recipient. Other information is best communicated informally by telephone or word-of-mouth, or more formally in a letter.

(f) **Clarity of presentation**

Information should be **presented in a manner suited** to the level of management which it is aimed at. Information suffers when it is too detailed and insufficiently summarised for the appropriate ODMs. If a great deal of detail has to be given a summary should precede it.

(g) **Concise**

There are physical and **mental limitations** to what a person can read, absorb and understand properly before taking action. An enormous mountain of information is counter-productive, as the ODM will not be able to absorb it all. **Information overload** can cause vital information to be missed, hidden within the massive volume of information. For example, the manager of a retail outlet that is part of a national chain requires a report showing the performance of his branch, as that is what his decisions can affect. If management feel local managers should also see the 'wider picture', national results should be supplied in a format that does not cloud the specific branch performance.

Conclusion

Even if these 'mechanical' features of good information are satisfied there is still a danger of the information provided to ODMs not being of good quality. This is because all organisations and ODMs operate in an environment **subject to constant change**. Information that is certain must be historical by definition, and may be of limited relevance to the future. **Forward-looking information** will always contain elements of uncertainty and risk.

11 TUTORIAL QUESTION: INFORMATION SYSTEMS STRATEGY

(a) **Reasons for having a formal IS strategy**

Information is now regarded by many organisations as something more than a useful by-product of commercial data processing. Instead, it is seen as a **resource** of an organisation, like the organisation's pool of human skills, fixed assets, goodwill and so forth. **Planning** in all these areas is widely regarded as desirable, so that an organisation can adapt to a changing environment.

As information is so critical to an organisation's success, then the provision of information must be an important organisational activity. Just as many organisations have a long-term plan covering sales and markets, production and so forth, so too **a long-term plan** is needed for **information provision**.

An organisation's **financial investment** in information technology is also **substantial,** especially with the proliferation of computing power around different departments. Moreover, information technology **spans** areas of management which previously would have been distinct: high volume data processing (a computer department); telecommunications (which may have been a general administrative function); office administration (as PCs replace dedicated word processors, which were themselves purchased to replace typewriters). Many organisations report dissatisfaction with the outcomes of their investments. Some **overall direction** is therefore required.

A **strategy** is a long-term plan, concentrating on the overall performance of the system, stating long-term objectives and goals, and outlining the measures to achieve them. Strategies are articulated **differently** in different organisations. In some circumstances, the organisation's very **survival** in a hostile economic climate is the long-term goal. The strategy contains the measures to achieve it. In other organisations the goal might be **growth** in market share.

Because information technology is pervasive throughout the business, and can significantly affect the relationship an organisation has with its customers, the **IT strategy** should be developed **within the overall corporate plan**. IT has to **compete with other investments** (eg other fixed assets) or expenditure programs for resources, and **implementing IT can be very disruptive**. Moreover, with the growth of **end-user computing**, it is important that there is at least **some central direction** to ensure that the IT resources are used to the best advantage of the organisation. This will not be the case if the organisation is plagued with **incompatible** hardware and/or software.

A **strategy for information systems** will therefore be **part of the overall organisational strategy** and will be geared to meeting organisational objectives. Equally significantly, it **demonstrates the importance of IT** to senior management and their commitment to it. Finally, it has the function of laying down the **plan for managing IT** in terms of **technical standards** and **organisational responsibilities**.

(b) **Developing an IS strategy**

Each organisation goes about the task of developing an information systems strategy in a different way. It may be carried out by a **corporate strategy department**. On the other hand, it may be carried out by a special team selected from **user departments** and the organisation's **computing professionals**. **Management consultants** may be involved, especially if the organisation lacks management time or expertise.

Making IT strategy part of the strategic plan for the organisation as a whole might involve a **culture change** for some organisations, especially those with long-established corporate strategy departments.

However, **all** strategy developments are likely to conform in some respects to the model outlined below.

A model

(i) Personnel devising the strategy are given **terms of reference**. The brief may be very broad, or quite narrowly defined. The terms of reference may be developed from the overall organisational strategy.

(ii) A **plan** is made for the strategy development exercise. This means defining in more detail what exactly is the subject of the study, from considerations of potential competitive advantage to purely technical decisions which need to be decided at strategic level. The plan would detail the timetable, required resources, and specify the outputs of the planning process.

(iii) **Strategy definition**. Three types of document are written.

(1) The **information systems** strategy. This details the long-term information plan to support business strategies or to create new strategic options.

(2) The **information technology** strategy seeks to provide a framework for the analysis and design of the organisation's technical infrastructure (eg communications, computing hardware, open vs proprietary systems).

(3) The **information management** strategy refers to the management of information systems, in terms of necessary resources, authorisation

procedures for systems development projects, cost control, and management of the technology (eg security policy).

(iv) **Strategy implementation**. The strategy is then set to work. To be successful, the exercise should have a **high profile** within the organisation and there should be suitable **commitment** to it from senior management. This means that any demarcation problems should be sorted out.

(v) **Review**. The success of the strategy should be reviewed on a rolling basis.

12 TUTORIAL QUESTION: COST LEADERSHIP

(a) **Overall cost leadership**

The factors which are important in achieving overall cost leadership are as follows.

(i) The implementation of a cost leadership strategy would call for **aggressive pricing** and a willingness to bear **large losses** initially in order to build up **market share.**

(ii) **Production facilities** must be set up for **mass production** so as to achieve economies of scale. This requires access to **large amounts of capital**.

(iii) A firm must be willing to **invest continually** in the **latest technology**, which also requires ready access to **capital.**

(iv) Management must concentrate on **productivity objectives** and their focus should be on seeking productivity **improvements** and **cost reduction** in various ways. For example efficient product design, value analysis programmes and zero base budgeting. **Rewards** could be linked to productivity where appropriate.

(v) The organisation must have **efficient cost control** systems with regular **feedback** of cost control information to managers.

(vi) The organisation must develop a '**cost cutting culture**', paying attention also to the **minimisation of discretionary costs** such as research and development and advertising.

(vii) Arrangements must be made to obtain favourable access to **sources of raw materials** supply wherever possible.

(b) **Risks**

An organisation which adopts a strategy of overall cost leadership faces a number of risks.

(i) The risk of **technological change** could result in even more capital investment to keep up to date and may **nullify all the cost advantages** so far achieved by experience and the learning curve process.

(ii) There is a threat of **competition from other countries** where costs may be even lower. For example the labour costs in Taiwan are very low compared with those in Europe.

(iii) There is a risk that **competitors** will attempt to **fragment the market** by building up a **high quality brand** image for their version of the product. An overall **low cost producer** would then have to compete on cost in each market segment it operated in and hope that cheaper prices can compete successfully with brand image.

(iv) There is a risk of **cost inflation,** especially if competitors in other countries are not affected in the same way.

(c) **Generic strategies**

Two other generic strategies are as follows.

(i) **Differentiation.** You make your product different from competing products in some way. Differentiation is an industry-wide strategy.

(ii) **Focus.** You only sell to a particular segment (eg geographical area, socio-economic position) of the market. Focus is not an industry-wide strategy.

13 TUTORIAL QUESTION: THE STAGE HYPOTHESIS

Nolan postulated that the six stages of an organisation's computerisation development are as follows.

(a) **Initiation**. This is the stage during which **computers are acquired** and initial systems implemented. The chosen initial systems will not necessarily be those which are the most cost effective, but are likely to be those whose proponents push the hardest. It is the **enthusiasts** who are likely to introduce systems to an organisation. **Technicians dominate** the operation and decisions are driven by **hardware and software** considerations. Planning and control are not important at this stage. **Cost growth** is relatively **slow**.

(b) **Contagion**. Due to a spreading of enthusiasm about the initial results of computerisation, **many more systems are proposed**. With management support the impact of computers is 'applied' to many other areas of the organisation. The **potential** of computer systems **becomes apparent**, and development commences on other applications. **Spending** on computer related items (staff and capital) **escalates** dramatically, but with a **low degree of control**. This stage is characterised by a high degree of **experimentation**.

(c) **Control**. Due to the increase in spending and lack of results in many areas, **frustration and disillusionment** set in. As a result **spending**, and the **management** of the runaway IT function, is brought under more direct control of **higher management**, and **constraints and controls are applied** in great numbers. These controls will include **committees** to 'manage' projects, **budgetary controls** on capital and project related expenditure and more effective controls on existing systems and infrastructure.

(d) **Integration**. The IT function becomes more a **part of the main organisation**. The committees introduced in the control stage become effective and the system adjusts from the level it reached in the Contagion stage. **Cost-benefit analysis** becomes standard. As **users** gain more confidence in themselves and in the systems with which they work their **active involvement in projects** increases.

(e) **Data administration**. The **data** becomes accepted as a **resource**, and steps are taken to administer it as such. The attention and focus of management shifts towards the data which the organisation has built up, and planning starts to take into account the existence of the **database**. Administration of the data may become **centralised** or **standardised**.

(f) **Maturity**. The **users** assume an **equal or dominant role** in IT projects; data **resources** are **controlled but flexible**; the **information flow** in the system matches **actual requirements**; the goal is to make best use of the data resources.

The first benefit of such a hypothesis is that it is **universally applicable** and can be 'fitted' to any organisation, so that development staff can ascertain where exactly an organisation is in its computer development. This assists in **understanding existing attitudes** of staff towards computerisation.

Secondly, once it has been established that an organisation has reached a certain stage, it may be possible to **plan for further development** by reference to expected experience in later stages. This may enable an organisation to **pre-empt certain problems** by for example, adopting appropriate **control procedures.**

Thirdly, it may help **users** who wish to become more involved in computer development, as it **supports their case** by showing that they are ultimately important.

14 JH LTD: IT STRATEGY

> **Pass marks.** This is a typical stage 4 question, asking you to look at things from the opposite point of view from the one that you have most probably learned. As the examiner's comments below indicate, just churning out pre-prepared lists is not sufficient at Stage 4. For part (b), you must think of other solutions besides training to overcome the barriers. The real problems are attitude problems: giving people the chance to learn new skills does not necessarily affect their attitudes, and may even harden them.
>
> **Examiner's comment.** In (a) a significant minority of answers turned the question around and explained the **advantages** of having a strategy, which tended to limit the marks awarded because it did not directly meet the requirements of the question. Similarly, answers that simply listed Earl's nine factors without trying to show how the **lack** of these would affect the company obtained little credit. For (b), poorer answers just repeated the information in the question without elaboration and scored very few marks. Slightly better answers provided some explanation but did not always show how the barriers could be overcome. Candidates tend to be weaker on questions that deal with the 'human' aspects of the syllabus, and there is still a lack of evidence of any answer planning.

(a) **Disadvantages of not having an overall IT strategy**

(i) One of the important aspects of the IS/IT strategy is that it **supports the business strategy** by fulfilling the information needs of the organisation. An important element of this is that the **information needs** are clearly identified before the actual IT (hardware and software) is decided upon. If the organisation has no strategy for its IT there is the danger that it can **spend a large amount of money** and yet **still not meet** managements' **key information requirements.**

(ii) As IT can involve high costs there is usually a **high risk** associated with the IT spend. This in part relates to the technical issues to be dealt with and the need to ensure that current IT and future IT is **compatible**. Without a strategy it is possible to invest in incompatible systems that increase the cost and complexity of working in the future.

(iii) Many companies are able to use IT to gain a competitive advantage, either by exploiting IT in their operations or by managing their information far better. It therefore follows that not having a strategy can lead to the company **losing advantage to its competitors** and falling behind in terms of technology used.

(iv) Not only do organisations rely on IT far more than they used to but **IT is changing the way many industries work.** For example the availability of information over the Internet is changing the way information is gathered and managed in many industries that are information-driven. Companies need to **build this into their future plans** and therefore plan IT to help them cope with the changes and remain competitive in the industry.

For example, retailing is becoming much more information-driven and many aspects of service industries such as travel agencies can do business over computer networks. The absence of an IT strategy will mean that the organisation is **not matching its future information needs** and **retaining its ability to compete** in a changing environment.

(v) IT is changing the **way** information is **collected,** the **amount** of information **collected** and **what is done with information** once it has been collected. For example, in retailing, EPOS systems and loyalty card schemes are allowing supermarket chains to build up vast databases of individual consumer preferences.

Companies that do not take advantage of this are liable to **fall behind the competition** and find it impossible to **reap the benefits** of using information as a strategic resource.

(vi) **Exchange of information** between various **stakeholders** is facilitated via IT and is also having an impact upon the **structure** of organisations making them more flexible, or softening the organisational boundaries. Where an organisation does not plan for this, it will **limit its ability to react quickly to changes.**

(vii) It is important for organisations to ensure they provide their **employees** with the resources (including IT) they need to do their jobs well and to keep morale high. Employees may see other organisations utilising the latest technology and become **demotivated**: the older technology will limit their own effectiveness and harm their career prospects.

(b) **Barriers presented by individuals**

(i) **The senior manager**

The senior manager has **little knowledge** of IT and is also **fearful** of it. Underlying his dismissive attitude may be a fear of losing face in front of his more IT-literate colleagues. He will therefore have little appreciation of the potential business benefits of IT.

He will also **fail to see the relevance of IT** to the industry in a wider sense which could result in **missing a strategic advantage**. The fact that he is good at producing overall policy may mean that he produces a general policy that skims the surface of the issues. His being task-orientated may also mean that insufficient time is taken to consider the issues fully. He is more likely to try and **push through his ideas** as fast as possible.

The first thing that needs to be done is to **increase his general awareness** of IT and its capabilities and relevance. He will then be much better able to focus on the benefits of IT for the company. Providing him with copies of **relevant, well-written articles** from non-technical journals (for example the FT's regular IT articles and supplements) should open his eyes to what his company may be missing.

Provided he is not totally resistant, the senior manager could be provided with a **desktop PC** and be shown how to use some **simple but useful applications** that will save him time from day to day. This may assist his confidence, kindle some enthusiasm and help to overcome his fear of IT.

(ii) **The IT professional**

The IT professional is probably **too close to IT**. She says she believes that IT is best left to specialists, yet her knowledge is **not as up to date** as one would expect a specialist's knowledge to be.

This may mean that she does not pay enough consideration to **user needs**. Many of the users may be familiar with PCs but she is unlikely to recommend devolving computing power into the hands of the user as she neither **understands** their needs nor **believes** they should be involved.

Her natural tendency will be to suggest an IT strategy that **preserves her empire** and revolves around the technical **IT department** rather than the **business needs**. There is also the danger that she will suggest continued use of technology within her own current knowledge, **ignoring current trends and developments**. Given that the Senior Manager may wish to rely on her knowledge to produce a quick solution, this could result in an inappropriate strategy.

These barriers may be overcome in a variety of ways.

(1) She needs to **update her knowledge** by reading computer journals and business press.

(2) She will probably need **further training** in topics such as client/server systems.

(3) She must be given top-level encouragement to look at the benefits of IT from the **business needs** viewpoint, rather than seeing IT as an end in itself.

(4) She must spend time with the **users** to realise that they have different needs and that their input can be valid in the development of the strategy.

(5) Visits to **other organisations** that are technically well advanced may also assist in overcoming her resistance to modern technology.

(iii) The trainee accountant may bring a lot of enthusiasm to the project, wishing to **prove himself** and bring all his knowledge to bear, but his desire to be the **IT champion** may well mean that he has a **private agenda** which could be **sub-optimal**.

He may have a **short term focus** to the problem as it will complement his studies.

His **limited experience** and position in the firm may limit his ability to see the **wider picture** effectively. However being a user of IT he will bring a valuable perspective to the project if his enthusiasm can be contained.

His input could also be **resented by the IT manager** who may try to blind him with science, especially as he is pushing for more end-user computing and less reliance upon her department. This could be a significant source of conflict within the group.

It will be important to **overcome any conflict** between the group arising from personal differences and background. This could be achieved by a careful **brief and initial discussion** by a board member ensuring that they all know why they have been included and **what their respective roles will be** expected to bring to the process. They all have a **valuable contribution** to make and making that clear to the group will help to understand the **objectives** of the group more clearly.

15 IT STRATEGY

Pass marks. We have used a fairly homely example of a small firm offering domestic services such as plumbing and electrical work. If you are stuck for material to illustrate your answer then remember that personal experience is always a good source, and, if appropriate, is likely to be more interesting to the marker of your script than examples lifted out of books. (For instance talking about whether or not banks have ATMs is really rather old-hat in 2000: ATMs have been fairly common since the late 1970s.) An answer that works through a number of Earl's reasons for having an IT strategy should be sufficient to earn a pass mark, but *only so long as it is accompanied by appropriate examples.*

Prizewinner's points. Our answer does not follow Earl's scheme religiously because we want to demonstrate one way in which a thoughtful student might have taken a different, but equally valid, approach. For the same reason (to give you some new food for thought) our answer is a good deal longer than most students could possibly have managed. Note also the layout of our answer and the approach of using an imaginary firm to provide examples.

Examiner's comment. Some candidates had problems finding five reasons. Some answers became quite repetitive or included points that did not appear to be relevant. Many answers failed to provide good examples, either because the candidate concentrated solely on the theory or because it was not clear how the example supported the reason why a company required an IT strategy.

Reasons for having an IT strategy

In this answer we identify five reasons for developing an IT strategy, using the example of a typical small firm offering domestic services such as plumbing and electrical work. For convenience we shall refer to this firm as **EG Ltd.**

(a) **Rationalising the existing investment in IT**

Because of the benefits it offers (speed, accuracy, and so on) IT has become a **key component of most aspects of modern businesses**. Most organisations have reached the stage in their IT maturity whereby IT has been used to automate tasks previously performed manually or by obsolete technology. Most organisations could **not now conceivably disinvest in IT**, and return to traditional methods of getting work done.

However, it is common in organisations, from small to large, for IT to have been **introduced piecemeal** to address specific requirements without due regard having been paid to the way that the individual systems **work together and communicate**.

Adoption of a strategy is therefore necessary to guide the direction and scope of the **whole** IT development of a firm allowing it to match the **resources available** to the changing **environment** and enable the firm to meet its **primary business objectives**. All of these matters - overall use of resources, environmental issues and overall objectives – are key issues in the formulation of business strategies.

The next stage of IT development is to **exploit the utmost that IT has to offer** by **re-engineering the processes** with the aid of IT rather than just automating current processes.

Example

EG Ltd originally invested in stand-alone PCs for basic administrative tasks such as writing letters to customers and keeping accounts. None of its systems were fully integrated, and much work still involves inefficiencies such as re-inputting of data, or manual searches for information that is held in computerised form but is not accessible by a computer search.

An **organisation-wide strategy** needs to be formulated if the **various systems are to be brought together**, enabling further gains, for instance, automatic generation of letters to debtors, proper accessible databases of customers, suppliers, materials, staff resources.

(b) **Beating competitors and enhancing relationships**

The **traditional** view of IT's role in competitive strategy is largely **reactive** - that is, a response to existing competitive strategy and business process, but not a critical factor in **shaping** that strategy and process.

A more sensible approach is to position IT in a **pro-active** role where the competitive strategy is not viewed as given, but rather as something that should be challenged, extended and perhaps modified, in light of **emerging technologies and applications.**

The perspective of IT strictly as a **support** function in competitive strategy is increasingly out-dated. Firms are now seeking ways to exploit IT to transform their basic businesses, **enhance their relationships** with suppliers and customers, and **create new market opportunities.**

Today, successful competitive strategy and corporate results are likely to focus on a small number of performance attributes including **speed, flexibility, quality** and **scale.** All four areas are **profoundly affected** by an organisation's **effective use of IT** to facilitate, enhance and accelerate strategic execution.

Example

EG Ltd's original investment in IT was made partly **because their competitors and suppliers** were clearly investing in such systems too, and EG's manually-produced communications with the outside world made the entire firm **look old-fashioned and inefficient.**

Greater use of technologies now available, or becoming available, could enable EG Ltd to **surpass** many competitors and **deal much more effectively** with suppliers and customers. For instance, **computerised scheduling and booking systems** could enable EG to respond more quickly to urgent call-outs and **make and honour promises** to customers about when work will be done and how long it will take (something at which the industry in general is notoriously bad). **EDI links** to suppliers could greatly simplify ordering and administration for both parties. A good **website** could generate a great deal of new business.

(c) **Getting the systems that are really needed**

In the past many organisations have found that information systems have **failed to deliver expected benefits** for reasons such as the following.

(i) There is no **commitment by the top management** of an organisation. IT strategy invariably involves some degree of **change**, and, unless top management is behind the strategy, its implementation can prove to be impossible.

(ii) The **users and providers of IT** in the organisation have not been fully enough involved. If new systems are simply imposed on such people and they are given no chance to explain their **real needs** there is a strong chance that the system will not reflect their needs.

The process of going through the planning stage in itself is extremely valuable as it provides a mechanism not only for determining what needs to be done but, if properly handled, it also ensures that the result is **achieved by consensus of all interested parties** and this means that the plan is far more likely to be put into effect satisfactorily. The formulation of an **IT strategy** should then result in a clear and **generally understood and agreed** document which sets out the relative priorities of each approved project together with the identification and allocation of the appropriate **resources, approval and delivery** dates, arrangements for **testing and training**, .and so on.

Example

EG Ltd originally acquired computers in cases where the manager of a function wanted one and had sufficient influence n the organisation to obtain funding. Other managers were either not interested or did not have the influence. Users, therefore, either had computers imposed on them or were deprived of them.

A **culture change** is needed: those who are opposed to computerisation or simply lack enthusiasm need to be persuaded of the benefits.

(d) **Continually improving the management of the organisation**

IT brings **ongoing** revolution in the way information is created, used and presented to management. After the strategy has been developed, it must be regarded as a living entity that the organisation needs to review on a regular and systematic basis as circumstances change.

Any strategic view of IT must take technical developments into account. For instance the **Internet** and **Intranet** popularity has forced many managers to rethink the direction of applications and infrastructure investments. The most popular applications use web publishing for existing documents, web forms for transaction entry or web-to-database links to access corporate data.

Example

EG Ltd could benefit from introducing an Intranet in ways such as the following.

(i) An organisation-wide phone directories that is always up to date, containing internal numbers and frequently used external numbers.

(ii) Sales information including price lists for jobs, staff availability for urgent call-outs, and supplier and competitor information, including links to suppliers' and competitors' Web sites

(iii) A technical database for staff such as plumbers and electricians showing how various jobs are done, how the latest tools and materials should be used, legal and safety requirements and so on.

(e) **Obtaining synergies and economies of scale**

If IT is not integral to corporate strategy a business is almost certain to be **spending too much,** if only because a sizeable percentage will be **spent on the wrong things**. If this goes unchecked there is very little chance that the company will realise the economies of scale and informational synergies that the business needs.

A company's IT architecture comprises **five different component architectures**: applications, technology, data, methods and management practices, and **spending needs to keep these architectures in balance**. For instance, if a large amount is spent on new technologies, but **nothing on training and data conversion** then at best there will be a lag before the new facilities are exploited to the full. The benefits of the IT expenditure might be delayed until the skills of users are available to produce them.

Example

EG Ltd is typical in that it has only computerised its administration so far: it ahs not considered benefits that could arise from using technology in **other areas of its business**, such as mobile phones and portable PCs for staff such as plumbers and electricians to use on site.

16 TUTORIAL QUESTION: COSTS AND BENEFITS

A proposed system may be in **competition for resources** with other projects in a company. A **monetary evaluation** provides at least a **common scale** by which different projects can be measured.

A distinction can be made between:

(a) **one-off costs**; and
(b) **recurring** costs.

One-off costs can be of a '**capital**' or '**revenue**' nature.

On the **capital** side, this may include the cost of **equipment, software** (if purchased outright rather than leased), and any new **buildings** or office installations.

'One-off' **revenue** items may include a variety of **systems development** costs. These include the cost of **management time**, the **salaries** of the systems analysts and a great deal of time spent in **implementation**. Other one-off expenditure will include **recruitment** of appropriate staff, training, and possible **redundancy** costs.

The distinction between 'capital' and 'revenue' is an important one. The project is likely to be justified in '**cash**' terms, whereas the costs most likely to appear in the company's profit and loss account relating to capital expenditure will be the **depreciation** of fixed assets over a number of years. Depreciation is not a cash flow at all, and so the effect on 'profit' will not bear an immediate relationship with the initial cash outflow. One-off revenue expenditure, however, is likely to be charged immediately to the profit and loss account. The decision to buy a new system will be made on the basis of '**cash flows**' (ie does the company have enough money?) rather than '**profits**'.

Recurring costs, apart from the non-cash items mentioned above, include:

(a) **salaries** for operational staff;
(b) data **transmission** costs (eg line rentals);
(c) consumable **supplies** (paper, disks);
(d) **power**;
(e) **rental**;
(f) hardware **maintenance**;
(g) software **support**;
(h) **leasing** charges for hardware and software if held under licence;
(i) **back up** or **standby** arrangements;
(j) **training**;
(k) **data preparation** work.

Benefits

The benefits from a proposed new system must also be evaluated wherever possible. These ought to consist of the following.

(a) **Savings** because the old system will no longer be operated, including:

  (i) savings in **staff costs**;
  (ii) savings in **other operating costs**, such as consumable materials.

(b) **Extra savings** or revenue benefits because of the **improvements** or enhancements that the new system should bring eg:

  (i) possibly **more sales revenue** and so additional contribution;

  (ii) better **control**: for example with a new stock control system, fewer stock losses from obsolescence and deterioration;

  (iii) further savings in staff time resulting perhaps in **reduced future staff growth**.

(c) Possibly, some one-off revenue benefits from **sale of equipment** which the existing system uses, but which will no longer be required. Second-hand computer equipment does not have a high value, however. It is also possible that the new system will use **less office space**, and so there will be benefits from selling or renting the space accommodation.

In addition, computerisation might produce a one-off benefit by making the company's operations **more efficient**. The information provided may allow more control over the detail of the company's operation, which will mean that the company's resources will have less chance of being wasted.

The relevance of NPV

These costs and benefits will normally be given a monetary value which in many cases may be the most appropriate way of treating them. An organisation might employ **discounted cash flow techniques** to estimate the **future costs or benefit**.

However, discounted cash flow techniques cannot accurately account for the **non-quantifiable costs and benefits** of any installation. As computer systems become more sophisticated, their applications in management become much more generalised. It is hard to put a value on the number of **improved decisions** a manager is supposed to make using a decision support system, for example.

A recent suggestion (by the Assessor for the Paper 15 paper :**CIMA Student,** August 1996) is that organisations should use a 'balanced approach', blending together NPV, payback and IRR along the following lines.

Project	NPV £'000	Ranking	Payback years	Ranking	IRR %	Ranking	Total score	Overall ranking
A	840	**2**	3	**2**	21	**3**	7	3rd
B	1,255	**1**	4	**3**	26	**2**	6	2nd
C	771	**3**	2	**1**	28	**1**	5	1st

The total score is obtained by adding together the scores in each '**Ranking**' column. The project with the **lowest score** is the one that comes top. The article claims that this method combines many different aspects of the components that go to make up an investment decision.

17 TUTORIAL QUESTION: PROTOTYPING

Prototyping is essentially the process of building a model of the envisaged system. Using a **fourth generation language**, the analyst constructs a **working model** which he then **demonstrates to the user**. They can then discuss and **agree any enhancements** or amendments. It is particularly relevant to the design of the **user interface**.

Analysis and design are a **dynamic** process; the **user** and **analyst** are in constant **consultation**. They have more opportunity to check each others' understanding of the problem, and this leads to **reduced misunderstandings**. On the basis of these checks, a course of action will be agreed upon as to whether to create a new prototype throwing away the current one, or to develop a more refined version of the existing one.

It should be noted that a relatively poor increase in programmer productivity as opposed to hardware improvements has led to a significant increase in the **applications backlog**; a situation aggravated by the large amount of time spent on existing system maintenance. This provides an obvious opportunity to **encourage the user** to take an **active part in the design** of 'his' computer system, with the analyst assuming more of an advisory role. In this environment an application prototype can prove invaluable, since it is an approach that **makes use of the expertise of both user and analyst**, in order to perform the difficult tasks of analysis, design and implementation.

The prototyping approach has **other advantages**, including an improvement in the **fact-finding** process, the **saving of human time** by using more computer time, an improvement in the **quality of analysis** generally and the encouragement of **user participation**. Users gain valuable computing knowledge and experience and hidden snags in the system can be discovered.

It is possible to obtain working versions of a system **very quickly**, often within days. This makes prototyping much **more responsive** than traditional linear methods. Linear methods also tend to **assume that there is a clear understanding** of current operations and of those that need to be computerised. Prototyping helps to develop a system specification where this is not the case. Prototyping also **increases the likelihood of a system being accepted**, indeed welcomed, by its users.

18 TUTORIAL QUESTION: STRUCTURED ANALYSIS AND DESIGN

(a) **Logical and physical elements**

The **logical** design of a system relates to the **processing** which is applied to the data in the system. It describes what the system is supposed to achieve. This would include details of the **timing of transactions** and rules regarding the **updating**. In other words the logical design is a description of what the system should do. **Documents are ignored**: the **data** in a customer order is recorded but the customer order form itself is not.

The **physical** design of a system comprises those aspects of the system which relate to physical, or **tangible** elements. These would include the computer **hardware, reports, screen formats** and **input media**. The flow of **documents** round the system is recorded. The physical design is a description of **how the system should achieve the logical design**.

(b) **Levelled dataflow diagrams**

A dataflow diagram (DFD) is a **pictorial representation** of the path which **data** takes from its **initial interaction** with the system until it **completes any interaction**. The diagram will describe the **logical data flows** without detailing the movement of any physical items.

The dataflow diagram is used initially as a tool by the analyst to **aid in understanding** the current or proposed system. The diagram gives insight into the **data** which is used in the system, **who** actually uses it and **where** it is temporarily or permanently **stored**.

Levels of dataflow diagram

The **complexity** of business systems means that it is impossible to represent the operations of any system by means of a **single** dataflow diagram. At the **top level**, an **overview** of the different systems in an organisation can be given, or alternatively the position of a single system in the organisation shown. This might be achieved by means of a **systems context diagram**.

Next, a summary of the **operation of a single system** can be shown by means of a **level-0** dataflow diagram. At this stage, a 'data process' symbol can be used to represent the workings of a whole department or of a series of related processes. This is in turn '**exploded**' by means of a **more detailed dataflow diagram**, known as a **level-one** DFD. **Further detail** can be represented on a **level-two** DFD, until all individual processes, sources and sinks and files are shown.

Level-0 - system input/output

A level-0 DFD describes the **system-wide boundaries**, detailing inputs to and outputs from the system. In the case of a sales ledger, for example, statements would be sent to the customer and payments received from him. Total sales figures and payment details would be sent to the nominal ledger. These are examples of inputs to and outputs from the system.

Level-1 - subsystem level data flow

A level-1 DFD describes the next level of detail within the system, detailing the **data flows between subsystems** which make up the whole. In the sales ledger, account details (name, address, credit limit, etc) would flow from the new customer authority to the sales ledger. Limit authorisations would flow from the ledger to the sales function. Sales ledger and sales day book updates would be examples of processes.

Level-2 - file level detail data flow.

A level-2 DFD details the **files to which the data is applied** in the system, and **from which data is obtained.** Each individual process is shown in detail. In the case of the sales ledger the account details would be applied to the customer master file, while the transactions would go into the transaction file. Transaction file data would then be used to update the master file.

19 WRF INC: SYSTEMS DEVELOPMENT LIFECYCLE

Pass marks. This question was set in 1996 so we have had to update the technical specification of the proposed system, to make it realistic. You were clearly meant to have doubts about the competence of the analyst and his recommendations. When referring to the SDLC be sure to relate the theory to the situation outlined in the question. The number of stages, and the naming of the stages of the SDLC will vary across models – this is not important. What is important is the planned, systematic approach the model describes and how you adapt the model to the situation.

Examiner's comment. The first part of the requirement was answered well by all candidates, but the second part produced answers of variable quality. Some answers gave detailed explanation of the theory of SDLC but nothing else: the lack of use of the case study information meant that few marks were obtained. Other answers gave excessive detail on the hardware and software requirements for WRF Inc, but not enough on other SDLC problems. The technology is important, but only to the extent that it supports the **information** systems or to show what the appropriate technology is.

REPORT

To: The Board

From: Management accountant

Date: 14 May 1998

Subject: Computer systems upgrade

This report urges the Board to adopt a **more formal approach** to the proposed systems upgrade than seems to have been envisaged up until now. The approach recommended is The Systems Development Life Cycle (SDLC), which is described in the next section of this report.

No action should be taken regarding the purchase of computer hardware and software until the **needs of the business** have been considered in more detail.

The Systems Development Life Cycle (SDLC)

The SDLC is a **disciplined approach to systems upgrades** intended to reduce the possibility of an end result that **does not meet the needs** of the organisation and **wastes time and money.**

There are six stages, although in practice the first three may overlap, and so may the fourth and fifth.

Feasibility study	Briefly review the existing system Identify possible alternative solutions
Systems investigation	Obtain details of current requirements such as data volumes, processing cycles and timescales Identify current problems and restrictions
Systems analysis	Consider why current methods are used and identify better alternatives
Systems design	Determine what inputs, processing and storage facilities are necessary to produce the outputs required Matters such as program design, file design and security need to be considered The end result is a detailed specification of the new system.
Systems implementation	Write or acquire software, test it, convert files, install hardware and start running the new system
Review and maintenance	Ensure that the new system meets current objectives, and that it continues to do so

The cycle **begins again** when a review suggests that it is becoming difficult for an installed system to continue to meet current objectives through routine maintenance.

Why WRF Inc should follow this approach

Arguably WRF has not even reached the end of the **first** of these stages, yet a purchase recommendation has been made for a highly standard system using hardware and software that is **already outdated** in terms of the fast-moving world of IT.

(a) A **systems investigation** is needed so that account is taken of the **specific requirements of users**. At present, users only know of a proposed change through the grapevine: they do not appear to have been formally consulted. This is particularly regrettable since they seem to be enthusiastic about change and would no doubt **have a good deal to contribute** to the specification of an ideal system for their needs.

(b) More **systems analysis** is required to determine what are the problems with the existing system. The upgrade is intended to improve the **speed** and **clarity** of information, but we have no details of how the design of the proposed new system will do this. The following points may be made.

  (i) Windows 98 is **hungry for hard disk space, processing power** and **memory**. The hardware proposed (basic Pentium PCs with running at only 75MHz) is **not adequate** to run Windows 98 versions of applications such as Microsoft Office.

  (ii) Is there a real **need for a LAN and e-mail**? Perhaps there is, or perhaps stand-alone PCs and conventional methods of communication would serve just as well, or perhaps a larger network would be more appropriate. **Other options** do **not** appear to have been **considered.**

(iii) Information in the company's **existing database** is likely to have to be **converted** in some way to make it compatible with the new system. What will this entail? Will data have to be entirely restructured and if so how. Will all the data have to be re-input, or is there software available to ease the task. Again the **full issues** do **not** appear to have been **considered.**

(c) Account must be taken of the **future needs** of the business. We trade in a dynamic environment and our information needs may well be significantly different in future years. Will the proposed system be able to cope with change and growth? Much of the proprietary software now being released (and no doubt being used by our competitors) is designed for a Windows 95/98 or Windows NT environment and requires a Pentium PC with around 64Mb of RAM and a large hard disk.

(d) The recommended system is reckoned to **cost** about $1,500 per user. Presumably this also includes a **shared element** for the network and communications infrastructure, for all the software and licences needed, and for peripherals such as printers.

However, we have **not actually been told what the figure includes**: we need a **detailed breakdown** of the **initial cost** and also of **ongoing costs** over the life of the proposed system. We should have similar details for alternatives within budget limits set by the Board.

(e) Arrangements need to be made for the **implementation** of the system. Even in the short term the analyst's contract ends at the installation stage: does this mean that we will be **without his support** during the early days of the system going live, when it would be unusual for there to be no teething problems?

Recommendation

The systems analyst should be asked to satisfy us on all of the above points, and modify his proposals as appropriate.

20 BKL PLC: NEW SYSTEMS BACKLOG

> **Pass marks.** There are a number of basic approaches to this problem which you could have described: using a bureau, subcontracting development to consultants, buying off-the-shelf application packages and encouraging end-user development. Applications backlogs are a serious problem, and prompted Blum to say 'Development is like talking to a distant star - by the time you receive the answer, you may have forgotten the question.'

Initial analysis

It would appear that BKL's **current policy on its computer service department's involvement** with all projects at the outset may be one of the prime causes of the applications backlog. The policy is clearly **well-intentioned.**

(a) It allows actual **co-ordination of computing resources** across the group.
(b) It **reduces the risk of duplication of effort** in different locations.
(c) It provides an **effective means of cost control.**
(d) It allows **economies of scale** in purchasing to be accessible.

However, it appears that there are a number of **problems.**

(a) Computer services does **not seem to have adequate resources** to carry out its function properly.

(b) The approach to **packaged/non-packaged software** may need to be reviewed.

(c) **Working methods** could probably be improved.

Any change should be preceded by an assessment of **how long** the backlog is, and how long some of the systems may have been awaiting development. An **initial survey** should be carried out to confirm that all the systems on the waiting list are **still required**. It is conceivable that some may no longer be wanted, and so can be removed from the list.

(a) **Resources**

The obvious change which can be made to affect the rate at which systems are introduced is to **increase the resources** allocated to the task. There will be an increase in systems introduction (although it will not be linear, or proportional to the increase in resource, in other words doubling the resources will not necessarily double the rate of introduction, due to a number of other factors). Resources which can be increased include **development manpower** (with the use of additional permanent or temporary **staff**, or the use of **external development organisations**), **equipment, training** resources, **time** (allow overtime or reduce other commitments) and **funds** (provide bonus payments for early completion).

If the computer services department is able to **charge its costs out** to the rest of the group, it should not have significant budgetary problems of its own in increasing headcount. Of course, there may be **'political' issues** to consider and the move would have to be justified: other departments would need to be **persuaded of the benefits** if their charges are to increase.

Hiring **more systems development staff** would be a **long-term solution** to the problem rather than a short-term solution because new staff would have to be found and then trained.

Using **external consultants** to help with systems development work is a **short-term solution** to the problem, because such expertise is expensive to hire. Consultants could be found:

(i) to develop systems, from **start to finish**; or

(ii) to help with a **particular stage** in systems development work - such as program development and testing.

(b) **Parameters**

Changes to parameters include modifications to a number of factors. **Packaged solutions** could be used in preference to in-house developments, the scope or **level of complexity** of the systems could be **reduced, large projects** could be **split** and introduced in stages, and **large projects** can be **re-scheduled** to the **end of the queue** (thus allowing more projects to be introduced in the short and medium term). It would also be possible to split development activities so that small projects are handled by a different team from large projects and to **give priority to small projects**.

It is now fairly common for companies which sell **off-the-shelf** software to be prepared to write some **amendments** into a software package to the specifications of a customer, so that the package becomes, to a certain extent, 'tailor-made' for the customer. Some of the systems on the waiting list might be suitable for the use of an off-the-shelf package with such **tailor-made amendments**.

(c) **Working methods**

Changes to methods of working include decreasing development times through the **use of different tools** (such as recent, more powerful design tools and better software writing tools such as higher or more structured languages), or the introduction of **prototyping**.

Consideration could also be given to **decreasing the amount of testing** performed on a system prior to its release or decreasing the **level of documentation** provided with the system, although both these options should be carefully controlled.

It may be possible to **involve users** in development teams, either as advisors (which has the additional benefit of obtaining their commitment prior to the introduction of the systems, and avoiding problems at the installation time) or as developers of small systems or sub-sets of systems which they can generate using tools such as **report generators** or **spreadsheets**.

Very often many factors are at play in such situations.

(i) One is the **number of projects** in the backlog. This can be reduced by completing small projects first; this would, though, create negative feelings among managers of the larger projects. However, it is often very useful to be able to register some visible progress.

(ii) A second factor is that projects which are **more than eighteen months old** often need to be **re-designed** due to altered circumstances anyway.

(iii) A third factor which should sometimes be considered is that workloads are often used as the **justification for the existence of a function**, and there can be a tendency for projects to be added to lists (and therefore affect delivery of other projects on the lists) simply in order to provide a continuing **reason to keep a department running**.

(d) **Fourth Generation Languages**

Fourth Generation Languages (4GLs) enable users to build systems without going through intermediaries, because the 4GL is designed for both **computing specialists** and **end-users**. They are used to build systems **quickly and inexpensively** and can therefore be considered effective development tools.

The **user** specifies the **data** to be used, the **operations** to be performed and the **output** required; all this is done through a fairly simple English-like syntax.

4GLs are best suited to end-user development of **reporting/analysis systems**, rather than the conventional transaction processing system. This allows the computer professional to continue working on major projects, whilst the user gets on with drawing data from the database in the manner he wants.

4GLs can be categorised into:

(i) information centre tools **extracting and presenting information** from existing databases, often unsuitable for development of high performance production systems;

(ii) **transaction generator systems**, specialist tools for programmers giving greater productivity to development of online transaction processing; and

(iii) **application generator systems**, which enable users to build multi-user production systems, and may also provide decision support facilities.

When used with a prototyping approach, 4GLs can much more readily incorporate new **user requirements**, provide **earlier feedback** to users, and enhance **user participation** and relationships, because user involvement is more or less continuous throughout the development process. 4GL use does however place **heavy demands on the user** to define his requirements and to envisage clearly how the system will work in practice.

21 MFS LTD: PROJECTS

> **Pass marks**. This question it is not as broad-ranging as a typical Section A 60 mark case study. Its purpose is to give you some experience at tackling these long questions, and to provide a thorough test of your understanding of the 'systems development' part of the syllabus.

(a) **The advantages of using a methodology**

It should be noted that there are two main areas of problem facing MFS Ltd. One is the **specific MIS project** currently under way and the second is more generally the company's **standard approach to systems development**. The first appears to be as much a **project management** issue, with perhaps some unfortunate decisions being made at the outset, as a systems development issue. However, the company's approach to development may have contributed to it and there is no doubt now that this problem is in turn lengthening the applications backlog.

The key features of a typical structured systems methodology are set out below.

Project management

The structured framework of a methodology **helps with planning**. It defines the **tasks** to be performed and sets out **when** they should be done. Each step has an **identifiable end product**. This allows control by reference to actual achievements rather than to estimates of progress. Users are able to see progress as clearly as systems professionals can.

The transition at **MFS** must be managed effectively, so that there is no further excess disruption and expense. It is obviously quite a difficult process, and there is a **danger of getting bogged down in sorting out current problems**, rather than looking ahead.

Techniques

There is an **emphasis on techniques**. As an example, three techniques are used in SSADM: dataflow diagrams, logical data structures and entity life histories. These allow information to be **cross-checked** between diagrams and ensure that the delivered system is close to the final system, in other words that the **necessity for later enhancements is minimised**. For example, an event in an entity life history will match data flows which trigger processes on the dataflow diagrams. These techniques and others are also available in different methodologies.

The specification

A logical design is produced that is **independent of hardware and software**. This logical design can then be given a physical design using whatever computer equipment and implementation language is required. The information that hardware installation is on course it is a little worrying, to say the least.

Users

Users are involved with development work from an early stage. Their involvement is a critical factor in the success of any development. A methodology encourages better communication between users and developers.

Documentation

Documentation is produced throughout the project. This gives a comprehensive and detailed picture of the system and helps understanding of the system. This makes the consequences of proposed changes clear and encourages user feedback.

Contractors

Several commercial methodologies are **used widely** enough to be known to many systems professionals. This is obviously an advantage, as it reduced dependence on individual suppliers or contractors.

Methodology

A methodology provides a set of **development standards** to which all parties can adhere.

Emphasis on graphical techniques

The emphasis on diagramming makes the system **easier to understand** for relevant parties, including users, than if narrative descriptions were used. Some narrative can be used; however if this is excessive, the advantage of the diagramming techniques is lost.

(b) **Why are projects time-consuming?**

The systems development lifecycle approach to systems development imposes a **disciplined approach** to the development process, it **encourages communication** between systems professionals and 'ordinary' users and it recognises the importance of **analysis and design**.

However, while it has some advantages, in **early forms** it had a number of **drawbacks**, some of which, although not in direct conflict with current views as incorporated into many methodologies, do not embrace the same philosophy.

Ignoring management

The SDLC is efficient at **automating operational areas** within easily defined processing requirements, such as payroll. Computerisation is seen as a means of speeding up high-volume routine transaction processing, not providing information for decision making. Therefore, the **information needs of middle and senior management can be ignored**.

Such an approach is not entirely appropriate at MFS, where a **management information system** is the main new feature. A methodology would encourage user involvement and invites management at all levels to specify their requirements. Of course, unrealistic requirements may not be met.

No radical rethink of current operations

When computer systems were first introduced, they were modelled after the **manual systems** they were replacing. All that happened was that **clerical procedures** carried out by people were **computerised**.

Where computerisation is **more ambitious**, it can lead to a potentially beneficial **rethink** of the way the organisation carries out its activities. As noted earlier, a methodology would produce a logical design independent of hardware and software requirements, encouraging a less constrained approach to developments.

User requirements poorly defined

Much systems design is based around what the **user**, at an early stage in the development of a system, has specified as to what **output** is required. This ultimately determines what is input to the system, the file structures introduced and so forth.

However, **output requirements can be altered**, even during systems development, and this can result in **substantial design modifications**. It has been estimated that a simple change in user requirements costs over 20 times as much to rectify after acceptance testing than after the design phase. Software maintenance consumes about 70% of the cost of developing a system.

This is likely to be a particular problem at MFS, given the lack of user involvement. If a methodology were to be used, the user is involved throughout the process and so the risk of divergence between requirements and actual development is reduced.

Documentation

Under earlier approaches to development much system **documentation** was written for **programmers and specialists**. It was **highly technical**, more of a technical manual than a guide for the user. Problems could also occur if inadequately documented modifications led to 'bugs' elsewhere in the system. The approach adopted should ensure that documentation is rigorously demanded and documentation standards are high.

Systems not complete

Many routine transaction processing systems could not cope with **unusual situations**, and so some complicated processing was still performed manually. With earlier approaches the system may be inadequately designed. A greater emphasis on logical design would reduce the problem.

Applications backlog

Time overruns mean that systems take a long time to develop. One of the causes is the time spent to **maintain old systems.**

At MFS, it is unlikely that there is resource available, either for other new systems or for systems maintenance. By encouraging **standardisation** on a single method, a methodology ensures that development is done in the same way each time and thus provides a basis for **estimation, management control** and subsequent **maintenance.**

(c) **MEMO**

To: Managing Director
From: Management Accountant
Date: 14 September 19X7
Subject: Systems development

This memorandum suggests ways of reducing the time spent on systems development, increasing user participation and developing quality systems.

Traditional systems development cycle

I do not consider the use of the traditional systems development cycle to be viable. I recommend that we switch entirely to a commercial methodology.

In the **traditional** systems development process the **user is isolated** from any close contact with the system during its development. Typically the user should be **intensively involved** during the design stage during which the system functions and requirements are defined so that a **system specification** is produced. This specification then serves as a **design document** during the system design and implementation phase so that the system analysts and programmers know what to produce.

The **weaknesses** of the current approach at MFS are manifold but two major ones are described here.

(i) Many users have **little real idea of what computer systems are** or how they operate. This ignorance is a very poor foundation for building a systems specification. This type of user typically **does not know what information is**

important for designing the system with the natural consequence that these systems are often incomplete or fail to achieve the required level of functionality.

(ii) A second drawback to traditional methods arises with even experienced users. Users often have **incorrect or unrealistic ideas** about what systems can do or how various functions might operate. In the traditional approach these ideas would not be corrected until the system itself was delivered. In these instances users would feel let down and often regard the systems as failures.

An additional problem arises because applications tend to **evolve over time** so that system specifications become less appropriate. If, as with many mainframe systems, the development effort takes a relatively long time the delivered system may no longer effectively perform the application it was **intended** to perform.

Prototyping

Systems prototyping can significantly reduce these problems by allowing the **user** to **participate actively** in the systems design and development process. Rather than producing a detailed specification the prototyping approach aims at producing a **simplified version of the system**, a prototype, which the user may then try out. Typically, the user might be able to try out **data input screens** or perform **file enquiries**.

The advantage of this approach is that the user actually **sees a system in operation** and can judge its usefulness and operation. This is extremely useful for users who are unfamiliar with information systems since they often revise their specifications as they become more familiar with the system's workings.

This approach greatly **reduces last minute system modifications** or enhancements - users can notice deficiencies before systems are delivered so that specifications may more fully address user needs.

CASE tools

Structured methods are reasonably widely used in a number of organisations. They are mandatory in many government IT functions. Their use, although standardising many results, does impose quite an overhead in terms of increased demands for correct **form filling** at stages of the software production process, as well as a requirement for larger amounts of other **paperwork** particularly in relation to updates and standards.

CASE tools can reduce the effort required to perform some of the stages of the structured methodology by **automatically producing the required stages**. Many CASE tools go some way towards producing working programs.

The CASE tool should provide the following facilities.

(i) **Support for the methodology** used by the IT function

(ii) Ability to **interface** directly to the central **data dictionary**

(iii) **Access and version control**, to prevent unauthorised use and to ensure the right 'master' is being worked on

(iv) **Graphical prototyping facilities** to assist in the production of reports, screens etc

(v) Ability to **assess the impact of changes** and also to **validate design work**

(vi) Facilities called **code-generators** to produce program output in a variety of programming languages

(vii) Ability to function on a **reasonable-specification PC** while maintaining control for a multi-member team

Conclusion

We should give serious consideration to the use of prototyping and CASE tools to speed up our systems development. Prototyping in particular will increase user participation, as will greater emphasis on a structured method. These measures should contribute significantly to the development of quality systems.

(d) **Project management**

The introduction of a new computer system can have a number of effects on the organisation. Some of the possible problems are clearly being experienced at MFS, particularly in connection with the **transitional arrangements** during the development of the new system.

(i) It can be **costly in terms of personnel** (requiring a team of system analysts or programmers if developed in-house, or consultancy fees if developed by outsiders). The extension from 18 months to 2 years suggests that personnel costs will be at least one third over budget.

(ii) Even if an application **package** is purchased, this can still be an **expensive** item.

(iii) The right **hardware** must be purchased

(iv) It is costly in terms of **management time** and attention. Managers from user departments inevitably get involved in systems development projects. Also different managers can have different ideas as to what is desirable. Here, it would appear that here is a 'black hole' effect in which increasing systems professional, user and management time is being taken up with the project.

(v) It is **disruptive**.

A **project** involves the management of a number of **disparate, yet interdependent activities,** within a **timetable** and a **budget** set in advance. A particular project is unique, in that by its nature once done it is never repeated.

Efficient management of the resources and process of the project is therefore important for the organisation and the achievement of the project's objectives. It would appear that this, more than the existence of an applications backlog, is the **key problem which MFS needs to resolve** as soon as possible in order to prevent any real damage being done to the company, for example through regulatory breaches or loss of customer goodwill and/or employee morale.

An approach to project management

A basic approach to project management would be as follows.

(i) **Delegation of overall responsibilities**. A steering committee comprising senior user department personnel, a member of the finance department and various systems professionals is appointed to oversee the project. If the organisation has an Information Director, this individual is likely to have a key role on the steering committee.

(ii) **Appointment of a project manager**. This individual plans, manages and executes the project and is responsible for its successful completion. The project manager presents the timetable and budget to the steering committee for their approval and authorisation.

(iii) **Project planning.** The **goals** of the project are identified, and the **activities needed to achieve them** are outlined. These are then matched to the manpower resources available, so that a project **timetable** can be outlined and agreed. The timetable will indicate **when** each activity has to be completed, and in **which order**. **Each stage** of the project is then planned in its own right. The stages of the project may be determined by the systems development methodology adopted.

(iv) **Controlling the project**. Actual outcomes are compared to the plan and any difficulties dealt with as soon as they become apparent. A position where the organisation falls six months behind and is only nine months into the project should never be allowed to occur and should in any case be forecast well in advance so that remedial action can be taken. **Regular progress meetings** should be held by the project manager with members of the project team to monitor performance. Specified **documentation** is produced at the end of each stage for review and approval, in accordance with quality control criteria established for projects of this nature. At the end of each stage, progress will be reported to the steering committee. **Users** should be consulted, as their approval is necessary to demonstrate that the project is meeting its objectives.

(v) **Output of the project**. This must meet any **technical criteria** of the organisation. This means that all the relevant **documentation** must be completed to an adequate standard, project files must be **cross referenced,** and there should be a clear relationship evidenced between the work done in the various successive stages of the project.

In summary, therefore, the project is controlled in **two ways**. Firstly the **technical quality** of the output is reviewed. Secondly, the **efficiency** with which the project tasks are carried out is also subject to management review and control.

Reviewing project effectiveness

The effectiveness of project management techniques used can be assessed during the life of the project and when it is completed. Participants should be asked for feedback, but, more formally, the project manager should estimate the **causes for each departure from standard**, and take corrective measures. This will require the establishment of a suitable management information system, so that the project manager can obtain feedback on the timetable for and success of stages of the development as each is undertaken. The monitoring process should take into account four criteria.

(i) **Time**, by reference to critical path analysis or Gantt charts.
(ii) **Resources**, by measuring available resources and percentage utilisation.
(iii) **Costs**, by reference to the MIS and budgets.
(iv) **Quality**, as appropriate.

22 TUTORIAL QUESTION: TRAINING

(a) **Expectations of the course**

A one-day course for clerical staff with no previous computer experience must inevitably be **restricted** in what it sets out to achieve.

(i) Obviously, there must be a **familiarisation** process, and an attempt to explain to the staff **how the change of system will affect them** in their jobs. This process must discuss:

(1) **why** the new system is necessary; and

(2) **what it means** for the staff. It will be important to explain how they will be retrained to do jobs in the new system, how they will not be left behind by the technological progress, and how the new equipment will

not disrupt the social fabric of their working relationship with colleagues.

The aim of this familiarisation process could be to begin to persuade staff that there is a **need for change**, and to give them **confidence** that they can handle the change.

(ii) There must be an **introduction to computers**, which explains in broad outline what a computer does, and how it affects office working. A training video or PC-based presentation might be available for show. The aim should be to give trainees a basic grounding in computer knowledge.

(iii) Staff should be introduced to the **physical hardware** that they will have to use. Keyboards and screens should be available to give staff some direct experience of what they are like. If possible, they should be given a few minutes' practice each, perhaps with the aid of an instruction program on the use of PCs. This will be part of the familiarisation process.

(iv) There must be a session on **how the new system will work** in some detail, in particular in the ways it will affect the staff directly. The explanation of the new system will undoubtedly give rise to numerous queries. These should be discussed at some length, to **reassure staff** that all eventualities have been foreseen.

(v) Since there is a limit to the information that trainees can absorb in one day, they should be provided with ample **documentation** and notes to take away with them.

(b) **Topics**

Topics to be covered are hinted at in part (a) of this solution. They would be:

(i) the **reasons** for introducing the new system;
(ii) the **new organisation**;
(iii) a **background in computer knowledge**, aided by a video or computer based training and training notes;
(iv) practical experience in PC operations;
(v) a discussion of the new system, based on questions from trainees.

(c) **Follow-up action**

Since the course lasts only one day, there must be follow-up to train the staff still further. The **momentum** started by the course should not be lost; rather, it should be built up.

Essential follow-up action must take the following into account.

(i) **Further training** in the new system operations will be necessary. Staff who will input data must be given a further course on using PCs.

(ii) Heads of clerical sections should **continue the process of explaining** the new system. Details introduced on the course should be explained again to ensure that they are understood. **Individual responsibilities** should be outlined in more detail.

(iii) **Testing** the new system should **involve the staff who will use the system**. A large-scale test would enable staff to gain experience in the system before it goes 'live' and to learn the codes, and error reports etc. Any teething troubles can be dealt with at this stage.

(iv) **Further comments and suggestions** should be discussed between clerical staff and the systems designers, perhaps in an open forum discussion meeting.

(v) Eventually, **further developments** to the system will need to be **explained**.

The **progress** of staff should be **monitored** throughout the training period. Staff with the job of inputting data should be checked regularly for input speed and error rates. Similarly, staff responsible for, say, coding input data should be checked for error rates and speed of working. Performance of staff should thereby be built up to satisfactory standards.

23 TUTORIAL QUESTION: SOFTWARE AND HARDWARE

(a) **Areas for computerisation**

(i) **Patient medical records** could held on computer, subject to the requirements of the Data Protection Act. A substantial amount of time and money would be spent on file design and set-up, but **savings in space**, and **file retrieval times** would be considerable. Additionally the introduction of **statistical information** would be easier as records displaying certain criteria could be selected.

(ii) The **appointments system** could also be computerised. Many software packages used in the 'electronic office' offer **diary software**, not only for individuals, but also to schedule meetings.

(iii) **General correspondence** could be word processed. It might be possible to access patient records directly if the word processing package was integrated to the database.

(iv) It would be quite easy to computerise the **accounting and staff records,** including the **payroll**, as there are accounting packages available for small business systems.

(v) The **statistical returns** report could be computerised. Data could be obtained from patient records.

(b) **Types and range of software**

(i) The Centre is likely to require a **database** for all the patient information. With 30,000 patient records, this is likely to be extensive. A suitable database management system could be purchased. Alternatively, one could be developed from scratch using a database application generator. It may be the case that the Area Health Authority has developed a **standard application** which can be implemented at Newtown.

(ii) The Centre could acquire **office automation software**. This could schedule meetings, provide a diary facility, and e-mail for the doctors and staff.

(iii) For the statistical analysis, a **spreadsheet package** could be used. A spreadsheet application could in theory be written to computerise the payroll.

(iv) Simple **accounting software** could provide automate any bookkeeping that is required. This may be needed if the Centre has to work to a budget (for example for drugs).

(c) **Hardware configuration**

The hardware choice will be made once the Centre's information and data processing requirements and the software to satisfy them have been identified. Ideally, then, the hardware is **only considered after the system itself has been designed**. In practice, the Centre might operate under **budgetary constraints,** and so the choice of hardware might be **restricted** by them. This in turn will affect the nature and extent of computerisation.

Assuming that the Centre has sufficient funds to meet its needs, possible hardware configurations are:

(i) several **stand-alone personal computers** with printers;
(ii) **networked** personal computers;
(iii) a small **minicomputer** with dumb terminals.

Additionally, data might be transmitted over the **telecommunications network** to the area health authority.

Stand-alone personal computers would be **unlikely to satisfy** the Centre's needs. Several users may wish to access the patient database, and this may be difficult with such a configuration.

The **disadvantage of a minicomputer-based system** is that if it goes wrong then the whole of the Centre's data processing requirements are impaired. However, it would use substantial storage space.

A **PC network seems to be the best option**, with one computer acting as a central file server. This can be added to very easily.

A **minimum specification** for the file server might include a Pentium III processor, 128 Mb of RAM and around 15 Gb of hard disk space. If possible the system should offer easy upgradeability.

24 TUTORIAL QUESTION: MAINTENANCE OF SOFTWARE

(a) Maintenance in the software context is the amendment of computer programs where they have been found to **contain errors** or where the computer user has decided that they ought to be capable of doing **additional processing** routines or should process some data in a **different way**.

Programs might also require adaptation to meet **new external requirements** eg new legislation, or because of **changes in the general hardware and software** of the system of which they are a part.

These various reasons are considered in a little more detail below.

(i) **Error correction**

Although all programs should be thoroughly tested before they are used for 'live' processing, it is sometimes the case that 'bugs' in the system are only revealed once live processing has been implemented. In this situation, it is essential that the errors are corrected as soon as possible, with every effort being made to ensure that all data records, reports etc affected by the errors are also corrected as part of the process of program maintenance.

(ii) **Changes in user requirements**

Most businesses will experience the need to change their systems in some way as they adapt to changed circumstances or simply because they have learned from experience that existing procedures could be achieved in a more effective way. Given such genuine reasons for change, it is essential that software maintenance is readily available to ensure that user needs are met.

(iii) **External factors requiring change**

Maintenance of software may be required as a result of such external factors as industry practice (eg metrication) or new legislation either fiscal (eg new tax rates) or general (eg The Data Protection Act). All businesses may have a need to respond to such external forces in the adaptation of their software.

(iv) **Changes in general hardware and software**

As more aspects of a company's activities are computerised, new user requirements are introduced etc, there may well be a need for additions to and/or replacement of existing hardware and software configurations. Such changes may well require the amendment of existing programs in order to cope with the new environment.

(b) As seen above, some **changes** in a company's software are almost **inevitable** at some stage. However, it may be possible to reduce the requirement for maintenance and ensure that it is carried out efficiently where necessary by always adhering to the principles of **good programming practice**. These include the following.

(i) The **program requirements** must be **specified in full and in writing**. These specifications will be prepared by a systems analyst. A programmer has the task of converting these specifications into a written program.

(ii) In developing a program, a programmer should keep **working papers**. He can refer back to these papers later to check what he has done in case:

(1) there is an **error in the program** for correcting;

(2) the user of the program asks for a **change in the program** - eg for an extra bit of processing on input data, perhaps to produce an additional report.

(iii) When writing a program, the programmer should try to **keep it as short as possible**, since this will make more efficient use of processing capacity in the CPU. The program should therefore be **logically well-structured**.

(iv) Programs should be **tested** when they have been written. A programmer should prepare test data and establish whether the program will process the data according to the specifications given by the systems analyst.

(v) Provisions should be made for **program amendments**.

(vi) A **record** should be kept of all **program errors** that are found during 'live' processing of data, and the **corrections** that are made to the program.

(vii) Each **version** of a program (eg versions that are produced with processing modifications or corrections to errors) should be **separately identified**, to avoid a mix-up about what version of a program should be used.

Other approaches to minimising maintenance include the following.

(i) **Prototyping**, which ensures user acceptance of key aspects of systems design.

(ii) A **contract with a software house** which commits to issuing upgrades and bug 'fixes'.

25 LDS: EVALUATING SUPPLIERS

> **Pass marks**. A variety of answers are possible. The six questions in the CIMA model answer concern: skills, efficiency, experience, reliability, cost and financial stability.
>
> **Examiner's comment.** The vast majority of answers could have been improved in two important respects.
>
> Firstly, by ensuring that appropriate questions were asked. A significant number of candidates did not actually provide a list of questions and therefore failed to meet the question requirement. Candidates also needed to ensure that the questions asked were actually appropriate. Many of the questions asked were fairly general concerning the system to be provided instead of concentrating on the supplier.
>
> Secondly, answers could have been improved by making the questions relevant to the specific circumstances of LDS. For example, a question might be asked concerning the training that the supplier would provide. However, the candidate would then fail to mention the fact that LDS was changing from a DOS to a Windows system, which meant that detailed training on an entirely new system would be needed.

Evaluating potential suppliers

Questions that LDS might ask of potential suppliers for its upgraded database include the following.

(a) **Reputation and stability of the supplier**

How **well established** is the supplier's company? Is it well-known for producing **good software solutions**? Has it been trading long? In the computer industry, it is quite common for small firms of suppliers or software houses to set up in business and then go into liquidation soon after. A firm with a **reasonably long history of trading** would be more likely to have some financial stability.

Certain **mainstream suppliers**, such as Microsoft and Oracle, are industry giants. They are highly regarded, and can be relied upon to produce a product that will serve LDS's needs well in the future. If LDS's original database software came from a source such as this it is probable that a **standard upgrade** based on Windows already exists.

However, although a **standard upgrade** will include functions to convert data from previous formats, it will **not reflect the modifications** that have been made to the original software. This means that **special tailoring** will be necessary, and any supplier of services in this respect needs to be checked. Ideally a supplier endorsed by the original software manufacturer, such as a **Certified Microsoft Solution Provider**, should be employed.

(b) **Benchmarking**

LDS's needs are likely to be unique to its circumstances, so suppliers will not be able to introduce LDS to any previous customers for the precise service that LDS requires. However, suppliers may have **other customers** whose software has been modified in other ways, and these customers may be able to **provide testimonials** as to how quickly and effectively the supplier did the work, how good they are at supporting it, subsequent problems if any, and so on.

(c) **Cost and timescale**

How do the **costs** of each of the suppliers compare? Do their tenders **break down** the costs so that it can be clearly seen what is and what is not included? For instance key issues are likely to be the **Internet-readiness** of the new system, and **32-bit** rather than 16-bit compatibility. Are suppliers providing a system that will work now, but will need **further modification**, at further cost, in the near future? Is new technology imminent that may render this system obsolete?

Is the supplier **able to meet the deadline** of six months for implementation of the new system? What arrangements do they propose to make in the event that the deadline is not met? If this possibility has not even been considered is the tender realistic at all?

(d) **Skills**

Do the supplier's staff appear to have a good **knowledge**, not only of **database software**, but also of the data **service** that LDS provides? LDS provides data of a highly technical nature about legislation, government proceedings and local conditions.

If the chosen supplier is **not familiar with the work that LDS does**, LDS will find it **hard to discuss any operational teething troubles** they might be having with the new database.

(e) **Hardware implications**

Windows-based applications are much hungrier for hardware power than character-based ones. What are the **hardware recommendations** of the supplier, **how much** will upgrading of hardware cost, and is this **in line with other objectives** of LDS?

(f) **Training and support**

At present a character-based system is used and it is quick and efficient. Windows-based systems are theoretically easier to use, because they are more intuitive, but if staff have never encountered such systems before then they will need a certain amount of **training in basic Windows skills** before they become as productive as they were in the past.

Do the suppliers undertake to **provide** any necessary training?

On-going support is also a major issue. It is most unlikely that all eventualities will be foreseen before the new system goes live. Moreover it is highly likely that further modifications will be necessary in the future, given the fast-changing nature of LDS's business. Do the suppliers **undertake to provide support** in the future, and if so **what level** of support and at **what cost**?

26 SWM LTD: IMPLEMENTATION

(a) **REPORT**

To: Departmental managers
From: Systems administrator
Date: 4 January 19X7
Subject: Recommendations for speeding up data processing

In response to the chief executive's memo of 31 December 19X6, I have pleasure in enclosing a report on SWM's information system. The report covers the topic listed above. Please contact me with feedback and/or queries by 7th January.

Information deficiencies

The following information deficiencies are apparent in the system.

(i) The **stock records** held on the mainframe and used by the sales order team will inevitably show **different positions** from the warehouse's own stock control system on the warehouse minicomputer. **Duplication** of stock records in this way should be **eliminated** if possible.

(ii) The listings sent to the warehouse must sometimes include **orders for out-of-stock items**, as the records used for sales order booking are a day **out of date** at all times. Customers might be unhappy not to be notified that there is a problem when ordering.

(iii) It is not clear whether there is a procedure for **same day despatch** of urgent orders.

(iv) **Keying in** of customer invoices in the accounts department is **inefficient** and provides a likely source of errors during input. Such **re-keying** of data should be **eliminated**.

(v) Provision of **management information** is, as noted in the company's own review, **poor.**

The first major issue is therefore for the company to ensure that the new database should hold a **single set of stock records**, available to all departments on both sites. **Telecommunications links** will eliminate the physical risks inherent in the use of couriers and will also allow all records to be updated at the same time. Similarly, billing details should be posted to ledgers **without re-keying.**

The second issue concerns management information. A system with a much **more flexible reporting framework** is required. A good database should allow this.

Speeding up processing

The comments above will enable all departments to have access to up-to-date data. Other suggestions for speeding up processing are as follows.

(i) An **upgrade to the existing processor** may be necessary. If the number of users or volume of transactions processed is higher than was ever envisaged when the existing system was purchased, it may be necessary to install a more powerful, and faster, processor.

(ii) An **increase in available RAM** (random access memory) would allow more relevant program files and data files to be stored in RAM during processing. This would reduce the number of transfers between RAM and hard disks during processing.

(iii) The system could be redesigned so that **more local processing** is performed using PCs and perhaps minicomputers at local sites. The mainframe could then be used for the stock database and for bulk storage and printing applications. Local terminals could be replaced by processors and used for small/medium-sized local requirements.

(iv) An analysis could be performed of **how time-critical** various processing operations are. **Batch processing** of non-critical operations could be scheduled for overnight/weekend running: this might improve processing speeds for higher priority operations done during working hours.

(v) A new **operating system** (perhaps an open system) might be appropriate. This would be likely to provide improvements in processing speed. Of course, this might require the mainframe to be replaced too.

(vi) A **separate processor** designed specifically to deal with **communications** and related issues could be installed 'between' the mainframe and the terminals. This 'front-end processor' would deal with protocols, sending and receiving messages, terminal allocation, security and related technical matters, leaving the mainframe free to continue with processing.

(b) **Controls**

Information is a **vital resource** of any organisation, and steps have to be taken to ensure its **security and integrity** as if it were any other valuable asset. Just as there are systems to ensure against theft or destruction of tangible assets, so too are measures taken to protect data and information.

Physical access

It is possible to enumerate any number of threats to the integrity and privacy of data held in any system. There are basic **physical dangers** such as **fire** which need guarding against. Controls to minimise risk include fireproof cabinets where important files are kept. Also, there are basic measures relating to **physical access** by **unauthorised people** to an organisation's premises. These physical controls relate both to the equipment and the storage media. In a database system like the one described, this is likely to be a random access storage medium. Both **backup** copies and **backup systems** can be maintained in case of disasters.

Particular risks at SWM Ltd relate to the use of **couriers and floppy disks** to transfer data between sites. Even assuming back-ups are available, it is still possible that loss or corruption of disks could retard processing by 24 hours.

In a new multi-user database system, the **database file will be held centrally**, and the problem of physical access to the medium on which the data is stored will not be multiplied over several sites. Also, it will be easier to keep backup copies of one set of files than of several.

Logical access

The database contains data relating to a number of different applications, some of which might be for **restricted viewing only**. Access to the entire database should be restricted also, for the same reasons. The type of control that will serve both functions is a **password system**, in which each user is given a unique code. The password can determine entry to the database, and also restrict users to specific views of it.

A further measure would be to **restrict an individual user to one terminal**, so that the password keyed in from that terminal could be checked to see that it corresponds in some way to the terminal itself.

For this system to work, **passwords must be kept strictly confidential** between users, and also as far as outsiders are concerned. Passwords should be **changed regularly**.

Communications

If data is transferred over a telecommunications link (as proposed earlier in this solution), controls should be made as far as possible to minimise the risks of **hacking**. Data sent over the link can be subjected to **encryption** and **authentication** procedures. **Dial-back** procedures can be used: they request callers to hang up and they then telephone the caller ensuring that the number is taken from a pre-set database.

Errors

The integrity of data can also be threatened by error. **Human error** can occur both in systems design and programming. Controls in the **design stage,** to avoid bugs, include adherence to programming standards, testing and so forth, before the database system is implemented. The same can be said for controls over **system maintenance and updating**. Proper **documentation**, **testing** and **authorisation** should minimise the risk of further design error.

Other forms of error can occur in the **operational stage**. There can be **programmed controls** over data input. These include **check digits, range checks, format checks** and so forth. The **user interface** can be so designed to make input of data strictly guided.

Personnel

Controls over personnel relate to a **separation of functions** as far as possible between programming staff and operational staff, so that operational staff do not have the opportunity to amend programs fraudulently, and so that programming staff do not get the opportunity to interfere with live data for fraudulent ends. For sensitive positions **strict recruitment procedures** should be followed.

With **end-user computing**, some of these controls are **hard to maintain**. In the situation outlined in this case, however, control over the database is maintained **centrally** so this is **not so much of a problem**.

(c) **REPORT**

To: Chief Executive
From: Systems administrator
Date: 11 January 19X7
Subject: Report on software maintenance

Software maintenance is necessary in three separately identifiable situations. Software maintenance may be required to **correct errors** which arise through normal operations. Software updates may be required following **changes in operating procedures** or from **external regulation**. Finally software may be enhanced simply to keep up with new **technical developments.**

Corrective maintenance

Faults may develop in applications software, often when consistently **higher than expected volumes of data** are processed. Volume limits are a key part of any software and it is important that these are reviewed regularly to maintain efficiency. Increases in volume may require software and hardware upgrades (such as additional RAM).

Testing procedures will identify most potential faults **prior to installation**. These may be caused, for instance, by incorrect programming or inadequate data validation checks. It is likely, however, especially in the first few months of use, that **further faults** will arise during normal operations. These will often be caused by a combination of **unusual data entries** or **operator errors**. Correction of these more obscure faults may be time-consuming and expensive.

Hardware failures can require changes to the operating system software. Additional warnings or error messages may be introduced. Procedures to **back up files automatically** when a system fails may be written into the software.

The **operating system** software may also develop faults if it is installed incorrectly or if it is not fully compatible with the hardware. OS faults are comparatively rare because development and testing of these products is necessarily more rigorous than is sometimes the case with applications packages.

Adaptive maintenance

Manufacturers may regularly **upgrade** standard applications or general purpose packages to **provide additional features** or make them **more user-friendly**. Customers need to decide **whether to accept the upgrade**, which is rarely supplied free of charge and will involve staff commitment to the new software. Non-acceptance of upgrades may lead to less effective support from the software supplier whose expertise is focused on the latest version of the package.

The **operating procedures and needs** of the user may change. This is very common with outputs such as reports and screen layouts which are often changed to suit user requirements. Data processing operations are less often changed because they are more likely to reflect standard procedures whereas computer outputs evolve to meet the needs of the business. Many applications packages now **allow users to make minor software changes themselves**; this usually takes the form of report generation.

Hardware upgrades are common in **larger** systems and this often results in operating software being changed or entirely rewritten. Hardware changes range from a simple memory upgrade to changing from multi-user to networked systems.

External regulation often leads to mandatory changes in software which can be quite extensive. A typically example is the change to various **tax rates** after the annual budget statement in the UK. These are normally straightforward and are often planned for in financial applications packages. However, the consequences of, for example, introducing multiple VAT rates would generally be complex and expensive for most businesses.

Perfective maintenance

Users may request enhancements to software which is not producing errors, but which could be made **more user-friendly** or improved in some other way. This may involve, for example, redesigning menu screens or switching to graphical user interfaces.

It may be possible to rewrite sections of programs to **improve efficiency and response times**. As noted above, output may be redesigned to provide better quality information.

(d) **Training**

> **Pass marks.** You do not need specific knowledge of Oracle to answer this question. It would help generally, however, if you could familiarise yourself with database software. Microsoft Access is a widely available package, with good on-line demonstrations and tutorials.

Oracle is a **relational database system** which provides a framework for the development of specific software applications. Complete financial and business systems can be developed on Oracle software. However, Oracle is a complex system and it requires a high level of technical expertise to develop and operate the database. By contrast the software applications developed for use on Oracle will be much more user friendly as they are designed to carry out routine processing, enquiry and reporting tasks. Oracle is the database that **holds and manages the data called on by the information systems** and as such is usually of no direct interest to the user.

Training on the new system

The training provided by software houses to SWM Ltd on the information system should be **agreed in detail prior to system implementation** as it must **cover a wide area of subjects** (for example, normal operations, error correction, printing, updating files etc) and be **flexible enough to react to users' needs.**

Training should be aimed at two key areas, firstly, **routine use** of the system and secondly, the **management** of the system.

(i) **Use of the system**

Training of system operators should have the objective of optimising system use at SWM. It should begin at the design stage where **users should be**

involved in the system specification; they will have a wealth of practical knowledge concerning the need for and requirements of the system.

Walkthrough techniques can be used, where system experts explain the proposals for the system and encourage users to comment. **Systems testing** is also a good training ground because operators learn a lot about a system in a short space of time; they learn how the system works and how it doesn't work. A useful discipline is to encourage users to attempt to 'break' the system during testing in order to thoroughly debug it and to learn as much as possible.

Intensive training prior to implementation may take several forms. **On the job training** allows users to operate the system for real, with close supervision. This is a sensible option when parallel running but not if the system is live. Training **courses**, with documentation, are often used; formality should be kept to a minimum so that operators are not nervous about providing an input and the courses should be aimed at the **practical operation** of the system. Training courses, especially those run by external training consultants, can often be rather theoretical and of little practical use. Training can also take place off-site, perhaps using a test environment at the software house.

Users should be **encouraged to learn about all aspects and features** of the system so that they can get the most out of it. The uses of each feature must be made clear at the time of training and **help screens** and **system manuals** should be available to allow users to maintain their knowledge during routine operations. One of the key reasons for the often disappointing results from information systems is the lack of user training.

(ii) **Management of the system**

Training in the **management** of the system should also be given a high priority. With larger information systems like this one, **several people** should be trained to manage the security and maintenance functions. Generally they should be sufficiently senior people who will not be involved in the day to day operations of the system.

Care should be taken that the training is **set at an appropriate level** because system management can be made into an overly complex issue. In the first instance training should only cover the maintenance of the information system, rather than managing the database, as the priority must be to **maintain efficient routine operations**.

Training should cover routine maintenance and software error correction; this will often be aided by detailed sections in the user manuals. Knowledge of the **security and backup procedures** is essential to reduce the risk and impact of system breakdowns. System procedures such as **file management** and **memory and storage requirements** should also be the responsibility of on site management. It is not good practice to rely too heavily on an external software house after the system has been installed.

Training in the use of Oracle

It is then a valid question to ask whether training should be given on the use of the database framework, in this case Oracle. This decision must be dependent on the advantages to SWM of understanding the operations of the database itself. Clearly training on Oracle would gain some **independence from the software house** and would allow at least **minor system enhancements to be carried out in-house**.

Major system developments would require a great deal of training and more than likely the employment of specialist IT staff.

Training on Oracle would be considerably **more expensive** than ordinary systems training because of the technical skills required. There is also the risk that contact may be broken with the software house leaving the company **exposed** in the event of system failure. It is true that some knowledge of the database system may be useful but it is **unlikely to be cost effective** to provide intensive and detailed training in this area. After all, the original decision to use an independent software house will have been based on the availability of expert skills in the system software.

27 TUTORIAL QUESTION: ON-LINE REAL-TIME SYSTEMS

(a) **Batch processing and real-time processing**

In a **batch transaction system** data is held in two types of file. The first type of file (the master file) contains the **cumulative transactions** which, like entries on a bank statement, make up the information about accounts. The second type of file (the transaction file) contains **temporary sets of transactions** which have been entered into the system, and are **waiting to be processed**. Periodically the entries from the temporary files are written to the permanent (master) file and actually applied to, or used to update these, main files, and when the transactions are applied the temporary files are then cleared (once their use as backups is complete) ready for the next set of transactions.

Batch processing is suitable for applications where **some delay in processing is acceptable**. Transactions can either be entered all at once, say at the end of the week, or they can be entered over a period of time prior to the processing run. In either case transactions will be stored on the transaction file and the master file will continue to reflect the position as at the previous update. This means that **enquiries will not provide up-to-date information**.

Batch processing allows a **high degree of control**. A header sheet is attached to each batch of invoices/clock cards/orders etc and the number of documents together with some type of control/hash total added. This is used to compare with output and ensure **completeness and accuracy**.

In a **real-time processing system** data is held in a single type of file, the main data file. Transactions are used to update the main files **as they are received** into the system. Enquiries on the system are generally performed in an on-line mode and so the **current position is always available.**

Transactions are input as soon as they are originated, verification/validation checks performed straightaway, processed against the master file and output is available immediately.

(b) **Accounting applications**

(i) An **on-line** input, real-time processing and on-line enquiry system would be suitable for a **hotel billing system**, where charges accumulated by guests need to be applied to their accounts speedily so that when they check out they are faced with the correct total. If a telephone call is made by a guest five minutes before he or she leaves, this must appear on the bill! A second often-quoted example is an **airline booking system**, where it is vital to know if any seats are left when a customer asks to make a booking.

(ii) A system using **batch** input, batch processing and batch output of the whole file at once would be suitable for the processing of the results of many **census** activities, ranging from the national population census to campaigns such as **opinion poll** surveys or **market research**. In these cases the data volumes are large, suggesting that the lower costs associated with batch input are appropriate, the time taken to process the data is not critical provided delays are not exaggerated and outputs should often be produced in batches for statistical, rather than individual, work. In an accounting context it is usually appropriate to operate a batch **payroll** system.

28 TUTORIAL QUESTION: REVIEW OF THE EFFECTIVENESS OF AN MIS

A management information system should provide information to management to enable them to **plan and control the resources of a business**. To be effective, the information must have a **purpose**, be **complete, relevant** and suitably **accurate** for its purpose, and **timely**; it must be delivered to the **right managers** (ie those who need it), and should be as **clear and concise** as possible; it must provide **value for money**; and it must be **used to positive effect** by the managers who receive it.

A review of the existing MIS should turn its attention in all of these directions. A detailed review should consider every category of management information (eg sales, accounting, production etc) and every report produced.

(a) The **purpose and scope** of the existing MIS should be compared with what its current purpose and scope ought to be for every category of information and every report. Any 'gaps' in the nature of the information provided should be identified.

(b) **Sources** of management information should be established, to determine whether sufficient information is gathered from both within the organisation itself (feedback) and also from the environment.

(c) **Channels of information** should be investigated, to ensure that there are no 'bottlenecks', whereby certain individuals block the flow of information to others.

(d) Having established the purpose of each individual report, an investigation should be made of its **accuracy**, the **relevance** of all the detail in it, and its **completeness,** both by:

  (i) assessing the **contents** of the report itself; and

  (ii) discussing with managers the extent to which they **rely on** the information in the report.

(e) The **frequency and timeliness** of producing reports should be assessed, to determine whether they are issued **often enough or too often**, and whether they reach managers **in time** to help with the decisions they must take.

(f) Discussions with managers should establish:

  (i) **what use** they make of reports sent to them;

  (ii) what information they **could** use, but **do not receive** (perhaps because a report is sent to someone else in the organisation);

  (iii) whether they **have time** to read reports, or whether they are too lengthy;

  (iv) whether they **understand** all the information contained in them.

(g) An assessment should be made of the **cost** of producing current reports, and the **benefits** obtained by using them. A similar assessment should be made of the costs or benefits of increasing or reducing the number/size/frequency/recipients etc of reports.

(h) **Duplication** of information should be looked for. Similar information might be prepared for different departmental functions (eg accounts and production). Occasionally, stories are told of departments that produce one set of 'correct' figures for themselves, and another set of 'doctored' figures for the management accounting section.

(i) The reviewer should look at the possibility of **integrating the data processing** of different departments, into a single system using **database** files. Alternatively the possibility of **distributed processing** to improve information for 'local' management might be considered.

(j) A major consideration in the review should be the extent to which the **requirements** for an effective MIS have **changed** over the years, and so the extent to which the current MIS has fallen short of what it should do (and the costs of having inadequate information). By implication, the design of a new MIS should look towards **changes in the future business environment**, and the review should therefore consider what **flexibility** should be built into an MIS to allow it to progress and **adapt to changing needs** in the future.

29 TUTORIAL QUESTION: MANAGEMENT SUPPORT

(a) **The decision-making process**

The phases which constitute the decision-making process were identified by Herbert Simon as follows.

(i) **Intelligence**. This involves a gathering of all the necessary data about the direct system, and about any associated or connected systems. It is a search of the environment for conditions which call for decisions to be made.

(ii) **Design**. Processes are implemented by which the problem can be understood. One or more solutions to the problem are formulated and their feasibility assessed. The consequences of each approach are calculated and comparisons between the various outcomes are prepared for evaluation.

(iii) **Choice**. The solutions and outcomes are studied and one solution is chosen as the one most favoured. This is then implemented.

Premises which form part of the Simon philosophy are that **multiple choices** will be available, that the choices will each have **specified outcomes** and that the decision maker has a **set of values** which will encourage him to make the correct decision.

It is important to realise that although there is a general flow from **intelligence** to **design** to **choice**, at any time there could be a **return to an earlier phase**. Thus a decision-maker in the choice phase who is unable to identify a suitable alternative may return to the design phase.

To the three phases noted above may be added a **fourth** phase.

(iv) **Review**. This involves an assessment of past choices.

(b) **Decision support systems**

A decision support system is a system which **processes and sifts data** in conjunction with a set of **decision rules and models** to arrive at **workable decisions**. It **presents** the results at such a time and in such a way as to **facilitate the decision-making process**.

Such a system is **computer-based** and allows the decision-maker to interact with the computer system.

Facilities which the system might include are:

(i) flexibility to allow **rapid, easy changing of requirements**;

(ii) **easy choice of different interpretations of the data**, allowing different styles of decision-making to be supported;

(iii) easy feedback of the decision, to allow for '**what if** investigations;

(iv) easy **changes to data requirements levels**, allowing use in different conditions;

(v) easy **changes to decision-making levels**, allowing use by different types of management;

(vi) ease of use, with a high degree of **user-friendliness**;

(vii) suitability in a **support** role, so that user's **judgement** is not supplanted.

Components which the system might comprise would include the following.

(i) A **database** including previous decisions and results. As with any database application, there should be minimum data duplication and the database should be independent of any individual applications. This is the **knowledge subsystem.**

(ii) **Analytical capabilities**. A complex software package is necessary to analyse the financial and statistical data which the system uses. This software must be able to manage and update the models used. This is the **problem processing subsystem.**

(iii) **Presentation facilities** for viewing results. This allows communication between the decision maker and the system. It is the **language subsystem.**

30 HS PLC: EPOS AND DATABASE

> **Pass marks.** In December 1997 Safeway introduced an experimental system known as ECR – Efficient Consumer Response – which allows suppliers to tap straight into Safeway's point of sales data live via the Internet. This seems to be the sort of system envisaged in this question. The CIMA model solution seems to have mainly in mind a loyalty card scheme, although this is only one possible aspect of the system envisaged in the question.
>
> **Examiner's comment.** A fairly typical answer began with about a page explaining how EPOS worked, before moving on to the benefits of the system itself. Only a minority of candidates perceived that this information was essentially irrelevant to the question and moved straight on to provide a summary of the benefits to be obtained.
>
> Many answers could have been improved by carrying out some initial planning of the points to be made (the level of repetition was very high) and by ensuring an adequate balance in the answer between operational and strategic benefits. There was some confusion as to whether particular benefits were strategic or operational. However, most candidates pointed out that the distinction was not always clear and gained credit for doing so.

REPORT

To: Managing Director, HS plc
From: IT Manager
Date: 25 November 1998
Subject: Proposed EPOS/database systems

Introduction

This report sets out the strategic and operational benefits that can be expected to arise from the proposal to introduce new Electronic Point of Sale systems and associated databases.

Strategic benefits

(a) **Competitive advantage**

Although we are aware that our **competitors** are considering similar systems, it will take them at least two years to implement them, whereas we can have the system up and running within 10 months. We will have a **head start** in learning to operate the new system and will start to realise the benefits more than a year before our rivals can, thereby helping us to maintain our competitive advantage. Early implementation is **in line with our corporate objective** of offering the best computerised sales service to customers.

It is likely that once the system is up and running, and becomes established with customers and suppliers, **further opportunities** will be identified. We will continue to be the **first to exploit such opportunities** and so we will be able to maintain competitive advantage in the **long-term** as well as the short term.

(b) **Stakeholders**

Public interest in consumer issues is high and the introduction of an innovative new system is likely to receive **considerable coverage in the media**. This will help to enhance our image with stakeholders such as **investors**, who will see us as a company on the leading-edge, with new ideas and a strong future.

As for existing loyal **customers**, they expect us to be in the vanguard of technological developments and this is one of the reasons why they shop with us. Media interest is also likely to generate **new** business, as potential new loyal customers, who are curious to see what the fuss is about, try out the HS shopping experience.

Suppliers will tie into **our** systems before they commit themselves to others. We have the opportunity to gain a significant degree of control over how the whole supply chain works.

Employees will have the advantage of being **highly trained** in the **most up-to date working methods**. More automation will allow them to devote less time to mundane, routine work, and more time to more satisfying work such as providing an outstanding service for customers.

Operational benefits

(a) **Stockholding costs**

Current levels of computerisation are **not effective** at minimising stock levels because **stock control is not integrated with sales processing**.

Using the EPOS system, **stock records will be updated by the second** as stocks pass through checkouts. If this is combined with EDI systems or Internet links and if Just in Time agreements are entered into, suppliers can be notified and take action the instant new supplies are needed.

This should result in **substantial savings in stock-holding costs**.

(b) **Sales forecasting and promotion**

The new system will give us the ability to **analyse sales patterns** in close detail. A key benefit is that we can then be surer that we are able to **meet customer needs** (that is, we can be surer that we have, say, enough cans of baked beans on the shelves at 3.30pm on a particular day). A second key benefit is that we can employ **promotional tools** such as displays and store layout in ways that more closely match what customers are actually interested in.

A famous example is the experience of Wal-Mart in the US, who found an unexpectedly close correlation between sales of disposable nappies and sales of beer, and were able to increase sales of both, simply by placing them closer together on the shelves.

(c) **Cash and cash flow management**

A higher level of technology is likely to have a number of benefits in this area.

(i) High-tech customers are more likely to use **high-tech methods of payment** such as debit cards, avoiding the need to handle cash at all.

(ii) Electronic scanning of purchases will help to **eliminate keying errors** at the checkout.

(iii) Following on from (i) and (ii) **day-end balancing of tills** will be a less laborious task, saving time and relieving an area of potential stress for check out staff.

(d) **Throughput**

The system should speed up the time it takes for customers to check-out and so **reduce queue lengths**. Long queues are often cited as a reason for avoiding supermarkets when doing small amounts of shopping. There is potentially a large amount of new business to be won if this problem can be overcome.

(e) **Conclusion**

The proposed new system offers considerable benefits from both a **strategic** and an **operational** point of view, and I strongly recommend that we proceed with the investment.

31 MIS AND EXPERT SYSTEM

Pass marks. The question is about information **provided by** the two systems, in other words information that they will generate, not information that will be input into them. Regarding hardware requirements, the examiner expects you to be able to explain **why** a 450 MHz processor may be needed. You will not get marks just because you can write down the figure 450! Remember that software requirements should dictate hardware requirements, not vice versa.

Examiner's comment. Management Information Systems and Expert Systems can be **complementary** rather than a substitute for each other. Producing a specification of hardware and software requirements should be straightforward. Candidates must **relate the hardware and software specification back to an Expert System**.

The main problem for some candidates lay in contrasting the characteristics of the information being provided by the two systems. A minority of answers provided information concerning how the Expert System was established and the different parts of the system, but provided very little discussion of the information being produced by the system.

A majority of candidates provided an **answer structure** which included information characteristics as main headings, and then commented on the two different systems under those headings. As well as covering a wide range of characteristics, this answer format also ensured that candidates provided the required contrast between the two systems. Most of these answers mentioned the structure of the information being provided, the accuracy of the information comparing mechanical accuracy of the MIS with probabilities of accurate information in the ES, and the use of the information within the hospital. These answers obtained good marks.

Answers to part (b) tended to be much more rushed and contain a lot less detail. Rushed answers resulted in candidates providing lists of hardware and software that could be used in an Expert System **without providing an explanation** of why that hardware and software was required. Thus, many candidates stated a need for a scanner as part of the hardware system. However, it was not clear what type of scanner was being suggested or how it could be used. In the context of an Expert System, it was difficult to see how a flat-bed scanner could be used; certainly, reading doctors' notes by OCR would be challenging and prone to errors.

(a) **Information provided by the two systems**

The **MIS** contains purely **factual** information such as name, address and personal details, historical information about illnesses and medical conditions that recur. Individual patient records will be updated as and when changes occur. This information will be available to doctors prior to and during appointments.

The **ES** will **use** some of the same information (medical history, recurring symptoms) but only to collate it with an **information bank** or 'knowledge base' that includes details of types of illness and apply a set of rules, so as to provide information in the form of diagnoses and recommended treatments.

For instance the ES will offer answers to questions such as 'Given that X (who the MIS says has a history of Y) is now displaying symptom Z, what is the likelihood of that X has illness A, illness B, illness C, and so on, and what is the recommended treatment in each case?'

Differences in characteristics between the information provided by the two systems are as follows.

Characteristic	*MIS*	*ES*
Accuracy and completeness.	Details of medical history and symptoms as well as personal information should be totally accurate, assuming they have been **input correctly** and the most **recent changes** have been input. The information **may not be complete**: the patient may have symptoms that he has not described to the doctor. He may have had an illness and recovered without medical treatment.	The information within the system (ie the knowledge base and rule set) should accurately reflect the current state of knowledge about different illnesses. However it may not provide accurate diagnoses or accurate treatments in an absolute sense, because current knowledge may be incomplete or wrong. Moreover, it is likely to take some time for new research findings and medical breakthroughs to be incorporated into the system and for rules to be amended accordingly.
Timeliness (recognising that hardware and software are described as 'the most up to date')	Information is likely to held in a relational database and will be **obtainable within seconds** on demand.	The ES may take several minutes to perform comparisons with what is probably a very large knowledge base, and to apply rules from a very wide number of possibilities.
User confidence	Subject to the points made above, users **should be able to rely on the information** provided by the MIS. **The patient** can be asked to confirm address details and the like during visits, and asked about their history when seeing a doctor. Any **discrepancies or omissions** should come to light then.	**If** the ES provides information that doctors find **believable**, then they will be able to have confidence in it. If, when it produces a range of possible answers, however, some of the options are **absurd**, this may undermine confidence in the system: it draws attention to the fact that the system is **not really capable of judgement** in the way a human being is. Worse, if the system occasionally produces a **wrong diagnosis**, then users will quickly lose confidence in it and probably **not use it at all**. **Some users** will almost certainly be keener on using of the system than others, who prefer to use their **own judgement,** just as some people in general are keener on the use of computers than others.

Characteristic	*MIS*	*ES*
Relevance and volume	The name, address and personal details will be of **approximately the same length** for each patient record (12 fields, say). Medical histories will **vary enormously in length**, however, and in fact it may be very difficult to read an entire history on screen. Much of what is there will **not be relevant** to the patient's current problem. It is not clear whether the MIS has any **sorting or search facilities**, though this would clearly be useful. It may also be useful to **categorise** aspects of patient history according to specialty (cardiac, ear, nose and throat, etc) rather than just in chronological order.	It is possible that certain combinations of medical history and symptoms will give rise to a very **large number of possible diagnoses** and/or treatments. However, they will presumably be **sorted in order of probability**, so doctors will not be overloaded with data and will probably ignore the least probable answers as irrelevant.

(b) **Hardware and software requirements for the Expert System**

(i) **Software**

The following software would be required.

(1) The **ES software** itself. An ES typically has the following components.

- A **knowledge base** that contains facts and a set of rules. This would be in database format.
- An **inferencing engine**, which is a program that would read in data from the MIS and from the knowledge base and applies the rules.
- Software to **present** the results of the enquiry.
- A **knowledge acquisition** program which is used to input new facts and rules.

It is not clear from the scenario whether the hospital's ES has been developed **in-house**, whether it is **tailor-made** software developed by a specialist software house, or (perhaps most likely) whether it is a **package**, perhaps provided by a local or national health authority and shared by many hospitals. If it has been developed in-house the hospital would also need a **programming language** such as CLIPS to maintain and upgrade the ES.

(2) A **network operating system** compatible with any ES software installed on the server. This would most probably be Unix or Windows NT. This is required because without an operating system the ES software would not function at all.

(3) The terminals referred to in the case study might be dumb terminals, but would more probably be PCs, in which case they would need the **operating system** for which the ES software was designed. This would probably be Windows 95/98 or Windows NT Workstation. Again this is required because without an operating system the ES software would not function at all.

(4) **Internet browser software** may be required: updates for the ES itself may be downloadable if it is a package; while information about the

results of medical research is published on websites or many research bodies.

(5) **Other software** may be useful for dealing with the results of enquiries, such as word-processing software for writing reports, letters and so on; possibly a spreadsheet program if figure-work is involved.

(ii) **Hardware**

The following hardware would be required.

(1) A **server** powerful enough to run the network. The precise specification depends upon how many terminals there are, the amount of storage required, and the speed of processing required.

The storage requirements are likely to be considerable, since the knowledge base will contain a large, and growing, amount of information (as will the MIS). Likewise fast results will sometimes be needed, so the processor should be very powerful, and there should be plenty of RAM available.

(2) As mentioned above, the '**terminals**' would probably be **PCs** of sufficiently high specification to run any part of the ES software that needed to be installed on client machines rather than on the server.

(3) **Cabling** is of course necessary to link up machines to the server.

32 IT DEPARTMENT COSTS: CHARGEOUT METHODS

Pass marks. Your answer to part (a) can be based largely on book knowledge but part (b) requires you to think quite hard about the specific scenario. This is a topic area that could come up in any Stage 4 exam, so this is another good question for practise purposes.

Examiner's comment. This question asks candidates to investigate this problem and provide a comparison of the two main charging methods for computer support departments. Candidates who manage to provide this **comparison** are likely to score more marks than those who simply explain the two different systems.

The standard of answers could be improved by providing a more detailed explanation in the area of lack of control over the costing systems that gave rise to demotivation. Few candidates explained the problem of the lack of control over the IT department and the concern that this would cause the individual departmental managers.

Part (b) provided some better answers. The main point to get across was that the charging method did not necessarily regulate network traffic, because users could not relate to the charging system. Most candidates referred to this problem although the reason for it, as in measuring network traffic, was not always fully explained. Perhaps due to lack of time, most candidates made only a brief reference to an alternative charging method.

The main weakness in many answers was suggesting outsourcing as an alternative charging method. On the face of it, outsourcing is not an alternative charging method unless the IT department itself is removed and outsourced. The most marks in this section were earned by candidates who correctly set about **identifying the cost drivers** for the IT department and then suggested methods of measuring these drivers and placing chargeout rates on them.

(a) **Charging IT costs**

(i) **Charging costs as part of company overheads**

Under this system IT is treated as a **general administrative expense**, and is allocated to user departments on the same basis as other administrative expenses, whatever that basis may be.

From the point of view of the manager of the IT department this approach is **simple** and **cheap** to administer, there is minimal **conflict** (at least between the IT department and user departments), and it **encourages innovation** and experimentation by the **IT department**.

From the point of view of other departmental managers this approach has a number of **disadvantages.**

(1) The IT department has **little day to day incentive to control costs** or use available resources efficiently, other than the enthusiasm of IT management. Other departmental managers may perceive the IT department to be inefficient or spendthrift. Fabulous innovations for Department X may be of no benefit to Department Y.

(2) Decisions regarding IT resources are taken at senior level in the organisation, and **funds may be limited**: both the sales and the production departments might require new IT systems, but there may only be resources for one of them. The departmental manager that loses out will resent this.

(3) **Managers** do not have the cost information to prioritise their requirements and so, through no fault of their own, may **not be making responsible use of the IT resource**. User departments which are inefficient in their use of IT will have no incentive to improve.

(ii) **Charging costs on the basis of individual department usage**

In general charging computer services on the basis of usage should achieve two results.

(1) It should **allocate scarce computing resources** according to economic efficiency.

(2) It should **regulate overall demand** for computing services within an organisation.

The problem, however, is arriving at a **fair** basis on which usage is determined.

Departmental managers are likely to desire the following.

(1) Chargeout rates should be based on a **tangible service to which the manager can relate,** for example cost per transaction processed or cost per hour of IT department staff member's time.

(2) **Standard costing** systems should be used. This is so that user departments are not penalised for inefficiencies in the IT department, and are not charged with long term fixed costs of the IT department itself (eg its office space) over which they have no control. Also the IT department is not penalised with variances caused by user departments' increased usage.

(3) Charges should be **lower** than those that would be charged by a **third-party** provider if one could be found, because of **internal economies** (for instance each department, presumably including IT, is a cost centre, not a profit centre). It appears that some departments have already obtained third-party quotes.

(b) **Assessment of the proposal to determine usage on the basis of network traffic**

(i) **Problems with the proposal**

The proposed chargeout basis has the advantages that it is **easy to measure** (presumably it can be monitored by the network software) and **easy to understand**.

However, the amount of data transferred **drives only some of the costs** incurred by the IT department, such as the cost of network hardware and software, and the costs of administering, maintaining and upgrading the network. Many other costs will bear practically nil relation to data transfer. Here are some examples.

(1) An individual PC may need **servicing or replacement** because someone spills a cup of coffee over it. Once it is repaired or once a new PC has been set up, it will simply be plugged back into the network. The cost of the repair or set up is **not related to network traffic at all**.

(2) A **physical problem with a printer** has nothing to do with networking.

(3) **Systems development work** is almost certain to be unique to **individual departments**, since they will each use different systems reflecting the work that they do, even if the data ultimately produced and transferred is compatible with other systems. During a certain period one department may incur substantial development costs while another may occur none. This will not be reflected in an IT charge based on network traffic.

(4) **Training needs** relate to skills within individual departments and have nothing to do with the amount of data transferred across the network.

Departmental managers will therefore perceive the proposal as quite **unfair** and unrepresentative of the cost of their use of IT.

(ii) **An alternative approach**

Although it will be more difficult to monitor and calculate it would be much fairer to **recharge costs under a number of headings** reflecting what **drives** them to be incurred.

Possible **drivers** include the following.

(1) **Systems development work**, perhaps charged according to the hourly rate of IT staff who do the work.

(2) **Equipment-related costs** could be charged at the actual cost of servicing, or a standard cost related to the number of PCs, number of printers, etc.

(3) **Network-related costs** could indeed be charged on the basis of network traffic. If the timing of transfers affects the costs then this could be built into the charging basis too.

(4) **Central file maintenance** (presumably database administration) could be based on the amount of storage space required by different departments if it is the volume of data that causes costs to be incurred, or again on a basis such as network traffic, if costs are incurred in relation to database updating and interrogation.

There may be **other headings**, as indicated, such as training (standard costs for different types of training), maintenance of a help desk (number of enquiries, or length of time spent dealing with each enquiry).

The **IT department itself** will also a user of IT, of course, and it should be charged in a similar fashion. Costs that relate solely to the IT department (eg repairs to its own equipment) should not be recharged to other departments.

33 10F GROUP: MIS AND OBJECTIVES

> **Pass marks**. Here, you are not asked to write about MIS in general, but about the **use** of a specific MIS in a **specific** business. This is typical of Stage 4. Note the second point made by the examiner below, and direct your learning accordingly. BPP Study Texts describe common commercially-available systems that you might encounter, or even use, in real life because otherwise you would think we were living in fairyland. But the examiner wants to know that you understand the **capabilities and uses** of modern systems in general, not that you can list all the bells and whistles in a particular package.
>
> **Examiner's comment.** Only a small minority of scripts actually described a MIS without any reference to the question information, suggesting that candidates are getting better at applying their knowledge. Some scripts lacked an explanation of why the output was relevant. To obtain more marks in (b) most candidates would have benefited from explaining why they considered the various items of hardware and software were necessary.
>
> 'Candidates and tutors should note that an understanding or description of particular protocols or hardware systems is not required in this examination. It is the understanding of what the hardware or software can do that is important, not that Unix must be used here, or that Windows '95 must be used there, and so on.'

(a) **Information from the MIS**

The MIS for the 10F group will provide the key link between the shops and the warehouses. With the flexibility of the shops to change the displayed merchandise, **stock management** is the key to profitability.

The **information** provided by each shop's MIS will be **used by**:

(i) the **shop** itself;
(ii) the **warehouses**; and
(iii) **group management**.

The **stock data** will need to be provided for each shop and for warehouses. Some stock deliveries will be straight to shops, eg newspapers and magazines from wholesalers. Stock should be recorded to include a unique identity for each product, including description, bar code, supplier, price, margin, and lead time.

Categorisation by shelf life is important. In the case of **newspapers** this is probably 'until midday same day'. **Magazines** fare better as sales continue until the next issue: monthly or weekly, although some will have a very sharp fall-off, for example TV listing for the week lose value to the consumer each day, and will therefore only sell in numbers on the first two days of issue. Many magazines will be **sale or return**, either when first published or if publishers wish to increase sales. Shelf life of **other products** will be longer.

Special information, for example, 'tie-ins' when a products is marketed alongside TV or film promotions, as 'Fred Flintstone's bubble gum', or 'Rugby World Cup crisps', will also be useful.

The shop-based **sales transactions** will be fed to the MIS, and the information provided by the MIS must include the following.

(i) **For the shop**:

(1) **sales patterns** by product within category. As a history of sales builds up the expected future demand of each product can be forecast with greater accuracy;

(2) present **stock levels**.

This information will provide the major input to the reordering quantity decision. It is the **objective** of the group to ensure that 98% of the goods the customers require are available. This objective will be **measured** by using a **statistical model** build from the sales data, then comparing ongoing sales against the average and standard deviation for each product.

Stock losses (when returns plus sales is less than supply, or from stocktakes) will be identifiable from the combination of sales and stock data.

Sales, profit and **market reports** for the shop against **budget** for the period and year to date will also be required.

(ii) **For the warehouse**:

(1) **consolidated sales patterns** from the shops serviced by the warehouse. The ordering decisions by the warehouse upon external suppliers require the warehouse to anticipate the shops' orders as well as taking into the equation supplier lead times and processing costs;

(2) **existing stock**, both at the warehouse and at the shops;

(3) **orders outstanding** from the **shops**;

(4) **orders outstanding** on the **suppliers**;

(5) **performance** statistics of **suppliers**;

(6) **recommended** and **alternative suppliers**, with **lead times**;

(7) **dates** by which **returns** must be sent back to publishers to qualify for credit;

(8) **performance** reports and **management accounts** of the **warehouse**.

The warehouse will require the information to be usable as '**picking lists**', ie in the same order as the layout of the warehouse. The **time** of receipt of the orders and of delivery to the shop should be recorded.

The warehouse will use this information **operationally** to facilitate the rapid supply of goods to the shops to meet the four hour target of delivery. It will also be used **strategically** for purchasing planning.

(iii) **For group management**:

(1) **sales** and **margin** data by product line;

(2) **performance of the shops** measured against the 98% satisfaction criterion using the statistical model;

(3) **performance of the warehouses** in meeting the four hour delivery time;

(4) **product trend and profitability** (by shelf space etc) analysis for marketing decisions;

(5) **management accounts** reporting.

The management will use this information for **control** of the company by measuring the **performance** of the line managers against the group's **objectives**, and then taking appropriate action. They will also be able to recommend **overrides** against pre-programmed EPOS master files, for example, to **increase discounts** or **raise prices**. Some local discretion to do this may also be appropriate.

(b) **Hardware and software**

The hardware and software will include the following.

(i) **At the shop**. The tills will be computer **POS terminals**, incorporating bar code readers. Products which do not have a barcode, perhaps because of their shape, will be recorded by manually keying in their stock code or by having a bar code book by the till that can be 'swiped' by the shop assistant. **Hand held scanners** with bar code reading heads will be used for stock taking.

Information from the tills and the scanners will be fed into a **computer** at each shop. Software on these computers will include **communications software** and on-line links to a centralised product **database** which holds stock price lists. On-line links will also update centralised stock records immediately.

The software will be **tailored** for the specific needs of the 10F Group to provide the management with the **information required** for the running of the business using a stock ordering model to meet the group objectives. These include not just the **98% satisfaction requirement**, but also maximising **shelf space profitability**, **stock turnround** and **return on working capital**.

The POS terminals will print **till receipts** and an **'audit roll'**.

Printers will also be required at the shop to provide hard copies of MIS reports and of orders. Managers would be expected to use their own initiative as well as the recommended computer figures when ordering, so the software will include the ability to **modify** and confirm the computer generated orders.

Modems and **communication software** will link the shops to the warehouses. Cost/benefit analysis will determine whether the volume of traffic will warrant permanent communications links or simple dial-up facilities. The communication will be two-way, with new products and marketing forecast information being fed to the shop data.

It may be appropriate to install a local **file server** at each shop. Since input to POS terminals is continuous, transactions will need to be batched regularly, say, hourly, ready for transmission to warehouses. This would mean that a **LAN** at each shop could be used to link server, POS terminals and bar code readers. Other hardware (PCs) and software ('Office' applications) could also be linked into the LAN.

(ii) **At the warehouse** there will be the need for several users to have access to the MIS. Thus a **minicomputer** with multiple user capacity, or a **local area network** with a **file server** will be required. The **memory and processing capacity** will be determined according to the volume of data being recorded and the length of time the data will need to be held. In view of the seasonality of many grocery and newsagent products it is probably desirable to keep at least two year's data on hand. The **software** therefore needs to be capable of summarising data and deleting detail, probably on a monthly basis.

A **wide area network** will link warehouse systems to shop systems.

The interface with the warehouse computer system will include:

(1) **workstations** - VDU, mouse, keyboard and personal printer - used for control of the MIS and various management functions such as purchasing;

(2) **bar code readers** and **printers**. All products within the warehouse will carry bar codes, which will include within the bar code information the **product code** itself, plus **batch details** such as divisible quantities (how many in each carton), **supplier** and **date of receipt**. Bar code technology

is necessary for **speed**, and for the possibilities for **further automation** which it opens up;

(3) **printers** to produce the despatch notes.

The heart of the warehouse **software** will be a **stock processing module** controlling a suite of **databases** holding the information by:

(1) product within **category**;
(2) **supplier**;
(3) **physical organisation** within the warehouse;
(4) trading by **outlet**.

The software must be capable of incorporating **stock control** models and **statistical analysis** and will be capable of downloading selected data into **spreadsheets** and private **databases** for specific analysis.

The MIS will include complementary **communications facilities** to the **shops**. Because of the openness to the public telephone systems and the value of the data held centrally, there must be **security procedures** built into the software. There will also be communications facilities to link the warehouse computers (or computer) to the **group management**. Direct link to the MIS is almost certainly the cheapest way of supplying the data. Finally, **EDI links** to **suppliers** will provide the quickest way of replenishing stocks.

34 JH PLC: INFORMATION CENTRE

> **Pass marks.** There is not very much to go on in the brief scenario. Consequently we stated one or two related assumptions within our answer enabling us add meaningful comments. We have also updated our answer. For example we have supposed that the organisation has just introduced Windows 98 and Office 2000. Care is needed with this technique, otherwise you may end up rewriting the question to suit yourself. Our assumptions made could alternatively be presented as valid examples of what an information centre might be doing in an organisation such as the one described.
>
> **Examiner's comment.** This question produced some of the best answers on the May 1996 paper, although those who left it until last tended to rush it, as indicated by poor handwriting, repetition of points and a lack of detail. Better time management would have produced a few more marks for many candidates. In part (b) some answers did not focus on the provision of an enhanced service, instead concentrating unduly on the Internet aspect of the question and repeating points made in part (a).

(a) **MEMO**

To: The Board, JH plc
From: Management Accountant
Date: 24 November 1999
Subject: Proposal to close the Information Centre

This memo sets out a justification for the continuance of the company's Information Centre on **non-financial** grounds.

JH plc, IT and the Information Centre

One of the main factors in the **success** of JH plc is considered to be its high **investment in modern IT systems.** The scale and complexity of the company's operations is such that it **could not function** without effective information management: this alone justifies the level of IT investment.

The Information Centre plays a key role in ensuring that this investment **continues** to be used to maximum advantage. This is essential if the company is to **achieve its mission** of being the most profitable freight forwarder in the country.

The contribution of the Information Centre

The IC performs its role in a wide variety of ways.

(i) The IC's **Help Desk** ensures that staff time is spent on customer service rather than on IT problems.

(1) It has sufficient **staff and technical expertise** to respond quickly to problems with hardware or software. It maintains **good contacts** and relationships with **suppliers** to ensure that they fulfil their maintenance obligations and their maintenance staff are quickly on site when needed.

(2) It maintains a **record of problems** and identifies those that occur most often. If the problem is that users do not know how to use the system, **training** is provided. If the problem is with the system itself, a solution is found, either by **modifying the system** or by investment in appropriate **hardware or software.**

(3) It considers the viability of **suggestions for improvements** to the system and brings these into effect, where possible, for all users who stand to benefit.

(ii) The IC sets, and encourages users to conform to, common **standards.**

(1) **Hardware standards** ensure that all of the equipment used in the organisation is **compatible** and can be put into use in different departments as needed. The recent upgrade of the marketing department's old Apple Mac computers to IBM-compatible Pentium PCs is an example of this.

(2) **Software standards** ensure that **information** generated by one department can easily be **shared** with and worked upon by other departments. The recent introduction of Windows 98 and Office 2000 throughout the organisation is an example.

(3) **Programming standards** ensure that applications developed by individuals to help them perform their jobs (for example word-processing macros or spreadsheets for data analysis) follow **best practice**, are **easy to modify**, and are **replicated to others** in the organisation where this is of benefit.

(4) **Data processing standards** ensure that certain conventions such as the format of **file names** are followed throughout the organisation. This facilitates **sharing** and **storage and retrieval** of information by as many users as possible.

(iii) The IC helps to preserve the **security** of data.

(1) It has developed a **utility program** and recommended **procedures** for company-wide use, to ensure that **back-ups** are made at regular intervals. Second copies of back-up files are stored off site and this system of archiving is operated and maintained by the Information Centre.

(2) The IC helps to preserve the company's systems from attack by computer **viruses**. The latest versions of anti-virus software are available to all users. Users are regularly reminded about the dangers of viruses and IC staff give training in the use of anti-virus software.

Conclusion

The IC is well utilised by staff. It fulfils a need that would still exist if the centre were closed. Staff will feel that they have been left to sink or swim, and they may very well **sink** if they have nowhere to go to obtain the support they are used to.

The idea that the IC has no discernible **income** does **not mean** that it has no positive impact on **profitability**. The annual **saving** of £4m from closing the centre needs to be weighed against the **costs** to the organisation if support is not provided (such as wasted time, ill-advised investment and sales lost because customers perceive inefficiencies in the system and receive an increasingly unreliable service), and/or the **cost of buying in support** when it is needed, as experience shows it undoubtedly will be.

The **costs of the centre could be re-allocated** on a fair basis to the departments that actually give rise to those costs - **the users of its services**. At the same time the centre itself could be subject to **performance standards** to ensure that it is giving the best value for money. Performance standards may be established by means of a **benchmarking** exercise with similar services in other companies.

(b) **How the network can enhance IC services**

The newly installed network provides opportunities for the IC to improve its services in a number of ways, including the following.

(i) **Training software** can be developed or purchased and made available over the network from a central server. Training applications often contain analysis software, drawing attention to **trainee progress** and **common problems** (the Software Toolworks **Mavis Beacon** typing tutor is a well-known example), and the availability of such information will enable the IC to identify and address specific training needs more closely.

(ii) **Help** can be made available directly through users' computers, using an **e-mail** system for queries and responses. Common problems and their solutions can be posted on a bulletin board for all to read (problems with using the Internet are an obvious candidate for such treatment). The network will speed up the process of sorting out problems and sharing knowledge.

(iii) **Remote diagnostic software** is available which will enable staff in the IC to 'take control' of a computer whose user is having problems and sort out the problem for them without leaving their desk, in the same way that they would if they paid the user a visit. Again this will speed up the problem-solving process.

(iv) The IC can take responsibility for **protecting** the system against possible abuses now that it is linked to the **Internet**. Anti-virus measures will become even more important in this environment, but network software should make it easier for the IC to **control the problem centrally**.

(v) The Internet link will also make **control over access** an important issue. The Information Centre can set up and operate '**firewalls**', which disable part of the communications technology that normally allows two-way communication.

This means that **internal** users can go out into the global Net to retrieve information but **external** parties are denied access to sensitive parts of the company's systems. (Clients will be able to visit JH plc's website and send in their requirements, perhaps choosing options from menus and filling in forms on screen, but they will not be able to interfere with the **processing** of their requirements.)

35 JS PLC: AN ACCEPTABLE STANDARD OF INFORMATION

Pass marks. Part (a) should have caused little difficulty because the problems in the system are pretty apparent from the scenario. However, you may have struggled to find 12 marks worth of material without repeating yourself. Regarding part (b), information centres are covered in some detail in the BPP Study Text and have been examined before, so again you should not have had many problems if you were properly prepared.

Examiner's comment. The mark-earning ability of many answers to part (a) was limited by two main factors. Firstly repeating the question information without adequate explanation of why the points were being made. Secondly concentrating on the update of the stock systems: the extent of detail of some answers was excessive. In part (b) most candidates showed a surprising lack of knowledge. The majority of answers assumed that the main function of an information centre was to process information from different departments and provide the relevant output back to users.

(a) **Why information could be incorrect**

(i) **Communication**

JS plc operates from 10 different sites which **cannot communicate with each other,** and neither can the various **functions** within each site. There is therefore little possibility that discrepancies between overlapping information in each system will come to light in the course of normal day-to-day operations.

(ii) **Piecemeal implementation**

It appears that the systems in use have been built piecemeal over the years and hardware and software are **not compatible** from one system to another. Given that there are certain to be significant **overlaps** between the data used by functions such as sales, production and stock control, this situation means that there will a considerable amount of **re-inputting of the same data,** inevitable leading to **inconsistencies** due to inputting **errors.**

(iii) **Approach to systems development**

Users of different systems in each department have **amended the systems** and this could mean that data and files are **not being processed as they are meant to be**. Again this will lead to inconsistent and inaccurate information.

(iv) **Systems overload**

Both computerised and manual systems are **working beyond the capacity** that they were designed for.

(1) For **computerised** systems this could result in the systems being **overloaded and crashing** frequently. Unless the operating system and the various applications offer strong protection in the case of a crash (which seems unlikely in this case) this will result in some **corruption and/or loss of data.**

(2) For **manual systems** it means that work will be rushed, shortcuts will be taken, and matters perceived as non-essential by tired human information processors will be neglected. Mistakes will be made, procedures will be ignored and information will be incomplete.

(v) **Co-ordination of decision-making processes**

Within departments it appears that managers follow the correct processes when reaching decisions, but because different departments are basing their decisions on different information they may **come to different conclusions**. Incorrect pricing and production decisions are specifically mentioned.

(1) **Prices** could be wrongly calculated by sales managers because they have inaccurate information about production costs and stock availability.

(2) **Production** departments may manufacture the wrong type or quantity of products because they have inaccurate information about sales orders and sales patterns and about stock availability.

Nobody in the organisation knows which department's information is the most accurate for a given purpose: indeed what must have been a long-standing problem has only recently come to light and has taken the company by **surprise**. This suggests that there is **little face-to-face liaison** between managers of different departments, which might at least **draw attention** to the fact that managers have a different understanding of the same situation, even if it does not sort out the detail.

(vi) **Manual and computerised systems**

Although the scenario does not give details, the fact that some systems are computerised and others are manual will lead to problems such as **time-delays**. Manual processes probably take longer than computerised ones, and this will cause problems if computer input depends upon manual processes being completed first. The system will never be fully **up-to-date**.

(b) **Information Centre**

An information centre (IC) is a small unit of staff with a good technical awareness of computer systems, whose task is to provide a **support function** to computer **users** within the organisation.

An information centre **alone** can do little to address the core problem faced by JS plc which is that the company has **no corporate-wide IT strategy**. The real needs of the business first need to be recognised by senior management, and there needs to be a commitment to addressing those needs.

Before an IC can be **fully effective**, therefore:

(i) there is a very clear need to examine the current operation of systems and find out where errors are occurring. This is probably a job for **internal auditors** rather than IT systems specialists;

(ii) it looks likely that some further **investment** is needed to make data and systems **compatible** with each other and to enable them to **communicate** with each other.

Once current problems are addressed an Information Centre (IC) could help in the following ways.

(i) **Standards**

The IC can set, and encourage users to conform to, common standards, which will ensure **consistency of data and processing** and save time.

(1) **Hardware** standards ensure that all of the equipment used in the organisation is compatible and can be put into use in different departments as needed.

(2) **Software** standards ensure that information generated by one department can easily be shared with and worked upon by other departments.

(3) **Programming** standards ensure that applications developed by individuals to help them perform their jobs (for example word-processing macros or spreadsheets for data analysis) follow best practice,

are easy to modify, and are replicated to others in the organisation where this is of benefit.

(4) **Data processing** standards ensure that certain conventions such as the format of file names are followed throughout the organisation. This facilitates sharing and storage and retrieval of information by as many users as possible.

(ii) **Applications development**

Part of the current problems are due to the fact that the systems have been subject to substantial amendment by users. Many users who develop their own applications have little or no formal training in programming, consequently their programs might be extremely crude and virtually incomprehensible.

An IC can help to remedy this situation by providing technical guidance to the developers and to encourage comprehensible and documented programs. Understandable programs can be maintained or modified more easily by people other than the system developer. Documentation then provides a means of teaching others how the programs work. These efforts can greatly extend the usefulness and life of the programs that are developed.

(iii) **Systems overload**

Problems in this area may be largely due to the fact that the system currently **holds vastly more data than it needs** (several copies of each piece of data) and that much processing simply **duplicates processing** being done elsewhere.

The introduction of **compatible** systems that can communicate and share data, and of **revised procedures** may alleviate the problem of lack of capacity without any further input from the IC.

In the future the IC can develop and maintain good contacts and relationships with **suppliers** to ensure that they fulfil their **maintenance** obligations and their maintenance staff are quickly on site when needed. It can also **monitor growth in system usage**, and recommend steps to ensure that extra capacity is available when needed.

(iv) **Problem solving**

An IC usually offers a **Help Desk** to ensure that staff time is spent on their real work rather than on IT problems.

The IC will maintain a **record of problems** and identify those that occur most often. If the problem is that users do not know how to use the system, **training** is provided, either in-house or via external courses.

Training software can be developed or purchased and made available over a network from a central server. Training applications often contain **analysis software**, drawing attention to trainee progress and **common problems**, and the availability of such information will enable the IC to identify and address specific training needs more closely.

36 INFORMATION SYSTEM INPUTS AND OUTPUTS

Pass marks. A logical structure to your answer will help you cover the points required. Do not repeat the same inputs and outputs in Parts (a) and (b). Ensure you **explain** the importance of the inputs and outputs you mention - if your answer lacks explanation the marks awarded will be limited.

Examiner's comment. This question investigates whether an organisation's information system is really supporting the objectives of the company or providing managers with the information that they need. To try and assist candidates place the information system that is required, Porter's theory of business was included in the question, although the question requirement is not on the theory. The Examiner has stated that questions **will not be asked on specific theories**. Many candidates failed to differentiate between input of data and output of information from the three systems. Some answers repeated the same items as being both inputs and outputs from the same system. The majority of answers tended to ignore the specific information in the case study regarding the lack of information on prices (for example, for inbound logistics). In Part (b), there was a tendency to simply list the outputs rather than **explain** them, which limited the number of marks that could be awarded. Most candidates tended to focus either on the production of garments by the MIS, or on the actual update of the technology itself. Either approach allowed the candidate to obtain good marks.

(a) **Introduction**

As a result of concerns raised at the recent board meeting a new Management Information System (MIS) is currently being considered. Output from the main transaction processing systems will **form the input of the MIS**. The MIS will manipulate this information into **summary level** information for **control and decision making** purposes to support the monitoring and control of the key functions of the organisation. The MIS will require inputs relating to the three key primary activities of inbound logistics, marketing and sales and technology development.

Inbound logistics

The inbound logistics function aims to ensure the **right materials are available, at the right price and at the right time.** A key element of this involves ensuring the best possible price for raw materials of the required quality is negotiated. Output from the Computer Assisted Design (CAD) and Computer Assisted Manufacture (CAM) systems will become inputs into the MIS. The MIS will manipulate and summarise this data, resulting in information that will enable the purchasing department to **plan** and meet its responsibilities in the most efficient manner. For example negotiations with suppliers can be faced with **improved knowledge** of the quantities of raw materials required in the medium term which should help win **improved prices.**

Marketing and sales

The MIS can provide information on the activities of customers and salespeople, showing who is buying and selling what. Over time useful **trends** should become apparent. The links with the CAM system will enable customers to be given accurate information relating to both orders in progress and finished goods. Forecast demand can be made available via the feeder systems to the MIS, and when matched with production scheduling information, instances of **spare capacity** should be able to be established and appropriate action taken.

Technology development

The new MIS should provide information that will allow the increased use of **Computer Assisted Design** (CAD) and **Computer Assisted Manufacture** (CAM). Use of CAD and CAM techniques will **improve efficiency**, resulting in the **faster** production of garments, and **improved garment quality**. **Prototypes** can be produced rapidly allowing customer feedback to be acted on at the design stage. The MIS can **monitor sales and production** information and when necessary provide **control information** to ensure orders are delivered on time. One difficult area to predict in the clothing industry is future demand levels for fashion items, as a change in consumer taste can often be rapid and on the surface unpredictable. The MIS will therefore require information feeds from '**outward looking**' sources such as fashion show trends and market research.

(b) **Outputs required**

Outputs from the CAD/CAM systems should include **performance measures** that show whether the design, development and production activities are **achieving their targets**, and how these functions are contributing to the overall performance of SFA. The performance measures should be available for on-screen viewing, and be included in control reports that highlight areas in need of corrective action. Reports from the MIS should also show supplier and buyer performance, including information on price, quantity and quality (including service quality). Marginal cost information should feed from the accounting system to the MIS, as this information is vital when negotiating prices relating to 'extra' production runs to utilise any spare capacity.

Conclusion

The proposed MIS will consolidate information from the main transaction processing systems. It will 'pull-together' information from the separate functions of SFA, allowing the **overall picture** to be seen more clearly. This will enable SFA to identify and respond quickly to circumstances that require action. The MIS will enable SFA to operate more **efficiently and effectively** and should be implemented as soon as possible.

37 OKR PLC: ACHIEVING OBJECTIVES

(a) The **objectives** of the computer department are as follows.

(i) **Recover the costs** spent on central computing services through appropriate charge out rates (given in the question). (**Note.** The issue of appropriate charge out rates is discussed more in part (c) of this question.)

(ii) Provide a **value for money service**, so that the market rate is used as a benchmark or price for a given quality of service. (**Note**. The cheap market rate may go with restrictions as to when the external suppliers' services are used, so OKR plc's users might still pay extra for the extra flexibility. Moreover, the market rate may apply only to routine processing and might be considerably more for specialised applications.)

(iii) **Provide information to management** which is **timely and relevant** to satisfy their existing information needs.

(iv) Assess, in consultation with user departments, the **future information needs** of management and staff, and endeavour to satisfy them.

(v) Ensure that the firm has an **adequate computer capacity**, improved where necessary in line with technical developments, and ensure that it is used at optimum efficiency and effectiveness.

(vi) Lay down **guidelines for computer usage** by departments. Although there is a centralised capacity, it is quite possible that each department will have its own PCs (eg for word processing, and perhaps spreadsheets).

(vii) Ensure all items of equipment and software purchased meet company **standards** and are **compatible**.

(viii) Regularly review the firm's information technology activities so that it conforms to the firm's **overall business strategy**.

(b) There will be a variety of **control procedures** to ensure that these objectives are met. The performance of some of the objectives will be easier to monitor than others. Not all objectives can be quantified.

(i) In order to ensure that the **costs** of the computer operation are recovered, an **accurate and realistic assessment** of what those costs are must be arrived at. This will include wages and salary costs, depreciation on equipment as a means of charging the department's capital costs and sundry other overheads.

An issue here must be the **charge out rate**. Most of the department's cost will be fixed. How much does the current charge out rate reflect the actual cost structure of the services provided? Some jobs may not require the same mix of staff or equipment. The charge out should reflect more exactly the type of service offered.

In order to check that the costs are being recovered, the department will need to set **budgets** covering both predicted expenditure, and likely usage of its services. This can be identified through consultation with other departments.

For routine tasks, it might also be possible to set **standard times** and **standard costs,** so any **variances** caused by sub-optimal performance, of staff or equipment, can be identified immediately.

(ii) Providing a **value for money service** to customers may be **easier said than done**. Although the price differential between the market rate and the department's charge out rate is very high, this may be because the department charges all services equally. We do not know whether the market suppliers provide all the services that the department does. For example, the computer department may be much better able to prepare special ad hoc reports, or 0reports at unusual times at short notice which would not be supplied by outsiders.

An **hourly charge out rate**, irrespective of the service provided, probably **does not reflect the true cost of the service** to the department (eg the time of one computer operator is charged at the same rate as that of four programmers).

The market price is a **benchmark**, but the department will charge **more** if it provides a **more flexible responsive service**.

If the department itself has **spare computer capacity**, it might try to recover this cost by letting it out to **external suppliers**. This will spread the fixed costs over a greater number of tasks and jobs.

(iii) Control measures to monitor information's **timeliness and relevance** can vary. **Timeliness** can be measured by the extent to which reports are printed within their deadlines. The department might like to ask management when they want their reports, and structure their activities around that.

As far as **relevance** goes, this can be monitored with regular meetings with user departments, and a log of proposed modifications which can be compared with what is actually achieved.

(iv) Assessing management's **future needs** requires a **strategic approach** to information. If sales are to increase, or if the company is to expand into new product or market areas, management will probably require information dealing with these issues. If the computer department knows these requirements in advance, it can prepare to provide the service.

However, the computer department should **liaise with user departments** on a **regular basis**, and there should be a system for noting down findings and a record of action taken.

(v) Ensuring the firm has **optimum capacity** and that it is used most effectively requires a review of the department's operations in **peak or slack times**, and the time in which user queries are dealt with by the system. **Standard response times** can be devised. The department should aim to make the most effective use of processor time. This might mean that routine number crunching operations are done at night, when there are relatively few other uses of a computer's time.

(vi) **Guidelines and standards** must be drawn up and circulated to the departments concerned. The computer department might even provide a consultancy service. However, the active **co-operation of user departments** is needed here. A system of **capital expenditure authorisation**, which ensured that all IT equipment and software purchases need to be authorised by the computer department, should ensure consistency.

(vii) Ensuring that the **IT strategy** conforms with the **business strategy** can only be achieved if IT issues are considered to be at the heart of the company's activities. Various monitoring exercises can be implemented to ensure that the IT strategy is derived from the business strategy (eg by seeing that IT based decisions have a wider **strategic justification** which is **formally minuted**).

(c) A **marketing-orientated department** would be one which identifies customer needs, and satisfies them within budgetary and other resource constraints.

The marketing orientation is both a **cultural** issue as well a set of **specific practices**. In this case, the computer department should look upon the departments it services as customers (the '**internal customer**' concept) rather than simply people working for the same firm. If user departments were able to use outside suppliers for some services, then a bit of **competition** might force a speedy introduction of this viewpoint. Moreover, if the computer department sells its services to external customers, the necessary market disciplines should spill over into its relationship with internal customers.

At the same time, the **true costs and benefits** of both policies should be estimated. Outside suppliers might appear cheaper, but there may be long term advantages in a centralised computer department, especially if IT is a critical success factor in the company's overall performance.

However, the real implementation of the marketing concept does not depend on these external factors. Instead the department should **research the needs** of its internal customers, and devise a service to suit these needs, rather than the other way round. It can then **promote** those of its services which are little known perhaps, but which users might find attractive. It will thus have to **communicate more information** about its skills to its internal customers.

38 TUTORIAL QUESTION: COMPUTER MISUSE

The three offences provided for under the Act are as follows.

(a) **Unauthorised access**

This would include both **physical access** to the **computer** and access to the **data** or **programs** contained on the computer. In order to process the crime the prosecution would have to show that access took place, that it was **unauthorised** and that the perpetrator **knew** he was accessing the computer or data and doing so without authority. It is not only hackers who are affected by the Act. Authorised users who **exceed their authority** can also be caught by the provisions of the Act. The penalty is a fine of up to £2,000 and/or imprisonment for up to six months.

(b) **Ulterior intent**

This makes provision for people who access a computer with the intent of **carrying out a serious crime**. This could include for example fraud or access to a hospital computer system to alter a person's treatment. The penalty is an unlimited fine or up to five year's imprisonment, or both.

(c) **Unauthorised modification**

This would include people who generate or write **virus software** and might also cover people who **alter physically** parts of computer systems. The penalty is again an unlimited fine or up to five years' imprisonment, or both.

39 SCP LTD: THREATS

(a) **Potential physical threats**

Threats to SCP's computer centre fall into two distinct areas - physical threats to the centre itself and threats to the software and data on the system.

Protection against natural and man-made disasters

(i) **Power problems.** The electrical supply should be set up so as to be immune from any foreseeable interruptions or fluctuations. This could be done with standby or continuously running generators.

(ii) **Flooding.** The facility should be constructed to be as secure as possible against the possibility of flooding, either from internal sources (eg fire control systems) or from external sources (eg leaking roofs, rain, rivers, and so on).

(iii) **Wind damage.** If the facility is in an area which might be susceptible to wind damage, or the building is not sufficiently solidly constructed, then precautions should be taken against the possibility of damage from freak wind conditions.

(iv) **Storm and lightning damage.** Both direct lightning strikes and lightning strikes on the power grid should be taken into consideration, particularly if the installation is in an area where electrical storms occur. Other storm damage (wind and rain) also needs to be provided for.

(v) **Fire.** Fire is an ever present threat. Smoking should be banned, and all electrical and heating apparatus should be checked to ensure that there is no likelihood of its being a source of fire. Smoke detectors, use of low-flammability materials and regular fire drills should all form part of control procedures.

(vi) **Intruders.** Both outsiders and disillusioned staff should be guarded against. Protection could take the form of security guards, levels of physical entry prevention and careful adherence to entry checking.

(vii) **Dust.** For some parts of the system dust can be a major problem. Access controls for personnel will aid in preventing dust intrusion, and proper air conditioning, with a system of sealed/double doors to important parts of the installation, will manage much of the rest of the problem.

Protection against unauthorised physical access

(i) Restrict the number of **entrances**. If the number of doors (taking into account safety requirements) is as low as possible the number of potential 'weak' access points which could cause a problem is restricted. Emergency exits should be fitted with **alarms**.

(ii) **Graduated access** to different parts of the facility. Staff and other visitors should only be allowed access to those areas which they need to visit. If different areas have different levels of authorisation requirements, then control becomes more easily implemented.

(iii) **Key card controlled access** to the facility. Using magnetic or electronic key card facilities allows for sophisticated control on the time and place of access, as well as more mundane aspects such as preventing double entry of a card before an exit.

(iv) **Time control** on access. Intelligent access control can limit access to staff to the hours when they legitimately would need it, and prevent access outside those hours except on override.

(v) Wearing of **ID badges**. Wearing of ID cards with built-in photographs allows both staff and security personnel to maintain a check on people who have access and those who have used the access power. Visitors should also be given badges and asked to wear them.

(vi) Voice, finger, palm or retina scan and **recognition systems** (if the investment warrants it). These systems can be expensive, but prevent card swapping and misuse.

(b) **Contingency plan**

The purpose of a contingency plan is to ensure that when a catastrophe happens, an organisation is **prepared** and is **able to continue working** in the face of a certain pre-determined level of interruption.

Catastrophes may have a wide range of causes. A contingency plan is usually invoked only in the event of a **'major' catastrophe**, typically fire, flooding, failure of the main processor or loss of a power supply. If a single system is 'lost', then an individual department must take appropriate action but this would not necessitate an organisation-wide contingency action.

The plan would be developed by establishing **how much interruption** could be tolerated in the system, what the **risks** of the various types of interruption are, what the **provisions** are that would have to be made for those interruptions and what **costs** would be associated with the failures and with the provision of the responses. Key to any contingency plan is **back-up** of data. However good the alternative hardware facilities, they will be of little use if SCP cannot load up with recent data.

Developing the plan

When a systems administrator sets out to ensure that the issues of security are fully covered, all these factors are taken into account. A team, led by the administrator, may be appointed to investigate the matter.

(i) The team should assess **how vulnerable SCP is in principle** to any of these problems. It may help to do an estimate of the likely **costs** of any particular threat identified. It is obviously easier to identify the costs of replacing hardware than the costs caused, for example, by a virus infection.

(ii) The team might review SCP's past history of security problems (eg any frauds discovered, and the **internal control** issues raised by them).

(iii) The team will then assess **how far current security measures are sufficient** to cope with the vulnerabilities discovered. This study might be quite a lengthy process, covering detailed technical issues (eg how easy might a hacker find it to enter the network? is there a proper lock system on new computer centre doors? fireproof cabinets? etc).

(iv) Some analysis will be made of the extent to which the security procedures **theoretically** in force are in fact being followed **in practice** (eg users might share passwords which they are supposed to keep confidential).

(v) Once some assessment of the risk, both qualitative and quantitative has been made, **additional security measures** may be suggested. These, too, will have to be costed, as far as possible, so that the costs of security do not outweigh the anticipated costs of the threats identified.

Standby options

Standby options would include some or all of the following.

(i) **Replacement hardware** to be installed. This clearly involves some delay and does not address short-term operational problems.

(ii) **Duplicate sites** to which communications links could be switched. These may be alternative sites already operated by the organisation, as in a distributed processing environment, or operated by a third party. **Third parties** may be either companies with which the organisation has some form of 'twinning' arrangement or dedicated companies providing standby services.

(iii) **Duplicate facilities** permanently installed. This is an expensive option, but one which should be considered for a mission-critical system.

40 TUTORIAL QUESTION: AUTOMATED OFFICE

(a) **Office automation** is the use of computer and telecommunications technology in creating, processing and transmitting information and data in the office environment. The goal of office automation is to improve the speed and efficiency of various office tasks. The paperless office has been touted as a goal of office automation, and while automation can reduce the amount of paper used, (for example memos may be transmitted as **e-mail attachments**), many people prefer a 'hard copy' and will print the document.

Office automation refers not only to electronic equipment linked to a communication network, but also to the changed social and organisational aspects of the work environment.

Some of the principal **hardware features** of the automated office are as follows.

(i) Wide use of **personal computers**. Office automation started when word processors were introduced to speed up document production. This was regarded as a way of saving money on secretarial salaries. Word processors were 'glorified typewriters' - not really connected with the mainstream computing power of an organisation. The arrival on the scene of financial modelling packages (spreadsheets) and information retrieval packages (databases) made the value of personal computing power more apparent.

(ii) **Networks and communications equipment.** Connecting computers and equipment means that they can talk to each other. It is easier, say, to send a spreadsheet file over a communications network to another floor in a building than to copy it on to floppy disk, leave it in the out-tray, and hope that it will wend its way through the company's internal mailing system to its destination. Data held on the network can be accessed by many users. Increasingly, centralised information may be accessed through an internal **Intranet**, with links to the **internet** if data held externally is required.

(iii) **Fax** allows the electronic transmission of documents over the public telephone network. The original hard copy is fed into a fax machine, which 'reads' it and converts it into electronic form so it can be transmitted over the telephone. It is printed by the recipient's fax machine. A PC equipped with a **fax modem** does not even require the document to be input in hard copy form. The computer communicates directly with the receiving fax machine.

(iv) The term **e-mail** is used to describe various systems of sending data or messages electronically via a modem and the telephone network or other data network and via a central computer, without the need to post letters - ie pieces of paper - or despatch documents by courier. E-mail is widely used both within and between organisations.

(v) **Integrated Systems Digital Networks (ISDN)** makes it possible to send voice, data, fax from a computer over telecommunication links without the need for a modem.

(vi) **Storage.** Much of an organisation's information can be stored on computer file, whether in magnetic form or on CD-ROM or as part of a **document image processing** (DIP) system which a user can obtain by calling it up on a VDU screen.

(b) **Benefits of office automation**

The adoption of networks based around personal computers can have major implications for the office environment.

Information distribution

It is easy to distribute computer files over a system. Technologies such as document image processing mean that documents (eg purchase invoices) can be stored on optical disk as they actually appear in hard copy, with notes attached. This means that **a number of individuals can consult the same file at the same time**. This also saves storage space therefore money.

Information generation and decision making

Office automation can support corporate decision-making. An example is the growth in usage of **executive information systems**, which provide senior managers with tools to drill down to the detail of an organisation's data to monitor performance and to analyse operations, eliminating the need for information requests to be passed through layers of management.

Office automation also enables links with **public databases** via the **internet** to be established so that '**environmental**' **data** can be easily assimilated into an organisation's information distribution system. This environmental data can be used to create information that affects corporate decision-making.

The use of word processing and graphics packages to enhance the **speed of production of hard-copy reports** can enable management to **react more quickly** where control action is appropriate.

Another improvement to corporate decision making can be the use of networks as 'bulletin boards', by which employees can **communicate ideas and opinions** in a relatively unstructured way, unhampered by the normal reporting hierarchies.

More productive use of human talent

A further consequence of office automation is that some **tedious processing tasks** (eg the endless retyping of memoranda for the sake of a few typing errors) **can be eliminated,** or performed by the machine. The management challenge is to employ the newly released ability of the work force in a constructive way.

41 TUTORIAL QUESTION: CENTRALISATION AND OPEN SYSTEMS

(a) The distribution of computer processing throughout SGI raises a number of issues, most of which centre on the **degree of centralisation** which the group wishes to employ.

As the directors have identified, distributed computer systems, either in the form of minicomputers or networked PC-based systems, imply that the organisation is willing to tolerate a **high degree of departmental or individual autonomy** in systems utilisation. Not only are the systems widely dispersed but the data/information held by the systems is similarly widely dispersed and used. In terms of organisational control this indicates a high level of trust and belief that the individuals will use the information effectively and responsibly.

(i) **Centralised** systems are typically employed for one of two reasons: there are often significant **cost savings** in using a single mainframe computer to provide the information service; and secondly, there are often concerns about the **security** of the information which make centralised processing necessary.

A further justification for centralised computer services follows from the **higher degree of control** which may then be exerted over the use of these services.

Centralised systems also mean that **specialised IT personnel** are in a **single location** and unit. This will reduce the risk of lack of necessary expertise at individual units.

(ii) In a **decentralised** system each department may decide its own computing investment and usage. This tends to weaken the control which might otherwise be imposed. However, the major drawback to centralised control is a tendency to **over-control** activities so that economically **justified actions are overruled** on technical grounds or the organisation **lags behind new developments**. Decentralisation promotes faster response to local problems.

The distribution of information processing throughout SGI is dependent upon a number of factors.

(i) At the simplest level only **economic considerations** are involved: is it cheaper to use PCs or minicomputers than a mainframe?

(ii) At a more sophisticated level consideration of **data control** and **systems development** are important: are distributed systems less secure or are distributed systems less controllable than are centralised systems?

(iii) At the most intangible level **organisational and internal political considerations** become significant: does the distribution of systems, information or the control of expenditure on them to individuals or departments reflect movements of power or influence within the organisation?

Distribution certainly gives **greater flexibility** to units and offers **greater operational efficiency**; the risk of **loss of control** or **excessive expense** must be balanced against this.

(b) **Open systems and distributed information systems**

At one time computer systems were developed on a **proprietary basis,** which meant that software was developed for use on specified hardware. In large organisations where a wide variety of computer applications were used, this led to inefficient generation and use of information.

An **open system** is a system that ensures that all of its constituent parts, hardware and software, are **compatible** and therefore can **operate together.**

The enormous increase in IT usage over recent years, in particular the development of PC technology, has resulted in demands from computer users for open systems. The compatibility allowed by open systems means that **different applications can 'talk' to each other.** Data processing is therefore made much more efficient and the information produced can be analysed and presented without duplication of work or other inefficiencies.

Over a similar period of time, **distributed processing systems** have also been developed and have become extremely popular. Using **networks** and local computers they allow a more flexible and efficient approach to information generation than do the more centralised options. In addition they are generally cheaper to purchase and operate and have allowed much smaller organisations to introduce sophisticated computer technology for the first time.

Open systems have made distributed processing and information systems much more freely available. Open systems technology means that distributed systems can now be developed using different types of hardware, allowing customers to choose on the basis of price and performance; in addition, customers can now develop information systems that match their needs rather than having to adapt those needs to match the system.

42 E-MAIL

Pass marks. You would have scored well if you addressed the question's specific requirements: describe the **impact of e-mail on work practices**, not just describe e-mail.

Examiner's comment. Candidates should provide wide-ranging answers, rather than simply mentioning that e-mail allows staff to work from home. Many candidates appeared to miss two important words in the question requirement, namely **work practices**. Many answers concentrated on the advantages and disadvantages of e-mail itself, rather than the effect e-mail can have on work practices.

Most candidates did include comment on speedier communications making decision-making faster within one location or even worldwide. Only a minority of answers provided information about the potential negative effects of e-mail on work practices. Areas that could have been mentioned in this context included: time wasted sifting through "junk mail"; slow response speeds on a network limiting the speed of communication; e-mail is less formal and therefore more difficult to understand and the absence of non-verbal communication.

Answers to part (b) were quite limited regarding the number of points covered. The vast majority of candidates mentioned the areas of: legal documents not being sent via e-mail, interviews requiring one-to-one or many-to-one dialogue and meetings where quick discussion is required. Most candidates would have gained more marks by including additional relevant points in their answer and ensuring that the points actually mentioned were adequately explained.

(a) **The impact of e-mail on work practices**

(i) **Speed** (transmission, being electronic, is almost instantaneous). E-mail is far faster than post (now sometimes called **snail mail**). It is a particular time-saver when communicating with people overseas.

This means that work can be completed **without the delays** associated with slower forms of communication: information requested, confirmation of an order and so on are received almost as soon as they are asked for. This may make **task completion** more efficient because it is **done in one go**, without double handling.

(ii) **Demarcation**. Conventionally, written office communications would be drafted by hand but sent out in typed form, so most offices employed trained typists.

A typical **e-mail client** (the software that enables users to send, receive and organise e-mail), however, uses a **rudimentary text editor** for composing messages, and this requires very little skill. The **usual essentials** of written communications (From, To, Cc, Date, Subject) are either inserted into special fields (linked to computerised address books) or are handled automatically. Conventions such as 'Dear ...', 'Yours sincerely' are ignored and written style is informal. Small **typing errors** are typically regarded as **tolerable**.

This means that the people who originate the messages using the PC on their desk now do work that would formerly have required a person with special skills.

(iii) **Economy.** E-mail is reckoned to be much **cheaper** than most other forms of communication over a distance. Money saved on postage and telecommunications costs can be diverted elsewhere and enhance other aspects of work.

On the other hand, e-mail is so quick and convenient that much more communication occurs, possibly counteracting savings.

(iv) **Efficiency.** E-mail client software such as Microsoft Outlook can help people to organise their communications.

(1) **Senders** of information have **documentary evidence** that they have given a piece of information to the recipient and that the recipient has picked up the message.

(2) **Receivers** are not necessarily disturbed by the information when it is sent (as they would be by face-to-face meetings or phone calls), but can **collect it later at their convenience**.

(v) **Sharing.** A message is prepared once only but can be sent to thousands of recipients at the touch of a button. For instance e-mail is a good way of canvassing opinions or pooling knowledge to solve a problem. A manager who has encountered a particular difficulty can e-mail other managers, alerting them to the problem and asking for suggestions as to how to deal with it.

(vi) **Teleworking.** E-mail facilitates working away from the office (whether at home or in the field) because staff can be kept informed about what is happening at HQ, can inform others of their own activities, and be provided with office resources that they may need (a particular file, say). They can also chat to colleagues, reducing the isolation that many people who telework suffer.

(b) **When e-mail is not appropriate**

In spite of its advantages e-mail may not always be the best medium for communications. Possible shortcomings are as follows.

(i) The nature of the **medium**. E-mail allows communication in the form of written words, numbers or graphics. Communication however entails more than just symbols of this type: it is estimated that perhaps 50% of the meaning that people are able to impart to each other in face-to-face conversation is non-verbal.

Meaning is conveyed by body language and **tone of voice** to a much larger extent than is generally realised. Some users have adopted what are called '**emoticons**' to try to avoid this: an example is the smiley face symbol (constructed thus: **:-)**), which is used, say, to indicate that the preceding comment is meant tongue in cheek.

(ii) The nature of the **message**. People may wish to discuss detailed operational problems, whereas e-mail is best suited to short messages. Immediate two-way exchange of information is possible, but it will be hampered by the need to type in messages on a keyboard, especially if the users are not particularly competent typists.

(iii) All exchanges are recorded. It may be possible for exchanges to be read by others, such as senior executives. This may be undesirable from the point of view of users since some of their exchanges may be '**off the record**', for example short cuts that get round organisational bureaucracy, but solve operational difficulties.

(iv) Senior managers may value **meetings** because they take place outside the main place of work, meaning that they are free of the usual daily pressures and better able to take an overview of the operations they manage.

(v) Large amounts of e-mail are likely to be received each day. Staff may quickly find themselves suffering from **information overload**. They will either spend excessive amounts of time dealing with e-mail or they will skip over much of the mail they receive and possibly miss important points.

(vi) It is **uncomfortable to read** much more than a screen-full of information. Longer messages will either not be read properly or they will be printed out, in which case they may just as well have been circulated in hard copy form in the first place.

(vii) **No distinction** is made between different types of communication. A short chatty message that might in the past have been scribbled on a Post-it note, is delivered in the same format and through the same medium as an important two page report.

(viii) Depending on the system in use, the facilities for **data presentation** in an e-mail message may not be as sophisticated as they are in a spreadsheet or word processing application. (Although this information could be included as an 'attachment'.)

43 SKO PLC: CENTRAL STORAGE AND DPA

> **Pass marks.** By 'critically evaluate' in part (a) the examiner means 'discuss the advantages and disadvantages of the proposal'. This is very much a question about managing information, not about using technology, as the Examiner's comment make clear.
>
> Part (b) looks easy, but for six marks at Stage 4 you should have produced a slightly more elaborate answer than 'no action is needed'. The question was set while the DPA 1984 which excluded paper based information applied. (The DPA 1998 applies to all personal information whether computerised or manual. We have **updated this answer in light of the 1998 Data Protection Act**.)
>
> **Examiner's comment.** The vast majority answers to part (a) missed the crucial point that the data being stored centrally was predominantly paper based, and therefore excluded from the 1984 DPA. Almost all answers set about explaining the computer systems and communication networks needed. In part (b) the majority of candidates were able to list the eight data protection principles (not required), but unable to **apply** their knowledge and show why the DPA 1984 was largely irrelevant to the question.

(a) **Information storage**

The transfer will have the following advantages.

(i) **Space** currently taken up by documents will be freed up for alternative uses. Given that it is retail space it is probably expensive to rent and can be put to profitable use, either for storing more goods for resale or as a sales area.

(ii) It will be easier to **collate and analyse** information, and specialist staff may be able to use more sophisticated methods of analysis. Besides the new outputs mentioned in the question, central storage will make it possible to provide information on various matters. Here are some further examples.

(1) The **performance** of each shop can be measured and compared. This will give central management the opportunity to analyse the reasons why some stores perform better than others and institute changes to bring the poor performers up to scratch. Publication of '**league tables**' may also increase individual managers' **motivation** to perform as well as, or better than, other shops in their region and across the chain as a whole.

(2) It will be possible to identify **good suppliers**, who can be relied upon to deliver on time and to the right quality, and **suppliers to avoid**. Such information would be useful to all but it may only be discovered locally, by accident, at present.

(3) It will be possible to collate information about **customers** and tailor marketing activity more closely to the needs of different segments.

(iii) The information can be kept more **securely** in a central location than it could be in a shop, which is necessarily exposed to the general public and so subject to greater risks.

(iv) A **consistent** system of document **storage** can be applied by specialist archiving staff to all the documentation produced, making **retrieval** much easier. This is unlikely to be happening at present: there may be as many different systems of filing as there are shops.

(v) **Storage methods** that are not feasible on economic grounds in individual shops may become feasible on the larger scale envisaged. These might include microfiche or, better, document image processing.

(vi) A policy for the **disposal** of documents that are no longer needed can be introduced and centrally controlled. It is likely that at present no such policy exists and that individual managers either hoard too much paper or dispose of it when it might still be of use.

(vii) It will be possible to **audit** the company's records (both internally and externally) much more quickly and easily. This may save a substantial amount of money.

Disadvantages include the following.

(i) The **physical difficulty** and (unknown?) **cost** of transporting large numbers of documents from all over the country on a regular basis. Besides the scale of the task there is a strong chance that documents will occasionally be **damaged** or **lost in transit**. It is also likely that **delays or omissions** will occur, which may prevent the central facility from producing complete information. Strong **controls** are needed and these may be **costly** to operate.

(ii) The difficulty of **sorting** documents which may be stored in a variety of different ways (date order, account number order, alphabetical order etc) into a consistent order.

(iii) Although **managers** are apparently to continue to produce their own 'normal' day-to-day operating information they will be deprived of the chance to **monitor longer term trends** and perform **ad hoc data analysis** tasks.

  (1) Collation of information and presentation in **summary** form may **smooth out** local trends so that they are not noticed, or else **exaggerate** national trends that happen not to apply locally. Inappropriate decisions may be made as a result.

  (2) The central facility may be unable or unwilling to carry out **unusual data analysis tasks** to order or within an acceptable time.

(iv) Managers of individual stores may resent the **loss of autonomy** that results from taking away part of their job (data management and analysis), and they may not welcome the idea of **closer monitoring** of the details of their performance.

(v) The central facility may provide so much information that managers suffer **information overload**, and miss important points.

(vi) A **disaster** such as a fire at the central facility would destroy **all** of the company's data unless back-up copies are held off-site. At present, a fire at an individual shop would only affect the data held there.

Assessment

The proposal must be looked at carefully from the point of view of the **costs** of acquiring new premises, and setting up and operating the central facility (as compared with the costs of carrying on as at present) and the **benefits,** financial and otherwise, that are likely to derive from it.

Although the question states that there are no plans to introduce any direct **communication** links between the shops, this approach would be of significant help in avoiding many of the disadvantages identified above.

(b) **Data protection**

The Data Protection Act 1998 applies to information about living individuals, not information about corporate bodies. The simple answer therefore is that SKO plc does not need to take **any** action. However, this depends on what information is held and how it is used. The 1998 Act includes provisions (applying to information in any form, even **paper**) that require consent to be given before 'sensitive' personal data can be processed, and that give the data subject the right to be told if personal information is obtained from a **third party**.

(i) If the information about other **corporate entities** is restricted to the entity itself there is no problem, but in practice it is likely that information will be derived from one or several contacts within that organisation. If **personal data** (including facts or opinions) about such contacts are held, SKO plc is a **data user** and the contacts are **data subjects.** Depending on the content of the data held, the company may be required to register with the Data Protection Registrar and abide by the Data Protection Principles.

(ii) Equally, if any of the **summaries** are derived from information about identifiable individuals there may be a need to register.

44 PC INC: INTERNET SERVICE PROVIDER

> **Pass marks.** This is quite a difficult question, based partly on economic theory, if you choose to answer it in that way. Good knowledge of current trends, for instance from reading the **Financial Times** IT Supplement, would be invaluable.
>
> **Examiner's comment.** In part (a) more marks could be obtained in most answers by including more relevant factors and explaining how each point was relevant to PC Inc, providing examples where appropriate. Part (b) was best approached by applying knowledge to an information resource which the candidate has already paid for, eg a newspaper or Study Text. Thinking in these terms would then provide reasons for the charge being made.
>
> Many candidates attempted to apply the mnemonic ACCURATE with varying degrees of success. An answer which explained why a charge could be made for timely information, for example, scored more marks than one which simply stated that information must be timely. Overall most candidates did not reach a pass standard in part (b) of the question.

(a) **Factors to be taken into account when setting prices**

(i) **Demand**

Internet use is increasing all the time, especially in developed countries, and predictions are that this is set to continue for the foreseeable future. The number of **different uses** is also increasing, as companies see new opportunities to offer services, or to benefit from interactive communications with customers.

A key factor influencing demand is the **extent of ownership** of the necessary hardware.

(1) A **PC plus modem** is becoming a common household item in developed countries such as the UK, and most people use a PC at work.

(2) **Digital television** (an alternative distribution medium) was launched in countries such as the UK and the US in 1998. Although initial take-up of the technology has been fairly slow, in the next decade it is expected the vast majority of the population will have access to digital television.

PC Inc produce **specialist information** that is not available from other providers. So long as this is **useful** information, the company will benefit from specialist demand, owing to the **scarcity** of this part of their service.

(ii) **Supply**

The ISP **market** has become very crowded. The dominant major players of the mid 1990s (America Online and Demon Internet) are now facing competition from many new 'free' ISPs. The sort of general information that

PC Inc is planning to offer is also available from **other sources** such as Reuters.

(iii) **Entry costs**

(1) **Development costs**

PC Inc will have invested time and money in developing their website. Costs that need to be recovered include the cost of **acquiring, and learning how to use, website development software** such as Microsoft FrontPage, and interactive tools/languages such as HTML, ActiveX and Java.

(2) **Hardware costs**

Powerful **servers** with high capacity storage will have been acquired, to allow PC Inc to offer its e-mail service. The investment here may be considerable, given that other ISPs often allow subscribers to have several e-mail addresses, and up to 10Mb of Web space as part of their basic package.

It is also likely that PC Inc will have invested heavily in specialised **communications hardware** such as ISDN links with other ISPs for high-speed exchange of mail.

All of these costs need to be recovered.

(iv) **Ongoing costs**

Once created PC Inc's website has to be **maintained and updated** on a regular basis, requiring further time and investment in the latest software and skills.

On-going **telecommunications costs** will be high, owing to the need to collect e-mail from and deliver it to other ISPs.

As demand increases further **servers** will need to be acquired.

(v) **Payment systems**

If PC Inc chose to charge a subscription, this would best be collected by asking customers to submit their credit or debit card details when signing up for the service. Regular monthly payments could then be collected automatically, keeping **administration costs** to a minimum.

Other customers, however, may wish to run **accounts** and subscribe on a company-wide basis.

Prices may have to reflect a **variety of structures**, taking into account issues such as the following.

(1) **Number of users** of a particular account.

(2) Whether an **unlimited amount of time** could be spent using PC Inc's services, or whether there would be a **flat fee** for, say, the first five hours and a fee per hour thereafter.

To justify charging a fee PC Inc will need to emphasise its **superior service**, and maybe offer reduced call connection rates.

PC Inc may decide not to charge a subscription and rely on **income from advertisers** and/or **agreements with telephone companies** giving PC Inc a percentage of user call charges.

(b) **Factors that make information a valuable commodity**

Many commentators have observed that an '**information society**' is emerging where information is a valuable resource.

Easy **access** to information, the **quality** of that information and **speedy methods of exchanging** the information have become essential elements of economic success. Mobility of, and access to, information have become key economic and social issues. In this climate the **demand** for information is likely to expand rapidly.

Organisations that make **good use of information** in decision-making, and which use new technologies to access, process and exchange information are likely to be **best placed to survive** in increasingly competitive world markets.

Unlike certain commodities the value of **information in general** is **not** based on **scarcity**: indeed the most frequent complaint of many modern managers is that there is **far too much of it** about.

Moreover, the value of information is **in the eyes of the beholder** to some extent: information about a new type of plastic may be of keen interest and value to a car manufacturer, but of no value whatsoever to a software house.

The factors which make information valuable are as follows.

(i) **The source of the information**

If the information comes from a source that is **widely known and respected** for quality, thoroughness and accuracy (Reuters, say, or CIMA) it will be more valuable to users than information from an unknown or untested source, because it can be relied upon with confidence.

(ii) **The ease of assimilation**

Modern methods of presentation can use not only words and figures but also **colour graphics, sound and movement**. This makes the receipt of information a **richer (and so more valuable) experience**, and it means that information can be more **easily**, and therefore more **quickly**, **understood**: again a feature that people will be willing to pay for.

(iii) **Accessibility**

If information can be made available in an **easily accessible** place (such as the Internet) users are saved the time and trouble of a trip to the library, say. If they just want a few sentences of information and they can find these (for instance using an Internet search engine) **without having to buy** a whole book or newspaper or magazine (which would mean that the information they actually wanted cost more than it was worth) then they will be willing to **pay for this convenience**. (This is why people have in the past been willing to pay more for TV sets with **teletext** facilities, for instance.)

45 TUTORIAL QUESTION: WORKING ENVIRONMENTS

(a) **Equipment and environment**

If the typewriter keyboard were invented today, rather than in the late 19th century, it is doubtful that the conventional shape or **QWERTY** arrangement of the letters would have been employed. The letters took this order because of the possibility for jamming by **adjacent mechanical keys** hit in rapid succession. There have been new keyboard designs which are supposed to be 'ergonomic'.

Equipment designed around people is more productive and safe, than if human activities were designed, as it were, to accord with the needs of machines and equipment. **Ergonomics**, then, is the design of operating machinery and work environments to **minimise physical (or sometimes mental) discomfort and injury** from working.

Moreover, the design of the **environment in which work occurs** (eg the noise levels, proper lighting etc) is a type of ergonomics as all these functions are important in making work a less demanding experience.

Recruitment

The importance of ergonomics specifically in recruitment is hard to gauge, for the simple reason that a person has many reasons for choosing one particular organisation over another, and the **type of equipment used may not be the dominating factor**.

However, for jobs requiring the exercise of skill, then the type of technology the organisation employs, even if it is not particularly user friendly, can be crucial. If, say, a systems analyst wishes to **gain expertise at particular database system**, then the software used by the employing organisation can affect his or her choice.

Likewise, some employees may see **benefits in training opportunities** on particular equipment or software provided by an organisation: in this case, information technology. Use of equipment which we have broadly defined to include software can be a vital part of the work experience necessary to a career.

It might also be the case that organisations using **old or dangerous machinery** might discourage some applicants, particularly if certain technologies have a bad safety record. Ergonomics, then, can be a matter of life and death.

Retention

As far as employee **retention** goes, it may not be so much the actual equipment, but the way it is used, and the work disciplines surrounding its use that are of most concern. At the most extreme example, abuse of VDUs can lead to **repetitive strain injury** in clerical workers, although the same condition also appears in industrial settings. If use of equipment causes acute or even mild physical discomfort, or if its procedures and routines are mentally frustrating this might **reduce the employee's morale**, and be indirectly a causative factor in leaving the job. It is thus a **hygiene** factor.

Again, to cite the example of information technology, it is widely believed that one of the advantages of the widely increased processing power available is in the field of **user friendliness**. The introduction of **graphical user interfaces** makes information technology easier to use.

Both the design of the hardware and the software can be influenced by ergonomics. In software, the employment of **Help screens** can make IT less threatening, so that the user knows what it is going on, and any **errors are clearly flagged**, together with suitable remedies.

Other features of ergonomics include designing **seats** which support the back and encourage **correct posture**.

In the overall design of the building, ergonomic features should encourage work, by **screening excess noise** (eg from computer printers) or providing the workers with earmuffs to enable concentration. Office buildings should be designed to avoid so-called '**sick building syndrome**' where a combination of poor ventilation, carpet dust, static electricity, and an atmosphere that is insufficiently humid conspire to cause headaches and migraines, which are bad for workers and reduce productivity.

However, the impact on workplace design is not simply restricted to physical health. If a **team spirit** is required, some **sociability** is necessary to encourage **good relations** and to **share information**. The use of IT does not reduce the necessity for social interaction. In some respects it enhances it. Also, if a sociable friendly atmosphere is necessary for morale, and more importantly for initiative, then the office layout should **discourage isolation**.

Performance

The effect of technology, especially information technology, on **performance** in part depends on how management treat IT-based work. Is IT simply used to automate procedures, or does it let employees use their knowledge and creativity better for the organisation?

(b) (i) Typical information technology equipment and resources required by a **home-worker** would include the following.

(1) A **PC** powerful enough to run all the software that the worker will require.

(2) A **modem** to provide a link, via public telecommunications links, or a private line if security is critical, to the main office computer.

(3) Possibly a **telephone line** in addition to the ordinary domestic telephone line. If urgent messages are sent regularly the computer will need a line and will need to be connected at all times. A similar link might be required for a fax machine, although fax facilities could be incorporated into the PC.

(4) Additional communications devices such as an **answerphone** and a **mobile phone** could help to improve the level of available contact between home-worker and office, reducing the office's possible frustration at not being able to get in touch.

(5) **E-mail** would allow a higher level of communication.

(6) A **printer**. If a laser printer is considered too large or expensive, a compact model such as the Canon Bubblejet might be considered.

(7) Links to **office services** such as on-line information retrieval systems and other technical **databases.**

(8) Contact names/numbers of **technical support staff**, in case of problems with hardware or software.

(9) Hardware and software user **manuals**.

(10) Supplies of **computer consumables** such as disks, paper, toner cartridges etc.

(ii) **Advantages** are as follows.

(1) **Saving of commuting time** (typically two hours per day, not only in the South-East of England but in many areas, particularly in times when employees have to look further afield to find work).

(2) The opportunity for home-worker to **provide services to more than one organisation** (assuming contract permits this) if the demands of the job allow this.

(3) Saving of **office accommodation costs**. If several workers work from home some of the time, then 'hot-desking' can be used in the office; if some workers work from home all the time, no space need be reserved for them.

(4) **'Flexitime'** advantages - employees can work to suit their own living patterns.

(5) **Greater motivation** of some employees given more freedom.

(6) **Fewer interruptions** from internal phone calls, colleagues etc. The 'mailbox' need only be checked a couple of times a day and urgent messages can be telephoned.

Disadvantages include the following.

(1) For the homeworker.

- A sense of **isolation** and being 'left out' of office life.
- **Domestic interruptions**.
- Availability of **space/accommodation** for self and equipment.
- **Overheads** are likely to be borne by the homeworker.
- **Tax implications** need to be considered (allocation of deductible expenses, risk of CGT liability etc).
- **Lack of backup facilities** (power cuts etc) and of on-hand **technical support**. Much technical advice can be provided by phone, with technician tracking on office PC, but sometimes a site visit is necessary.
- The **constant presence** of 'work' at home may be a negative factor.

(2) For the employer

- **Lack of control** and ability to **monitor and supervise** work. The employee must be reliable and trustworthy.
- '**Team spirit**' may be lost among staff.
- There may be a greater risk of **hacking, sabotage**, and **system faults.**
- There will be a good deal of **administrative effort** in dealing with 'ownership' of domestic phone lines, recharges of invoices etc.
- The **risk of theft** of equipment is greater.
- **Quality control** is more difficult.

46 YK PLC: E-MAIL

Pass marks. This question is as much about communication as it is about e-mail. So long as you are well prepared and were able to apply your prepared knowledge to the scenario it should have caused few difficulties.

Examiner's comment. Answers tended to score fewer marks where the candidate spent a lot of time explaining potential problems with the hardware requirements. The focus of the question was on e-mail as a communication system. Others explained the advantages of e-mail only and made no mention of the 'human' aspects. Some seemed to confuse e-mail with the (much faster) 'chat' forums provided between members of the same ISP. **Future candidates who are uncomfortable with the 'human' aspects of the syllabus should note that this is certainly an area that will be returned to in future examinations.**

E-mail is a method of **sending data or messages electronically** via a network. Typically information is 'posted' by the sender (who might click on a 'Send' icon) to a central computer which allocates disk storage space as a **mailbox** for each user. The information is subsequently 'collected' by the receiver from the mailbox, again probably by clicking on an icon. The system may use **sound or a pop-up message** to indicate to users when there is post waiting to be collected.

(a) **The problems of using e-mail**

The new e-mail system is clearly not fulfilling its purpose of replacing travel and face-to-face meetings. Possible reasons for this are as follows.

(i) The nature of the **medium**. E-mail allows communication in the form of written words, numbers or graphics. Communication however entails more than just symbols of this type: it is estimated that perhaps 50% of the meaning that people are able to impart to each other in face-to-face conversation is **non-verbal**. Meaning is conveyed by **body language** and **tone of voice** to a much larger extent than is generally realised.

(ii) The nature of the **message**. Directors wish to discuss **detailed** operational problems, whereas e-mail is best suited to **short messages**. Immediate two-way exchange of information is possible, but it will be hampered by the **need to type in** messages on a keyboard, especially if the directors are not particularly competent typists.

(iii) E-mail is a **relatively formal** means of communication. It is likely that all exchanges are **recorded** and may be readable by others, such as the senior executives. This may be undesirable from the point of view directors since some of their exchanges may be **'off the record'**, for example short-cuts that get round organisational bureaucracy, but solve operational difficulties.

(iv) Directors are likely to value meetings because they take place **outside** the main place of work, meaning that they are **free of the usual daily pressures** and better able to take an overview of the operations they manage.

E-mail is not the panacea that YK plc hoped for: it has a number of drawbacks, besides those already mentioned.

(i) Large amounts of e-mail are likely to be received each day. Directors will quickly find themselves suffering from **information overload**. They will either spend excessive amounts of time dealing with e-mail or they will skip over much of the mail they receive and possibly miss important points.

(ii) It is uncomfortable to read much **more than a screen-full** of information. Longer messages will either not be read properly or they will be printed out, in which case they may just as well have been circulated in hard copy form in the first place.

(iii) **No distinction** is made between different types of communication. A short chatty message that might in the past have been scribbled on a Post-it note, is delivered in the same format and through the same medium as an important two page report.

(iv) Depending on the system in use, the facilities for **data presentation** in an e-mail message may not be as sophisticated as they are in a spreadsheet or word processing application, or the senders of messages may **take less care** over presentation.

(b) **Benefits of using e-mail**

In spite of the above, e-mail does offer many benefits if well used. It is to be noted that the new system had the approval of directors initially, and it is likely that they do find it **useful for many purposes**.

(i) Transmission of messages is almost **instantaneous**. Previously messages would have to be printed out on paper, addressed, and physically transported to their destination. Using e-mail none of this is necessary and **urgent information** that cannot be adequately or conveniently conveyed over the telephone can thus be **instantly placed in the recipient's hands**. This is likely to be a significant benefit in a company such as YK plc, which is highly subject to changing market forces and needs many daily decisions on operational matters.

(ii) It is a highly effective way of **sharing information** amongst many interested parties. A single message can be sent to everyone on a particular 'mailing list', or even to everybody in the company with a few clicks of the mouse. Given that the directors are all doing the same job in different locations, there are likely to be many occasions when this facility is of use, say, for share pricing information.

(iii) It is a good way of **canvassing opinions** or **pooling knowledge** to solve a problem. A director who has encountered a particular difficulty can e-mail other directors, alerting them to the problem and asking for suggestions as to how to deal with it.

(iv) E-mail **saves money**. In YK plc it is intended to avoid travelling costs. It should also bring about savings in postage and stationery costs and in post-room staff time.

(v) **Security of confidential information** passed between the directors should be enhanced. Paper can be read or damaged while in transit. E-mail allows **access** to data to be **restricted** by the use of **passwords**.

(vi) E-mail is **less intrusive** than other methods of sending quick messages such as the telephone. It will allow directors to deal with non-urgent matters at a convenient time rather than being interrupted by calls at the time when the matter occurs to the sender of the message and when they are busy on other matters or away from their desks.

(vii) E-mail provides a **written record** of information exchanges, and this may be very useful to avoid ambiguity and, where necessary, to ensure that the reasoning behind the decisions taken by the directors is fully documented.

(viii) Senders of e-mail messages have **documentary evidence** that they have **sent** a message in the first place and they can check to see if the intended recipient has picked up the message, in which case they can expect a **reply**.

47 CP LTD: HOMEWORKING

Pass marks. Some people like to come to work to **escape** from the pressures of home life! Homeworking is not suited to everyone, and is still more the exception rather than the norm. Some companies and individuals make it work very successfully.

Examiner's comment. Common problems in (a) were: providing examples of benefits to the company (not asked for); not discussing staff concerns or IT solutions; and not recognising that IT cannot solve all of the problems. Some candidates made unrealistic suggestions like setting up video-conferencing or a WAN, both of which would be very expensive. For part (b) many candidates failed to include sufficient examples. Many answers tended to repeat points already made in part (a).

REPORT

To: Managing Director
From: Management Accountant
Date: 22nd May 1997
Subject: Homeworking

1 **Introduction**

1.1 This report sets out the potential **benefits** to the staff that will be gained by homeworking and the **concerns** they may have together with an assessment of the help that can be provided via the IT infrastructure to alleviate these.

2 **Potential benefits**

2.1 **Savings in travel time and cost**

The staff will not have to travel to work, which could be a significant advantage to those who have long or difficult journeys. They will also save the cost of travel to and from work.

2.2 **Flexibility**

Staff can be more flexible about the hours they work (eg 7 to 3, 8 to 4, 9 to 5, or whatever suits them) and about the timing of breaks. It would also make it easier for them to **contact customers outside normal office hours**, giving them the satisfaction of providing a **better service** and increasing their potential **sales bonuses** (this is, of course, a benefit to the company too).

2.3 **Work environment**

There are many **disruptions** at work which can hinder or distract employees: examples are constantly ringing telephones, printer noise, loud conversations. These would not be present at home, and although there may be **other distractions** these are less likely to be stressful ones.

2.4 **Quality of life**

More generally homeworking should provide a better quality of life for the individual working at home. The home is likely to be **better lit, heated** to suit individual taste, more **comfortable**, and have **more facilities**. It will not be necessary to cram domestic chores such as shopping, cleaning, washing into evenings and weekends. It may be possible to adapt working hours to accommodate **family commitments**, such as taking and collecting children from school.

3 **Staff concerns**

3.1 **Employment relationship and legal implications**

Staff may be concerned about their **employment rights** if they work from home and whether there are any implications in terms of **health and safety** regulations, **insurance and tax**, mortgage and council tax.

A further concern in this area is whether they will have enough **space** to work effectively at home.

I suggest we clarify these matters and then **brief the staff** about any potential implications on an individual basis if necessary.

3.2 **Isolation**

Staff currently have a great de al of interaction in the office, so a concern of staff could be that they become **cut off from their colleagues** and will miss the social contact. This could engender a feeling of uncertainty in staff which could affect their ability to provide an efficient service. They may also fear that being out of sight and out of mind will damage any **prospects of being considered for advancement** within the organisation.

3.3 **Exchange of information**

Staff help each other by **exchanging information** about work-related matters and **sharing the problems** they have experienced. There may be fears that they will lose this mutual support if working at home.

4 **IT infrastructure**

4.1 Much of the information that is required for the staff to carry out their jobs is on the computer system. It is fairly straightforward to provide a connection to the computer system to each employee in their homes and provide them with the necessary hardware.

There will obviously be an associated **cost** to this which we will need to quantify to ensure that it is not prohibitive.

The link could be a permanent link or a dial up facility. The **dial-up facility** may be more appropriate if it is possible to download the files staff need to access onto a local PC. This could then be updated at intervals avoiding the need to be permanently connected.

4.2 The same link could also be used to provide **e-mail** and **bulletin board** facilities to enable the staff to keep in contact and exchange information.

4.3 Access to the **VAN** would also be possible using the same link, but again the **cost implications** would need to be investigated in more detail.

4.4 Local copies of **software** such as word-processing packages and spreadsheets can be provided to produce the necessary documents and letters.

4.5 IT is only part of the answer, however: telecommunications links are a poor substitute for the actual **direct social contact** currently enjoyed. A carelessly worded e-mail, for instance, can easily be misunderstood.

5 **Overcoming the concerns of staff**

5.1 It will be important for us to ensure that the staff are **kept informed** of developments and that we consult with them to **identify any worries** they may have. This will enable us to prepare them for the change and to alleviate their key concerns. The key **benefits** to them and the organisation should be **stressed**. It is important that they realise that both the individual and not just the organisation will benefit. This will hopefully enable them to **own** the change and buy into it.

5.2 Consideration could be given to **piloting** the method of working with a few individuals who are already pro homeworking. They will **champion the change** later if we decide to implement it throughout the sales staff. Asking for volunteers and for suggestions on implementation will ensure that staff feel that they have been properly consulted.

5.3 Consideration could also be given to setting up a **demonstration** to impress upon them that they will still be able to perform their jobs and keep in touch with each other. A visit to (home and office) sites of an organisation that already uses this method of working may also help staff to realise its benefits and its operability as well as its ease of use. It will also help us to assess the **level of training** necessary which must be given to support the staff.

5.4 **Social contact** could be retained to a limited extent by providing **regular meetings** at a convenient place. This could be used to update staff collectively of developments, organisational matters and reinforce the commitment and cultural aspects of the organisation whilst providing the opportunity for social contact.

5.5 The company will **save** a considerable amount of money (90% of £3,500 to £4,000 per employee per annum). Part of this could be **offered to staff** as an incentive to work at home.

48 PDY LTD: HOW DO YOU DO IT?

(a) **Review of the product delivery system**

The systems development lifecycle includes as part of its last stage a requirement that a new system be subject to **review.** This is usually referred to as a **post-implementation review**. In certain methodologies, the review stage is not included. This does not mean that it should not be performed, it simply means that the particular methodology does not address the later stages of development, being more concerned with analysis and design.

The review should **evaluate the success of the project**. The system should have been designed with clear, specified **objectives**, and justified in terms of **cost-benefit analysis** or other **performance criteria**. Post-implementation review should establish whether the objectives and targeted performance criteria **have been met**, and if not, why not, and what should be done about it.

Planning the review

Such an evaluation must be planned, so that suitable measurements can be made on the basis of the **old** system. The post-implementation measurement should **not** be made **too soon** after the system goes live, or else results will be abnormally affected by **'teething' problems, lack of user familiarity** and **resistance to change**.

Performing the review

In appraising the operation of the new system immediately after the changeover, comparison should be made between actual and predicted performance. This will include (amongst other items) consideration of **throughput speed** (time between input and output), use of **computer storage** (both internal and external), the number and type of **errors/queries** and the **cost of processing** (data capture, preparation, storage and output media, etc).

It should be the **steering committee's** responsibility to ensure that post-implementation reviews are carried out, although the **internal audit** department may be required to do the work of carrying out the reviews.

Just as during the feasibility study the feasibility of a project is assessed by reference to **technical, operational, social and economic factors**, so the same criteria can be used for evaluation. For example, a **technical** evaluation might ask the following questions.

(i) Is the **throughput rate** from data capture to receipt of output acceptable?

(ii) Is there sufficient **secondary storage** to keep the necessary data, including back-ups and archive data?

(iii) Are **response times** acceptable for given processing volumes?

Reporting on the review

The findings of a post-implementation review team should be formalised in a report.

(i) A **summary** of their findings should be provided, emphasising any areas where the system has been found to be unsatisfactory. The report should recommend what action(s) should be taken.

(ii) A review of system **performance** should be provided. This will address the matters outlined above, such as run times and error rates.

(iii) A **cost-benefit review** should be included, comparing the forecast costs and benefits identified at the time of the feasibility study with actual costs and benefits.

(iv) **Recommendations** should be made as to any further action or steps which should be taken to improve performance.

(b) **The stock controller**

The situation described is a rather extreme example of the types of **problem** which may occur when a new computer system is installed.

There are two types of issue to consider here.

(i) Firstly it is **not clear how well staff have been prepared** for the idea of computerisation in general terms: for example, its likely effect on their working practices and the benefits it can bring.

(ii) Secondly, it is clear that the stock controller has **not been trained** in what he is supposed to do.

Effect of computerisation

Any systems development brings a great deal of **change** to users - the familiar, however unsatisfactory it may be, is replaced by the unknown, so that a user's **working practices** and **environment** may change beyond all recognition. Users may not therefore embrace the systems development process wholeheartedly. Many people are averse to change. Change brings **disruption** to working practices and **effort** is required on the part of the user to **understand** and **adopt** a new system.

Users may be reluctant to become involved through **fear of loss of their job**; computers are seen as replacing people as tasks become automated. Even if the individual does not fear redundancy, it is unlikely that a whole department will continue to operate without some kind of re-definition of roles of redeployment of resource. Established **teams** may become **broken up**. The stock controller may have a number of concerns.

Analysts must use appropriate skills to involve users. A belief that analysts are 'techies', ruthless in their approach and themselves having all the characteristics of a computer and none of a human being, may discourage users from involvement. Analysts require an **understanding of user concerns**, so that these can be understood and overcome.

Training

It appears that the stock controller has not been adequately trained. First of all, some **basic computer literacy training** would have been of benefit; this could have dealt with such matters as the following.

(i) Switching hardware **on and off.**

(ii) Basic **printer troubleshooting**, giving an awareness of the difficulties of actually connecting an 'intelligent' printer and convincing it to stay on line.

(iii) How **menu systems** work.

(iv) **Password** discipline.

(v) **Back-up** procedures.

(vi) **Office regulations.**

(vii) **Health matters**, such as maintaining a good posture.

(viii) Basic **keyboard skills.**

Benefits of proper training include the following.

(i) **Best practice**. Formal training ensures that users follow good working practices. This is particularly important in the area of general policy and procedure, eg computer security, back-up routines etc.

(ii) **Software capabilities.** Since the organisation is likely to have spent considerable amounts on software, it is worth making users aware of the software's capabilities on more than some kind of assumed 'need to know' basis. This will encourage users to make best use of systems and operate them in the most efficient and effective way.

(iii) **Confidence.** Users will be given confidence in their ability to use the system - without formal training they may be reduced to flicking through manuals and left with a feeling of uncertainty as to what they are doing.

(iv) **Assistance.** Formal training is important if only to point out the user-friendly features of a system and the existence of 'help' screens. The user will be given some indication of where to turn for assistance.

(v) **Feedback.** It is easier to monitor the success of formal training than informal training. Follow-up procedures will identify the aptitude of trained staff for the tasks they do, and changes can then be made where necessary.

(vi) **Surroundings.** Users can be given an awareness of how their jobs fits into the whole system entity. An understanding of how tasks are related may lead to suggestions for improvement.

49 WEBSITE DESIGN

Pass marks. The Examiner has indicated that the IFM examination will be forward-looking and involve questions on newer technology where appropriate. The focus is expected to be on how technological developments have affected (or may affect in the future) organisations and people - rather than an explanation of the technology.

Examiner's comment. Candidates' knowledge of the Internet appears to be very good. However, areas of weakness included: inappropriate comments such as taking longer to find items in a paper-based catalogue due to the lack of an index, lack of colour in a paper catalogue, company information would only be given away on a web-site although presumably competitors would also obtain copies of the paper catalogue, only about 30 per cent of answers actually mentioned lack of personal service as a problem with using the Internet. Most answers provided a lot more information on the advantages of a website rather than the disadvantages.

The range of advantages and disadvantages included customers not having an Internet connection, losing the paper catalogue, customers not having powerful enough computers (or not being able to access the Internet due to company policy), on-line ordering, customisation of the 'home page' to individual customers and customer perception that payments via the Internet are not secure.

(a) **Advantages and disadvantages of SK Products Ltd providing information on a website.**

A website has the **following advantages** over a paper based catalogue.

(i) In the **long term a website is cheaper**. Paper, printing and postage costs are avoided.

(ii) Once set-up, a website is available **on demand to a world-wide audience**. This would enable SK Products Ltd to reach customers in foreign markets cost effectively.

(iii) A website can utilise a greater variety of communication methods. A paper catalogue is restricted to text and images but a website can add moving **pictures and sound** to enhance the customer experience. Websites can be interactive encouraging two-way communication.

(iv) **On-line ordering** can be provided. Ordering this way may encourage customers who would not make the effort to fill in a manual catalogue form.

(v) Website registration and 'cookie' technology will enable the site to recognise users and **personalise** the site. (eg 'Welcome Joe Bloggs').

The main disadvantages of a website are:

(i) A professional and productive site utilising multimedia and on-line ordering features will incur **significant set up costs.** In the short term a site is likely to be more expensive than a simple catalogue reprint. (Once the initial set-up is complete, the savings explained earlier will offset the initial costs.)

(ii) Keeping the site up-to-date is a task that must be resourced and properly documented. The danger of ad-hoc site development by IT orientated staff should be guarded against.

(iii) An **out of date** website will show the organisation in an **unprofessional** light and discourage rather than encourage potential customers.

(iv) Some potential customers **may not have the equipment,** ability or inclination to use the Internet. Others may be unwilling to order on-line because of the **perceived dangers** of Internet payment technology.

(b) **Information SK Products can provide on its website to help customers**

(i) **Installation instructions.** Engineers may need help with installation, so instructions should be provided. These could take the form of video clips showing installation steps, and pages of text with diagrams. The required pages could that could be printed by engineers to take 'on-site'. A 'frequently asked questions' section would be useful.

(ii) **Video clips of new products** in action in a 'What's New' section. This should enable users to establish whether a new product would be of benefit to them without requiring a product trial or demonstration.

(iii) **Detailed product specifications** and performance statistics could be provided in a 'Technical' section. This should reduce the need for customers to telephone with technical queries.

(iv) **Links** to related sites such as general industry standards and related trade associations.

50 HUMAN PROBLEMS

Pass marks. It is not clear whether the management accountant is responsible for personnel management throughout the company or just for his own department. We have assumed the former, just to make life even more stressful for poor MO'B! There is a good deal in the question to get your teeth into, but you must not simply repeat the question material without providing comment and analysis on the situation described.

Examiner's comment. Although the question (particularly the second part) was reasonably well answered, very few answers showed the depth of analysis expected at this examination level.

Human problems that the management accountant is facing

(a) **The scope of the job**

MO'B's responsibilities are **far too wide.**

(i) **Financial Accounting** is a responsibility that requires constant learning of **new standards, disclosure requirements and techniques.**

(ii) **Taxation** is likewise a specialist area subject to frequent **changes in legislation.**

(iii) **Management accounting** in a small company may not be too demanding in itself, but this depends entirely upon the **demands of management**.

(iv) **IT and personnel management** are areas in which MO'B probably has **little specialist knowledge** other than what he has acquired on the job. The world of IT is one of **constant change,** while personnel management requires, at the very least, specialist **people skills.**

Attempting to maintain adequate standards of work in all of these areas is likely to be stressful, to say the least, and it is not surprising that Board reports, for instance, have suffered.

(b) **Inability to delegate**

According to the scenario, the **two junior accountants** work hard but do not feel that they have enough responsibility, given their level of knowledge. If this is correct it implies that MO'B is attempting to do too much higher level work himself rather than delegating it to his assistants, perhaps because he **does not have the time or patience** to **train** his staff properly, perhaps because he **does not trust them** to do the work to the required standard, or perhaps because he feels **threatened** and is **protecting his own job.**

Alternatively, it may be that **more than two staff** are needed to complete the work-load. Possibly MO'B is **not prepared to admit defeat** and request more staff, or feels that it will **undermine his authority in preparing budgets** if he goes beyond his own departmental budget.

(c) **Overtime and holidays**

Most people can work long hours for brief periods (even for quite long periods, if there is clearly an end in sight, such as a **holiday**). In general, however, it is agreed that human effort is subject to the law of **diminishing returns**: extra hours worked at the end of the day will not be as productive as hours worked at the start of the day.

Moreover, tiredness and lack of time mean that **mistakes** are more likely to occur, and **shortcuts** are more likely to be taken. The arithmetical errors and the use of ou-of-date information suggests that this is precisely what has happened in the case of the recent Board reports.

It seems likely that sooner or later a **very serious mistake** will occur, and that MO'B will become ill and be **forced to take time off,** perhaps at a time when it is highly inconvenient (eg a year end) for the work of the company to be without his expertise and input.

Human solutions

(a) **The scope of the job**

Financial accounting and taxation matters could be handled by the company's **external auditors**: this is very common for small companies, precisely because of the level of expertise required.

IT could be outsourced to a computer consultancy or support company.

Some aspects of personnel management could be handled by **recruitment consultants**; others could be passed across to **another member of staff** (perhaps one of the Directors; perhaps a person in another administrative position).

If it is felt that re-allocating work to third parties will be **too expensive** or will entail too much **loss of control and expertise** within the company, new **permanent staff** could be appointed to tackle each of these tasks, or several of them. (For instance, a member of the **Institute of Chartered Secretaries and Administrators** would have far more specialist knowledge in IT and personnel matters, and some knowledge of accounting and taxation matters.)

This would free up the **management accountant** to concentrate on what he does best, which is presumably **management accounting**.

Whether any of these suggestions are acceptable depends, of course, on the relative **costs and benefits**.

(b) If MO'B needs **more staff** then this option must be considered, again in the light of costs and benefits.

If, as seems more likely, the problem is one of **lack of delegation**, the following action could be taken.

(i) **Discuss** the problem with MO'B and with his staff, both separately and in a group meeting, and hammer out the issues. The group meeting could possibly be chaired by a person who is perceived by all parties to be **objective** and to **understand the issues** (again, perhaps, by a representative from the company's external auditors).

(ii) Establish the **actual level** of knowledge, experience and ability of the two **junior accountants**, and provide them with any extra **training** that they need. A sensible way forward would be for one to **specialise** for a time in financial accounting and tax and the other to specialise in management accounting and IT. The **roles could be reversed** after a suitable period to ensure that both accountants developed the full complement of necessary skills.

(iii) MO'B may even then be reluctant to relinquish work into the hands of the junior accountants. He too needs to be provided with training: in this case management **training in delegation skills**. He may also need to be provided with reassurance about the **security of his own position** within the company.

(c) Specifically with regard to **MO'B**, the following measures will be beneficial.

(i) Urge him to take a **proper break** of at least two weeks, and **discourage excessive overtime**.

(ii) Provide **further training** in time management skills

(iii) Consider whether any aspect of his **work can be eliminated** entirely, not just re-allocated. This is only likely to be in the area of management accounting, but it may well be that management are demanding information that they do not strictly need to do their jobs, or that they could obtain easily for themselves.

IT solutions

(a) **Integrate** systems as far as possible, for instance link the EIS to the transactions processing system rather than maintaining two separate systems.

(b) **Consider whether accounting software is adequate**, and if not upgrade it. For example, the software should allow sufficient analysis of data and have a good enough report generator to allow the required reports to be **generated by the system automatically**. (This may require a completely new system, in which case it can be an aim, but would only put more pressure on the management accountant in the short term.)

(c) **Software packages** are available to assist in the preparation of **tax returns** and with **administrative personnel matters.** A variety of packages should be assessed to see if they will fit the company's requirements.

(d) **Access to information** may need to be improved throughout the organisation through more through deployment of a network, networking software, and databases. This could allow managers to obtain for themselves information that they presently have to request from the accounts department.

51 FMF LTD: SHAKE THEM HIPS

(a) **Overcoming resentment and opposition**

New systems can generate **hostility** from the staff who are to **operate** them, from **middle management** who must **control** them, and from **senior management** who are ultimately **responsible to shareholders** for the use of a company's assets.

All businesses are **social systems**, and the computer system has to **fit into that context** in FMF. The degree of hostility which a systems analyst encounters will partly depend on the **culture** of FMF. If it has had **good experiences** with computerisation in the past, new systems are more likely to be **welcomed**. However, if there have been one or two disasters, then the prospect of a new system will be greeted with **scepticism**, at the very least.

At **senior management** level, there is **competition for resources**, and questions might be raised as to whether it is worth spending money on computer systems as opposed to other projects. Some senior managers may be less friendly to information technology than others. This may be because they are **unaware of its potential** to offer competitive advantage. A way of coping with this is for an **IT strategy** to be developed and **senior management approval** to be gained by a process of education.

Commitment from senior management is an important factor in persuading **middle management** to be positive towards computerisation. Middle managers are often **threatened** by computerisation, as some of the control mechanisms which they exercise can be built into the computer system. Also, their **subordinates** will **learn new skills**, which management might not possess.

Both management and staff at FMF will have a number of fears related to computerisation.

(i) **Redundancy**. This fear may be justified, but in many cases it is not. New jobs are created, and staff can be trained or redeployed.

(ii) **Change in work practices.** It is sometimes felt that computers will eliminate boring and routine work. In many cases this is transparently false, but there are still gains of this nature to be made from computerisation. However, it might interfere with some of the working networks that have evolved.

In fact, the opposite is true at FMF. Staff think that the computers will leave them with only the **boring and routine work** of actually operating the computers. They should be re-assured that a computer system could not, at present at least, replicate the wide range of **external knowledge** which they possess. A database of the type imagined, if it were to be developed, would in any case give staff **greater opportunity to develop their knowledge**. In addition, **computer operation is itself a new skill**.

(iii) **Change in organisational structure**. Some computer systems (eg executive information systems) might have the effect of **thinning out the layers of middle management**. There will always be 'winners and losers' where this is the case; it is a well-observed fact that in general the proportion of middle managers has reduced in recent years.

Some writers have argued that these problems are not inherent to computerisation as such, but in the **management culture** behind it. If computerisation is seen simply as a means of automating current procedures, it can remove autonomy and fulfilment from work. Alternatively, if it is used as an opportunity to **expand the skills of staff**, it can encourage a more dedicated work force. This might require a change of attitude by management, who might even benefit if they listen to the concerns and experience of those directly involved in computerisation.

The analyst's task will be made if easier if the following conditions exist.

(i) There is a **clear commitment by senior management** to the computerisation project. This will include a promise of appropriate training of staff.

(ii) **Staff are aware of the purpose and consequences of the computer system.** This can be communicated through staff magazines, lunch-hour video presentations, seminars, personal briefings. Any false rumours regarding redundancies should be scotched. The necessary training schemes should be publicised. Secretarial staff should have their fears allayed if they are told about password systems.

(iii) During the systems analysis phase **end users should be consulted frequently** and their views taken into account. In some systems development methodologies, this is a required phase.

This latter requirement can be a real benefit as users are a source of invaluable information as to how a system works in practice. Users are likely to **support** a system more if they have been involved in creating it, as **their own suggestions** will have been incorporated in the plan. Also, users are best able to discern the ideal man/machine interface, although this sometimes might impede operational efficiency.

User co-operation is essential in the implementation phase, as users have to **transfer the old data** to the new system. Again, the involvement of users in planning implementation can make matters much easier, and reduce hostility.

(b) **Is the system a compromise?**

It is a basic principle of general system theory that every system should have a purpose or **objective**. A system designer or planner at FMF should therefore attempt to specify and quantify what the objective is. The objective of the whole company, for example, might be to **maximise the return on shareholder capital**, and a planner would consequently need to **quantify what the target ROCE should be**. Similarly, a computer systems analyst should be able to recognise the purpose of any computer system he intends to design, and to **establish quantified targets** for it.

Constraints are factors which put a limit or restriction on how far the system can go in achieving its objectives. Constraints on the new computer system would include **resource restrictions** (for example the money, hardware and the number and quality of staff available) **time pressure** (for example the time period allowed for system design and operational procedures) and constraints imposed by trying to **adapt an operational system to computer methods** (for example imposing conformity of procedures on a hitherto non-conforming clerical system). There is also an **economic constraint**, that the achievements of the system should not cost more than the benefits they provide.

A systems analyst does not so much **establish** objectives and constraints; rather he is **told** by the **system user** what the objectives of the system are, and he might also need to **accept** constraints that already exist **within the system** itself, or within his terms of reference.

However, he may be given some **scope to elaborate on the objectives** of the system. For example, he may be told that the objective of a computerised payroll system should be to provide weekly wages for wage-earners, paid up to the Friday of each week, by the end of the following Tuesday. The systems analyst might then add the further objective of providing fuller information on wage slips.

Constraints will be identified through an **investigation** of the current system, and an **assessment of the resources** available for the new system. A key aim of the systems analyst should be to **minimise the effect** that the constraints have on the achievement of the system's objectives.

(c) **Personnel management issues**

The IS manager needs to **appoint, train and retain skilled staff** at as low a cost as sensible or practical. However, because of the nature of the function performed in the IS area, particular **human resource problems** faced by IS managers include the following.

(i) The **tendency for IT staff to change jobs** more frequently than staff in other occupations. Those who are familiar with new technology are extremely 'marketable'. Conversely, changes in technology may be too challenging for some.

(ii) The perception among many that the **seniority structure** involves a **move** from programming to systems work and then to management, while these are in fact three different skills.

(iii) **Recruitment problems** relating to finding staff who are good at their various roles but who **fit into and complement the team** and the department requirements.

(iv) **Retaining staff** after they have been through what is often very **expensive training**.

Many of these problems are similar to those faced in other high-tech areas. Some of them do not have solutions - for instance most programmers do move away from programming at quite an early age. In times of redundancy programmes, and of pressures on companies as a whole, some of the problems cannot realistically be addressed.

(d) **Software**

There are two aspects which need to be taken into account by FMF when planning for compliance with copyright law. These are the copyright **law itself** and the **restrictions** placed on the use of the software by the **author** and possibly various **governmental agencies**. The US government, for example, restricts some software for sale in the US. Using it outside that country might breach copyright laws even though the number of licences was correct.

Options for FMF using software in a multi-user environment include the following.

(i) A **single copy** of each software item to be purchased for each user.

(ii) Users allowed to make (typically) **one extra copy** on another machine on the basis that they could use only one machine at a time - say one at home and a different one at the office. This is also permissible sometimes to ensure a (non-operational) back-up is available.

(iii) **Multiple copies** of the single-user software - one per user, if terms permit.

(iv) A **network copy** of the software for as many users as will use it at any one time, the number being set in advance.

(v) **Site licences** from the copyright holder.

(vi) **Company-wide licences.**

Copyrights are designed to protect the **expression** of ideas. Thus copyrights apply to creative works such as stories, photographs and paintings. The **ideas themselves** cannot be copyrighted (and this was used as the argument for a long time in the Far East as to why programs should not be able to be copyrighted). However, the expression of the idea in the form of the program can be copyrighted.

The work being copyrighted **must be original to the author**. Some expressions are general public knowledge and are not subject to copyright. These are in the public domain, and this applies also to some software (notably publications from the US Government). This differs from 'shareware', where users are allowed to use software for an evaluation period, but are then required either to stop using it or to pay for it.

Copyright law indicates that the copyrighted object **may be reproduced subject to 'fair use'**. Specifically the law allows for the use of the work for criticism, comment, news reporting, teaching, scholarship and research. This would not include commercial use.

Copyright relates to copies: if a copy of a program is placed on a network and other users obtain access to the program then, so long as a new copy of the software is not created, **copyright** has not been infringed, although **other regulations or contract terms** may of course be infringed unless such software is used with care and according to contractual terms.

52 TRAVEL AGENCY

Pass marks. The examiner is careful not to base scenarios on industries which are extremely specialist or unusual. This allows you to use a certain amount of common sense and draw on your own knowledge of the business environment in writing your answers. Make sure, though, that you do not do this to the exclusion of demonstrating your competence in applying knowledge of specific syllabus topics. Finally, what does 'contrast' mean? See the official 'Meaning of Examiners' Instructions' at the front of this Kit if you don't know!

Examiner's comment. Answers to (a) were of a high standard, but it was 'difficult to describe the standard of answers' to part (b): the vast majority of candidates appeared to have no idea of what Human Information Processing is, or of the problems faced by Human Information Processors. For instance, answers contained lengthy discussion on subjects such as EU directives and poor screen design but failed to explain how these subjects were relevant.

For (c) the requirement was to 'contrast' but most candidates wrote about VANs and EISs in isolation. Also many candidates seemed to know little about VANs. For (d) many candidates failed to explain the features of a good screen design, and many just listed the qualities of good information rather than asking themselves what they wanted from an MIS. Many attempted to describe the use of the MIS at operational level rather than as a reference and support tool.

(a) (i) **Vision and reality**

There are a number of aspects to the vision of the manager, both stated and implied, which are not being achieved in reality. Given the approach adopted by the manager, it is unlikely that any workforce could have done any better.

High quality service

The manager believes that consulting a computer would be more efficient than asking colleagues and consulting brochures. In time this may well be true, however at close of business on the first Monday, the staff would have been **struggling to find any information at all**, given the lack of training provided and the complexity of the system. The requirement to obtain authorisation from a senior manager would also have delayed office activities.

Friendly, highly-trained and knowledgeable staff

There was no computerisation in the office at all before this date. This means that, even though the system may not need much provision of training, the staff still need **training in basic computer literacy**. Even with the best graphical interfaces, the computer is still a daunting tool to use by a complete novice. Simply finding out how to use a keyboard, when to use Alt and Ctrl keys, operating the mouse and using printers, are all extremely difficult at first.

Staff may well have been **friendly** *before* computerisation, . The manager has not identified the effect of such dramatic change on the staff. Instead of being a 'nice surprise' the effect is to **demoralise**. There will undoubtedly be a degree of **friction** in the office.

As the means of obtaining access to information on the VAN was not explained to the staff, the assumption can be made that this **information is not available at all on day one.** At least previously the staff were able to call upon the help of colleagues. They will no longer be perceived as **knowledgeable.**

The **vision** may well be of a working environment where the staff member taps the holiday requirements into the magic box, and out comes an immediate set of possible holidays, at which point the customer chooses one, smiles with pleasure and hands over his or her deposit.

The **truth** has been a confused consultant, bravely attempting to search the databases with one finger tapping heroically at the keyboard, lacking all confidence and desperately wishing themselves anywhere but sitting in front of an impatient customer.

Competitive prices

The third objective will have been impossible to achieve. **Staff will simply not have known how to access all relevant areas of the VAN** and will probably have missed some operations and been **unable to recommend holidays from the full range available.**

Staff need access to:

(1) **late availability** holidays;
(2) **up-to-date prices;**
(3) ruling **discount** structures;
(4) all **alternatives** such as special deals for midweek or night travel;
(5) **alternative carrier** details.

(ii) **Implementation**

The manager has failed to carry out all of the following stages of implementation.

(1) **Consultation with the users**. There has been no consultation with the staff and no attempt to 'sell' the new system to them. Failure to obtain willing user participation is probably his biggest 'crime'. Staff are the people who actually have to use the system; it is nonsensical to ignore their views.

(2) **Systems analysis.** This has been ignored. Although the desire to computerise is a commendable one, it should only be done on the basis of a detailed **analysis of existing operations and of business needs.** Several aspects of the new system are problematic, in particular the way it addresses the three operators of information search on one terminal, updating records on a second and actually making a customer booking without one at all.

(3) **Pre installation training.** This has been ignored.

(4) **Implementation**. Even if the system is completely reliable from a computer point of view, which is unlikely, there is also a requirement to **pilot the effect of the change of systems** within the travel agency. No contingency plan in the event of failure appears to have been considered.

(5) **Post installation training** This looks unlikely, given the manager's stated view.

(6) **Tailoring of menus to individual users.** The two screens need rationalisation.

(7) **Best use of facilities.** Given that operators' systems are being accessed for information purposes, it would seem logical to use them to make bookings as well instead of using telephones.

The **actions the manager should now take** are as follows.

(1) Stop use of the system and **revert to prior methods** at once and **admit his or her mistake.**

(2) Do the **installation** properly, starting with **consultation with the staff.** The system may not be optimum for a travel agency - it is certainly not the norm to find that operators in travel agencies have to use two VDUs at once.

(3) Assess the **staff skills** and aim to introduce a **pilot installation** with key members of staff.

(4) **Analyse the pilot run** and use this time as a means of introducing the benefits of computerisation to the other staff.

(5) **Plan a timetable of roll out of the installation** compatible with the ability of the staff to cope with the change, say two months.

(6) **Train the staff fully** and be prepared to **pay for outside training**. For example, local colleges provide suitable computer familiarisation courses.

(7) Introduce the **VAN** early as a **resource available to all the office** via a **trained user**. Soon the other staff will be asking to have the facility, not fearing its introduction.

(8) Do **not try to introduce all the changes at once** (for example the requirement for bookings to be checked by senior management).

(9) **Put someone in charge** of the system to be a **help** to the others, and to look after the **housekeeping** of the VAN, so that the staff are not inconvenienced by having to work late and will have someone to turn to when problems arise.

(10) Have a **fallback plan** for those days when the system is down.

(b) **HIP problems**

The staff will encounter various human information processing problems with the system including the following.

Data capture

It will be **difficult to know where to look** when processing customer requests. The staff must deal with two VDUs, brochures, the customer, colleagues and the telephone in the course of arranging a holiday booking. Ideally they should be able to refer to the customer and a single screen only. This applies equally to output.

Efficient operation

Without **proper training and explanation** the staff will not use the system correctly. This aspect, and its solution, has been discussed in part (a) above.

Noise in communication

The wide range of data capture avenues identified above means **staff may filter information excessively,** and consequently **miss important details.**

Over reliance on the system

When the system has been implemented, there is a danger that the staff will consider their job finished once the computer 'oracle' has been consulted. Proper training will **emphasise that the computer is only part** of the arsenal available to each member of staff. **Informal communication** must still be encouraged.

Information overload

Because there will be so many databases available (the agency's own data, the VAN and the third party databases), there is the possibility of **spending too much time** searching every avenue. To avoid this situation, the agency needs to formulate a policy with regard to the more frequent types of enquiry. Adroit set up of front end menus can assist greatly with this objective, so for every enquiry the staff member should have the **shortest route to the information required.**

Human information processors and hardware problems

There needs to be a **rapid response to hardware problems,** from the simple everyday problems like paper jams in the printer, to the complicated like modem and phone link failures.

It is recommended that **someone within the agency** should be responsible for the housekeeping of the system, and should be able to help with everyday problems. For more complicated areas, a **service agreement** should be arranged with a local computer maintenance company, possibly the supplier. Staff must be able to deal with simple issues if processing is to continue.

Human information processors and software problems

Software does not stand still. The agency is using a number of platforms, the external databases and its own LAN as well as the VAN. Any or all of these will change in time, and the front-end program will need to be compatible and be able to **take advantage of new facilities.** The agency would be wise to use a software supplier who will continue to provide upgrades and software support. This will provide **challenges for the staff** in keeping up-to-date with changes.

Health

Physical strain will distract the HIPs and result in errors in their work. It is the recommended that certain health issues are addressed by the agency, including checking the **ergonomic arrangement of the equipment**, lighting within the office and reflected glare, and recommended practise for VDU users. Advice in this area is available from local councils or the usual health and safety organisations.

Knowledge

It is possible that the system will be seen as a **de-skilling** device, with staff becoming **computer operators** rather than purveyors of a **caring and personal service.**

(c) **VANs and EISs**

The facility of a local VAN, as implemented by Voyager, and an EIS are very different. These differences can be categorised as follows.

Source

The **VAN** supplies **external information,** in this case about other agents' specialised holidays.

An **EIS**, on the other hand, is usually almost entirely focused on **internal information**, for example details of customers, sales, products and management accounts.

Time scale

The **VAN** is supplying **up to date or future** information, whereas the **EIS** is **historic**.

Presentation

The **VAN** is bringing information from **different sources**, which will possibly have **different presentation** according to the type of holiday and its speciality.

The **EIS**, on the other hand, will have information in **consistent formats** in order to facilitate drill-down enquiry and side by side comparisons, ratio analysis and so on. Typically **comparison** will be available between **versions** of the data (actual, budget prior year), or **classes** of data such as product groups (in this case perhaps, groupings of holidays by destination or customer profile to compare profitability, cancellation rates and other key data.)

Cost

A third-party **VAN** is accessible on **payment** of a regular subscription.

The **EIS** is '**free of charge**'.

Access

Anyone who pays the subscription can join the **VAN**. This means that **other travel agents** might sign up to it.

The **EIS** is restricted to **internal users** only.

Level of user

The **VAN** is intended to be used at the 'sharp end' of the business, so the information will be geared to the **selling function**, with subjective information included alongside bare facts.

The **EIS** is intended for use by the '**executive**' and will not contain any subjective information. The figures will be interpreted by the user. They could be used to plan where to concentrate efforts, for example in identifying popular resorts or high commission levels.

Degree of summarisation

The **VAN** is concerned with **individual transactions**, the **EIS** with **summary** data. It is possible to 'drill down' with an EIS to focus on individual (historic) data, but this is usually only required on an exception basis. For example, the VAN assists with making an individual booking, while the EIS summarises previous periods' total bookings etc.

(d) **Design issues**

A well-designed human/computer interface and management information system will **integrate the various information requirements** of the staff at Voyager. To obtain the maximum benefit from the system, all the usual **financial** functions, as well as the **sales** information already discussed, will be included within the MIS.

The proposed **human-computer interface**, as envisaged by the manager, is the use of **two VDU's** per member of staff, with associated keyboard and mouse. The manager may consider whether multitasking software could remove the need for the second VDU.

Screen, keyboard and mouse constitute the conventional 'interface', but in addition input to the computer could be by **magnetic swipe**, for reading credit cards, and **scanners** for reading in pictures and diagrams, for example resort maps, and documents.

A well-designed human-computer interface should help in the following ways.

(i) **Elimination of superfluous processes.** The system should be designed with the user in mind, so that menus and program groupings are arranged to match actual usage and offer quick routes to relevant areas of the system.

(ii) **User-friendliness.** This covers on-line tutorials, on-screen help and clear menus/icons. It also should offer suitable dialogue boxes such as 'Please confirm you wish to ...' or 'Are you sure?' when commands are input. Basic design features such as readable fonts and colour highlighting of key items should be evident.

(iii) **Alternative options.** Although icons are user-friendly, they can hamper speed of operation. An experienced keyboard user will find it quicker, for example, to select 'Ctrl P' or similar than to click on a 'printer' icon then on a 'yes' button.

(iv) **Ease of learning.** A well designed system with a good HCI should be easy to learn. Training costs will be reduced (although not to nil, as here!)

(v) **Mirroring human processes.** A system should appear to 'know' what the operator wants to do next and offer appropriate prompts and dialogue boxes.

(vi) **Output.** A well designed screen could use windowing to display all the information required by the travel agency staff. Output in the form of graphs and charts may be easier to use than tables of figures.

A **well-designed MIS** would help the staff obtain information which they need in the following areas.

Product information

This is the area that has been covered in the above evaluation of the databases made available by the manager. Once the implementation has been conducted properly the staff will have on-line, categorised information at their fingertips.

Credit control

Immediate access to commercial VANs specialising in credit information will enable staff to make immediate credit control decisions in respect of corporate customers. This information will typically include key results over recent years, ownership, court decisions relating to companies, and directors' names and addresses.

Marketing

The marketing staff can obtain **lists of potential customers** from data agencies for use for mailshots and telesales, if appropriate. For example the 'MOSAIC' geodemographic data is available via VAN. As enquiries and sales arise, the MIS can summarise this data to assist in forward planning. **Customer satisfaction** can be measured by post-holiday surveys and questionnaires. Again this information will be processed by the MIS and summarised for use by the management, both in report and graphical form.

Sales ledger

Information will be immediately available relating to **customer turnover** and **payment** records. **Trend analysis** will identify customers whose business is growing or has fallen away.

Supplier information

In this case, airlines and holiday operators are key suppliers. Useful data such as **turnover spent** with each supplier, and **reliability indicators** (cancellations by the supplier, satisfaction of the customers) will prove useful when negotiating and making strategic decisions.

Accounting

Because the transactions of the company are on the system, information will be available to **trial balance stage** of the nominal ledger. This will be available to the accounts department with comparable **budget and prior year information**, through drill down enquiry and also available in report formats.

Commercial

The MIS can link with commercial VANs to download industry-wide information, particularly useful for intercompany comparison.

Modelling

Key data from the above areas can be combined into reports, possibly via spreadsheets, to create **strategic** and '**what if' models**.

53 CHEMICALS PRODUCTION

Pass marks. Part (a) of this question is an excellent illustration of a point made repeatedly in BPP study material for this paper. Mere knowledge (in this case the qualities of good information) is not enough at Stage 4: you have to be able to apply it to the scenario you are given and think about what the recipient of the report is likely to need.

There are further Pass marks and Examiner's comments later in this answer.

Examiner's comment. A minority of answers to part (a) tried to explain the attributes of good information without reference to the case study.

(a) **The production report**

There is no question about the **relevance** of a report of this nature, at least under the current system of sharing out responsibilities. Senior managers need information about the progress of projects for which they are responsible.

However in its present form **this report has little relevance to the purpose for which it is used**, for the reasons set out below. Each of the points overlap to an extent.

(i) **Completeness**

It is **not possible to see how the figures link up**: there must be some correlation between sales value, cost and profitability, but there is nothing to explain, for example, how many batches are produced, how production cost and manufacturing cost are related or how profit for the week is derived from the overall sales value and cost figures.

As for the technical details, the report is clearly incomplete because **senior managers have to obtain additional information** from production managers and technical journals.

Presumably different projects use the same **materials** but there appears to be **no overall summary** of usage, cost and stocks of, say, material X.

Progress seems impossible to judge because there is **no budget information,** such as standard costs and weights and variances, and **no comparative information**, such as last week's figures. There is **no indication of how many weeks** the project has taken to date.

(ii) **Accuracy**

Some figures are stated to two decimal places and yet sales value appears to be rounded up to the nearest 50,000. Input tonnes and stock appear to be rounded (if stock is stated in tonnes - this is not shown) while the cost of materials is stated to the penny. This is **highly inconsistent and confusing.**

(iii) **Clarity**

Inconsistency with decimal places means that within individual columns figures are **not properly aligned.** The project B Cost to date, for instance could very easily be misinterpreted. It is not clear if the **units** reported on are in millions or thousands. Some figures are stated 'per batch', others 'per week' and others 'to date'.

The **layout** means that although Project A's financial details can be compared at a glance with input mix data for Project A, products use a large number of chemicals and the input mix data for project D is likely to be some way down the page or on a separate page, **making at a glance comparison impossible.**

(iv) **Volume**

In spite of the fact that it does not contain all of the information that senior managers need to collect, in *this* format the report as a whole is likely to be a **mass of figures over several pages,** because of the number of projects and the large number of chemicals used. This will be extremely **difficult to read** and **impossible to take in at a glance.**

It may be that **some of the information given,** such as sales value, is **not necessary at all** in a production report.

(v) **Timeliness**

The report relates to the week to 30 April but it is dated 19 May, by which time the information it contains is **nearly three weeks out of date** and may bear no resemblance to current operating conditions. Yet we are told that adjustments are required frequently to maintain quality. It is **difficult to see how this report can form the basis of such decisions.**

(vi) **Channel**

The format in which the reports are sent is **not compatible** with the format used by senior managers, so the information has to be **input again manually, wasting time** and increasing the **risk of error.**

The **medium** of email and on-screen viewing is **not appropriate** for information of this volume and complexity. It irritates senior managers, again increasing the likelihood of errors, and their time is wasted printing out material that could (especially given its lateness) have been sent to them in hard copy form.

Proposed amendments

Amendments should **take account of the use to which the information is put** by production managers on the one hand and by senior managers on the other. Allowing for different information needs, it should nevertheless be as easy as possible to turn production report information into senior management report information.

(i) The **purpose** of the report should be defined: if it is to judge profitability, to assess manufacturing cost, to effect stock control, and to measure progress, both of single projects and overall, it is probably trying to fulfil too many purposes at once. Perhaps **several shorter reports** would be more effective.

(ii) Information that is **needed but not reported** should be included.

(iii) Information **collection and analysis** by production managers needs to be **speeded up** considerably, probably by the introduction of better information systems.

(iv) Production managers and senior managers should be using **compatible systems** to produce their reports.

(v) The problems of level of accuracy and clarity of presentation referred to above should be resolved, leading to a '**house style**' that is agreed and adhered to by all.

(vi) **Alternative methods of presentation** should be considered, such as **graphs or charts**, to make it easier to review the information **at a glance**.

(b)

Pass marks. The examiner commented that 'a number of candidates were confused by the distinction between parts (a) and (b)'. This is not surprising: part (a) is about format and transmission and part (b) is about decision making, but it is very hard to produce 20 marks worth of material for part (b) without either repeating points made in part (a) or anticipating points that belong more properly in part (c) (as the CIMA suggested solution does). We have addressed this problem by cross-references.

Examiner's comment. Few candidates recognised problems such as noisy environment or verbal reports being misunderstood. A number provided a surprising amount of detail concerning the calculation of individual items on the report itself. Some went into excessive detail about how to set up and use a MIS.

Weaknesses in information provision affecting decision making

The problems are as follows.

(i) Decisions are impaired by all of the problems with the production report identified in **part (a)**.

(ii) Senior managers' decisions have to be **authorised** by the Chief Accountant, even though they appear to be closer to the matters in hand and they 'collate' all the information needed for decision making. (The Chief Accountant, incidentally, is likely to be suffering severely from information overload.)

(iii) Collation involves bringing together information from **several different sources**: information manually transferred from computer screen (or from a print-out), information obtained over the telephone from production managers, information from technical journals, and information arising from discussions in meetings.

Given the variety of sources and the way in which information is obtained the whole process is **extremely error-prone**: it seems almost designed to give rise to failures of communication, particularly because of the extent of **reliance on verbally reported information** to supplement the written reports.

(iv) Senior managers have a **large number** of projects to keep track of over a **long time span** (4 months). It is highly likely that matters will regularly be **overlooked** because of the piecemeal nature and slow pace of information provision.

(v) Inappropriate use of the **email** system means that it is **neglected** and the telephone (which is far more intrusive), is used instead.

(vi) The technical **database** is **difficult** for senior managers to **access** and **presents information badly**.

(vii) The office environment is **noisy and crowded** and this is unlikely to be conducive to highly detailed information analysis.

Suggested changes to overcome these problems

The following action needs to be taken.

(i) **Improvements** to the production reports and systems such as those suggested in **part (a)** should be implemented. This will help to address problems of completeness, clarity, accuracy, and timeliness of information provision, and problems of incompatibility between the formats in which information is provided.

(ii) A **more appropriate decision-making structure** is needed. Senior Managers should be **empowered** to make decisions about input mix and quality of inputs. Decisions about day to day matters that could be dealt with by production managers should be delegated to them. This should **improve motivation** throughout the organisation.

(iii) Information **gathering** and **collation** of information is essentially a clerical activity that could either be **delegated to less senior staff or automated.** Senior Managers could then concentrate on their management role. Managers should **not have to buy their own technical journals**: the company's own technical database should be the single source of such information (see point (vi)).

(iv) The **ordering and production process** is highly inefficient and needs radical change. This is the subject of **part (c)**.

(v) **E-mail** should be **more widely used**, but **in a different manner.** It is an ideal medium for circulating **small amounts of non-urgent information**; managers can review it at their own convenience rather than being constantly interrupted by the telephone; it can be used to canvass opinions on how to deal with a problem and it provides a written record of any matters discussed.

(vi) **The technical database is a wasted resource**. Whatever is needed to make it accessible should be done. This might include **better networking** and database **software**, a **more powerful server**, a **better database structure, training** in the use of the database, and **regular updating** to include information from the latest and best technical journals.

(vii) **The working environment could be improved** by installing printer hoods or buying quieter printers, and by partitioning (so long as this does not impair communications). **Improved layout** or relocation of managers closer to the production managers they deal with may reduce the need for constant phone calls, and may provide extra space away from the area of main activity, which could be used for meetings or as **'quiet havens'** when concentrated, undisturbed work is needed.

(c) (i)

> **Pass marks.** You are asked to 'describe' CSFs not simply 'list' or 'identify' them, so some extra detail is needed, but only six marks are at stake so don't get carried away. By 'ordering and production process' we take the examiner to mean the **four** stages described under that heading in the scenario, not simply the material ordering and production stages. The CIMA suggested solution has cost reduction of the process as a whole as its second CSF. The two we give are those that the examiner expected.

Critical success factors

Possible CSFs against which the success of the change can be judged include the following.

(1) **Order fulfilment**

Presently the time between receipt of an enquiry and delivery of the product is **four months**. Changes could be considered to have been successful **if this time is reduced.**

Time is wasted on over-bureaucratic purchasing procedures, there is a disproportionate ratio between production time and post-production quality checking time, and activities that could be done concurrently (for instance production and arranging production and shipping) are done sequentially with no overlap.

Reporting techniques might include **Gantt charts** to monitor progress towards fulfilment of an order over time and **exception reports** identifying stages where unexpected delays occurred. Since there are a large number of projects, **project management software** might be used to ease the administrative burden.

(2) **Product quality**

Production takes only one week, but quality control takes three weeks, suggesting that there is a **major quality problem**. It seems likely that the problem is caused by inadequate systems for ensuring a **consistent quality of inputs** and for adjusting the input mix as required.

Changes could be considered to be successful if material ordering and production **'get it right first time'**.

Reporting will require **exception reports** detailing instances where rectification work is needed and giving the cause (to what extent it is due to inaccurate specification of input requirements, poor quality materials, or failure to adjust the mix in time). **Adverse comments** from customers and **returned products** must also be taken into account.

(ii) **Benefits of the changes**

> **Pass marks.** It is a shame the question does not ask about drawbacks, too, because it is a bit of a struggle to find 14 marks worth of material that you have not already mentioned. The CIMA model answer waxes lyrical about the dynamic new company that is about to emerge. Our answer is a little more cynical.
>
> **Examiner's comment.** The number of marks obtained was limited in some cases because candidates mentioned benefits without reference to the case study information, or simply explained what BPR is, without attempting to isolate the benefits of BPR.

Benefits for the company

(1) The principal benefit from the point of view of the company will be that it can give customers a **much faster service,** whilst maintaining or even improving the **quality** of the product. Processes throughout the company will be geared to satisfying the customer rather than to maintaining a cumbersome bureaucracy.

(2) It looks as if an order could be fulfilled about four times faster than at present. In theory this ought to mean that the company has the capacity to fulfil **four times as many orders.** If the demand is there **profitability** will increase dramatically.

(3) There is some potential for **reducing costs,** notably in the areas of material ordering and rectification costs avoided. Again this will impact upon **profitability.** It may be possible to drop prices, which will help MQS to **compete more effectively** in its market.

(4) **Staff** appear to be frustrated by the current methods of working and are likely to **welcome change and offer more commitment** to the company's mission and objectives than they do at the moment. Barriers between different departments (for instance material ordering and production) are liable to be broken down, improving staff's communication and understanding of the task of the company as a whole.

(5) New systems and better recording and storage of information should mean that the company's ability to reach ever **better-informed decisions,** to **measure its performance,** and to **identify areas for further change** will improve.

(6) **Some problems are only brought to light when change is proposed** and resisted. In the material ordering area, for instance, where redundancies are likely (see (c)(iii)), it could emerge that there are very good reasons for operating in the present way, but these had not previously been considered. The Chief Accountant may be exercising certain essential controls that should not be dispensed with, even if he does not implement them himself. In other words resistance may lead to **useful insights and adaptation of the change program.**

Benefits to the staff

These are likely to include the following.

(1) As mentioned previously, changes in the decision making structure will give **more responsibility** to staff at a lower level, which should make work **more rewarding** for Senior Managers and Production Managers.

(2) Projects will be completed more quickly which will make it **easier for managers to keep track of them** (they are not having to remember issues that first arose three or four months ago). This benefit may be lost if MQS attempts to take on many more projects.

(3) New information systems will also help managers to do their work more effectively and spend **more time on challenging work** rather than pen-pushing and paper chasing.

(4) The **working environment** will be more pleasant.

(5) **Relationships will improve** (senior managers are at present 'hostile' to the information provided by production managers).

(6) Increased productivity and profitability should mean **increased pay** for staff.

Caveat

Although the question asks about benefits it ought to be noted that change is never put into effect without some **resistance.** It seems likely that the company will have to deal with opposition from the **Chief Accountant** and from the **purchasing department**, and these staff have the potential to **undermine the effectiveness of changes** if they cannot be persuaded of the merits of new practices.

The company **must maintain good communication with staff**, provide **training** in new ideas and skills, and offer **fair deals** for **staff who are no longer needed** if the changes are to be successful.

(iii)

> **Pass marks.** It does not matter precisely what your estimate of the time saving is, so long as you recognise that a substantial amount of time can be saved in certain areas.
>
> **Examiner's comment.** Poorer answers provided an estimate of the time that could be saved, but without explaining how this time saving would be achieved. A surprising number of examples included almost excessive detail on potential computer links. The point is made again that the IFM exam is about information, not about technology.

How time could be saved

Here is a suggested revised timescale for order fulfilment. Notes are appended to explain the figures.

Stage	Note	Working days
Initial input requirement and pricing	1	2
Assessing processing requirements	2	2
Drafting quotation and internal authorisation	3	1
Sending quotation to customer and confirming order	4	5
Ordering and obtaining materials	5	3
Production/obtaining containers/organising courier/quality control checks	6	14
Total working days		27

Notes

1 The information provided tells us that this stage takes two days. **No information is given about whether this can be improved.**

2 Each order is made to individual customer requirements and it is therefore likely that some **time needs to be spent working out the implications of tailoring the processing to meet these needs.** We have assumed two days, in the absence of further information. This may be an underestimate, given that the quotation process currently takes about one month.

3 Some care is needed in **drafting the quotation**, given that the company may be tendering against competitors. Some **liaison** between production, purchasing and marketing will be needed to ensure that one department is not making undertakings that other departments cannot meet and that considerations such as the likelihood of repeat orders are taken into account. One day is allowed for this.

4 This time is likely to be very variable, as it **depends on customers' decision making processes**. One day is allowed for the quotation to reach the customer, three for the customer to consider it (more time may be needed if the customer is obtaining and comparing several quotations), and one day for confirmation of the order. **Fax or email would speed up this process**, of course, if this is acceptable to customers.

5 **Major time savings** can be made in the area of **ordering and obtaining materials.** The savings achieved by negotiating prices only amount to £25,000: this must be far outweighed by the cost of employing ten staff. The process of obtaining three quotes, looking for discounts and accepting the lowest quote should be dispensed with.

JIT purchasing is clearly possible, since goods are available from stock. The material ordering department should identify reliable suppliers of good quality materials, perhaps negotiating long-term contracts in return for guarantees about quality and delivery quantities and time.

There is **no need for a quote to be authorised** for acceptance by the Chief Accountant. Expertise in this activity resides in the purchasing department. **Authority limits** could perhaps be set at an appropriate level, if controls are felt to be necessary.

We assume three days from placing of the order to receipt of the goods. This assumes that suppliers are reasonably local so that delivery times are fairly short. **EDI links** with suppliers may reduce this time still further.

6 Production need not hold up ordering of **containers** or organising of a **courier.** All of these can be **done concurrently** over a maximum time span of two weeks, the time it takes for containers to be delivered. We assume that this time cannot be reduced because the containers are 'specialised', but this should be **investigated further** to see if time savings can be made.

The time taken to perform **quality checks** can be reduced by using **better quality materials,** by using **better information systems** and **devolving authority** to allow faster decisions on input mix, and by substituting **in-process quality controls** for post-production ones. The latter may mean that production takes longer than a week, but time will be saved overall because **less rectification work** will be needed. Fourteen days, overlapping with the packaging and shipping arrangements, is assumed to be sufficient.

54 ARG INTERNATIONAL AIRLINES

Pass marks. Part (a) (i) should not prove too difficult. There are many possible reasons - as long as you provide a logical explanation of each reason you provide you will score well. Don't be afraid to 'think on your feet' when faced with questions like this. The marks are there for the taking, even if you 'don't think this was covered' in your formal studies.

Examiner's comment. A significant number of answers were hindered by the provision of lengthy introductions explaining the work of various theorists such as Earl and Porter. Whilst this information is not inappropriate, the answer must also explain why it is relevant to the situation of ARG.

A number of other answers provided an explanation of the overall strategy setting process for a company including the use of critical success factors. However candidates did not always explain how the IT strategy fitted into the overall process of setting the company's goals.

In (a)(ii) some candidates provided a detailed explanation of systematic and unsystematic risk: while this was not irrelevant, long detailed discussion was not called for. Other answers tended to be too brief.

(a) (i) **Why large companies should have an IT strategy**

A strategy for IT is justified on many grounds, including the following.

(1) **IT involves high costs.** The scenario does not give specific details, but we know that the system is **large scale**, that it is **state of the art**, that it has **excess capacity** and that an additional fixed capital amount is to be available for **upgrades each year.** This is clearly a major investment that needs care over planning, control and co-ordination.

(2) **IT is critical to the success of many organisations.** Information access and provision is the **key service** offered by ARG's local offices and the most up to date computer and telecommunications technology will allow ARG to **access and provide information more effectively**. It will not be possible to meet the business objectives set for ARG's services unless the appropriate IT infrastructure is in place. Conversely, future developments in IT are likely to lead to **ever more ambitious objectives.** A properly devised strategy is essential to allow the company to **grow in a co-ordinated way.**

(3) IT is seen by the Board of ARG as essential to produce a sustainable **competitive advantage.** ARG needs to be able to make more effective use of information to serve its customers' interests than any of its competitors.

(4) IT involves many **stakeholders**, not just management. **Staff** at ARG, for instance, appear to have welcomed the new system and adapted to it very easily. A less careful approach to development and implementation by the board might have impaired the effectiveness of staff - and therefore the whole business - for months.

Again, the opportunities presented by the new system's excess capacity are leading the company (rightly or wrongly) to diversify away from its main mission, and this impacts upon **shareholders**, who originally chose to invest in an airline, not a computer services company.

(5) **The detailed technical issues in IT are important.** The Board of ARG recognised that the pace of change in technology meant that its system could be obsolete in a very short space of time and their strategy therefore included easy **upgradability** as one of the key points of the system specification. On the other hand the controls proposed over

future investment indicate that they intend to ensure that upgrades are not undertaken merely because the technology has become available. Presumably the intention is to **take advantage of technical developments when they judge the time to be right**, which may depend on many other factors in the business environment. This matter is addressed in more detail in **part (c)**.

(ii) **Comment on the diversification strategy**

The opportunity presented by the WAN's **excess capacity** leads one to wonder whether the Board was persuaded to **invest too heavily** in the new system at too early a stage. Post-implementation review has found that the capacity made available at the outset will not actually be needed for another 7 years, and this should have been realised at an earlier stage in the development of the system

Could other options be considered, such as **renting the excess capacity** to an existing network services provider, and gradually taking back capacity as it becomes needed?

Advantages

The most obvious advantage, and the one that appears to have influenced the Board, is that the proposal will **make use of an idle resource** and give a **positive contribution** to profits.

Given that ARG's core business is **susceptible to events quite beyond its control** (such as wars or terrorist activity) that have in the past led to marked reductions in air traffic, there is **some logic in diversifying** into business **telecommunications**, a growing **competitor to business travel**, thanks to improvements in technologies such as video-conferencing. The new strategy could be seen as a **safety move**, making the future of the business as a whole more secure.

Arguably, ARG's business is **carrying things** from one place to another: being an **information-carrier** could be seen as an extension to being a people-carrier and a freight-carrier. If ARG is perceived as being a market leader in the latter fields, this may inspire potential users' confidence in its ability to deliver information.

ARG's **brand name** can be attached to a device used for communications by other businesses (perhaps even by competitors). Assuming it is successful this will provide valuable publicity.

Disadvantages

ARG has **no experience** at operating the sort of service proposed. The **risks of total failure** are high, and anything less than a service that equals that of ARG's core business will **damage the core business** by association.

If the IT division concentrates on providing this new service it may **lose sight of its responsibilities** regarding the existing business, with the result that the new system **fails to fulfil its original purpose**.

Many other organisations specialise in providing this sort of service. ARG may find it **difficult to establish enough of a presence in the market** to justify the extra investment involved.

Markets may react badly to the new venture. A general business trend is to **outsource** non-core activities, especially those of an IT nature, but ARG is **moving in the opposite direction**. It is likely to be criticised by stakeholders who, like a minority of the Board, see potential conflicts between the strategies.

The company has **already over-invested** in its WAN and the proposed 'fix' for this is to invest even more. **Other possibilities** do not appear to have been considered.

The additional investment is based on what ARG 'expects' users to require. Users may, however, **require considerably more services** and support than ARG envisages. The IT director **does not have a good record** at determining what is required.

Conclusion

On the basis of the information available the disadvantages appear to outweigh the advantages. At the very least, **other options** should be considered. If there is **more work** to be done regarding investigation of the new market and its customers, and detailed costings and revenue forecasts, this should be done before the proposal goes ahead.

(b)

> **Pass marks.** Choose the most appropriate qualities **in this case** and show **why** the qualities of good information are relevant to ARG.
>
> **Examiner's comment.** Many candidates were good at identifying the characteristics of information, but fewer were able to go on to show how these characteristics applied in the scenario. A minority of candidates misunderstood the requirements and concentrated on the system rather than the information.

Characteristics of information provided across the WAN

ARG offices **use** information on flight times and destinations, passenger and freight bookings, and **have access** to information on aircraft locations, servicing history and personnel details.

The information provided across the WAN should have the following characteristics.

(i) **Completeness and timeliness**

Full, up-to-date information on **bookings** needs to be available instantaneously, otherwise an office might, say, book a passenger onto a return flight from another country only to discover that the flight is already fully booked.

Similarly, if an aircraft is due for a particular type of **service** when it lands in a country, the office concerned will need timely warning so that they can make advance preparations and ensure that staff and resources are available immediately. **Servicing cannot be put off once it its due**: it is crucial that ARG operates a safe service.

Servicing information needs to be **complete** in the sense that **any** details that servicing staff might need to know about a particular aircraft must be available to them on demand.

(ii) **Accuracy and clarity**

A high degree of accuracy is required: people will miss their flights if they are told the wrong time for checking in and take off. Flight durations and arrival times will also be key issues to customers. Inaccurate servicing information could quite literally be fatal.

Data is to be passed between 200 offices worldwide, so there is clearly **huge potential for errors** in transmission and for data, or parts of it, to get lost in or corrupted by the system. Communications **protocols** such as TCP/IP should be adopted. These govern the switching of data, detection and correction of errors and so on.

(iii) **Relevance to those it is communicated to**

It is **not immediately apparent why each office needs salary details** of staff not based in that country: this is sensitive information that should not be available to all. If it is necessary to send these details (for comparative purposes, perhaps, or for planning cost-effective use of cabin staff), it should be **transferred in an encrypted form** to prevent it falling into the hands of those not authorised to see it.

(iv) **Trustworthiness**

Offices will be reluctant to **make promises to customers** if they do not feel they can trust the information provided. Customers will not be amused if, for example, an item of freight needs special handling equipment and they use ARG because a local office claimed that these facilities could be made available at the destination, only to find that this was not true.

As another example, since customers appear to be allowed access to the booking system, **some method of ensuring the integrity of a booking made by a customer is needed**. This might consist of passwords or identification numbers for individual travel agents and requirements to submit details in a prescribed form.

(v) **Cost**

It should not cost more to provide the information than the value of the benefits derived from the information. ARG's excess capacity indicates that, **at present, it probably does cost too much to provide the information**: hence the decision to diversify, discussed in part (a).

(c)

Examiner's comment. Many answers were quite limited in scope. Relatively few answers went on to consider the effect on the core business of the decision not to upgrade from the point of view of either service to customers or the ability of the company to continue trading in its present form.

Upgrading the IT infrastructure

We are told that ARG is assuming that its WAN infrastructure - including such items as cabling and communication hardware - will remain unchanged for the next ten years. This **assumption may be questioned** for a number of reasons.

(i) The previous ten years have seen phenomenal change in computing and telecommunications fields and there is **no sign that the pace of change is slowing down**, particularly in telecommunications.

ARG may find that it is not in the position to take full advantage of new technologies as they become available, especially as its supplier, AP Ltd, does not always use industry standard systems.

(ii) The previous ten years have also seen a huge **change in the business environment** many industries. A **customer focus** is now held to be essential for success; many organisations now have radically **different structures** and job functions compared with the past; **competition is fierce and global**; and there is a worldwide trend towards **deregulation**.

Again there is no reason to believe that the next ten years will not bring equally dramatic changes that could have a major impact on the way the ARG wants to use IT.

(iii) In any case ARG's strategy is aimed at 'sustainable competitive advantage', and if it is successful this will inevitably mean **growth and change, possibly in unpredictable ways.** Competitors may introduce new services that do not form part of ARG's current plans, and ARG will need to match these or better them to maintain its position.

Such growth and change will **not** be sustainable, however, unless core activities are **supported by whatever changes in the IT infrastructure** are needed to keep up with or ahead of competitors.

(iv) Upgrades in computer hardware tend to be **led by developments in computer software.** For example, to be used effectively each subsequent version of Windows, from Windows 3.1 to Windows 2000, has required more RAM and hard disk capacity than its predecessor. Many organisations find they need to upgrade their hardware (eg from 486 PCs to Pentiums, or from Pentium II to Pentium III) to accommodate the new software.

This consideration does not seem to form a clear part of ARG's strategy: they are only thinking in terms of improvements in chip technology and the like, and of **capital** expenditure.

(v) A **fixed** capital amount for upgrades may not be appropriate: huge developments may occur in year four, say, followed by small changes in years five and six. If applied as rigorously as the scenario suggests, the upgrading strategy **may be too inflexible** to take proper advantage of developments as they occur.

(d)

Pass marks. Our part (i) is longer than your answer should have been, to ensure that you are aware of the range of points you could make. This topic is highly likely to be examined again. Try to get some hands-on Internet experience.

Examiner's comment. Many answers were hindered by the lack of explanation provided with the points they made. Hopefully candidates will be less concerned about at least attempting to apply knowledge in this area in future examinations.

(i) **The dangers and benefits of providing Internet access**

ARG is proposing to offer users of its WAN Internet access to transfer data to customers and receive information back from customers. ARG itself will also be able to use the Internet in this way.

Advantages for ARG and other businesses fall into three categories.

(1) **Access to vast amounts of information on computer databases.**

This includes information that may be highly useful for both **day-to-day management**, such as government department Internet sites, and for **environmental scanning** purposes, such as sites of customers and competitors, and sites devoted to industries and markets.

(2) **Ability to send electronic messages to individuals or groups.**

Internal messaging is, of course, the primary purpose of ARG's WAN, but Internet access means that email messages can be sent (for the cost of a local telephone call) not only to others connected to ARG's WAN, but to **anybody in the world** connected to the Internet. This could save businesses large amounts of time and money that would otherwise be spent on more conventional methods of communication.

(3) **Marketing and sales benefits.**

To date Internet **marketing** activity has mainly been a matter of **providing information about products and services.** The Internet offers a speedy and impersonal way for customers to find out the basics or the details of the products and services that a company has to offer. This saves time both for customers and for the provider, who has less need to employ and train staff to man the phones on an enquiry desk.

In ARG's case many enquiries will be received about flight times and availability, and this information can very easily be made available on an ARG Website. Virgin Atlantic Airways site, for instance, has an area called 'Flight Plan' that allows the browser to find out the flight numbers and departure and arrival points and times on any of Virgin's routes, and offers the chance to find out more about Virgin's services such as 'Upper Class'.

The provider of the information can also **collect information about potential customers** who contact their Website. The *Electronic Telegraph*, for example, allows free access to the Website version of its daily newspaper, but users are required to fill in a form on screen giving personal information such as income level, address, job title and so on.

Purchasing on the Internet was relatively slow to be embraced initially, but is now expanding at a rapid rate. ARG could provide a **booking service** that allows customers to fill in a form on screen giving all the necessary details, and allows payment by recording a debit or credit card number.

Dangers exist, however, unless proper safeguards are put in place.

(1) The full **legal implications** of doing business on the Net have not been fully worked out, and are highly complex because although it is a worldwide medium it is subject to the different domestic laws of each of the countries in which business is done. ARG or one of its WAN users could easily fall foul of local trading or advertising standards by inadvertently including or leaving out some item of information from their Website services.

(2) People may be able to get access via the Internet into ARG's **internal systems** or those of its WAN users. A mischievous user, for instance, could make **false bookings**, or **delete details** of others bookings, or launch a **virus** that disrupts internal systems, or obtain confidential information, or alter aircraft servicing information.

(3) Internet browsing tends to be compulsive: it is in the very nature of the medium that users are offered the chance to explore topics related to their original enquiry. A common business fear is that **staff might waste time and money** 'surfing the net' for non-business-related information and entertainment in office hours.

(4) Although access to the Internet is priced at the cost of a local call, finding and downloading data can often be a **painfully slow** process. An innocuous enquiry might turn out to cost the price of a **hour long** local phone call, which is clearly much less of a bargain than it might have seemed when the enquiry began.

(5) **People are reluctant to give credit card details** or other sensitive information to a computer and telecommunications link because they

fear the information may be **intercepted and used fraudulently**. This is a problem, but it is one that is likely to disappear over time, since it is clearly in legitimate users' interests to make the data transfer process secure. For example, 'secure payment sites' have been developed that encrypt card numbers during transmission. Public confidence in such systems is essential to the growth of e-commerce.

(ii) **Data security**

There are numerous measures that ARG can take to provide the required level of security. A **security policy** should be developed and regularly reviewed, identifying and quantifying risks, identifying, selecting and implementing counter-measures, and formulating **contingency plans** to be operated in the event of a breach of security.

Protocols should be adopted such as the TCP/IP, which includes layers ensuring that individual messages are **switched and routed properly** through the network, that there are **standard formats** for the interpretation of data, and so on.

WAN customers and ARG's airline customers

Users of ARG's WAN must be **prevented from accessing each others' systems** or intercepting data transmission unless they are authorised to do so. Likewise ARG customers should not be able to gain access to all parts of ARG's system. This is likely to entail the use of '**firewalls**', which allow levels of access to be controlled.

(1) Firewalls **disable** part of the communications technology that normally allows **two-way** communication, so external parties are denied access to parts of the system.

(2) **Access can be controlled by various electronic means** so that one set of users cannot see information exchanges between members of another set of users.

Access control may be effected by **disabling certain terminals**, so that they are not capable of receiving or copying confidential data, by **user-identification procedures** (different users have different levels of access), and **password procedures**. The normal rules concerning passwords should be applied and monitored: passwords should not be disclosed to others, should be in a prescribed format, and should be changed regularly. **Access control logs** should be maintained, recording unauthorised attempts to gain access.

Encryption of data is a possibility that should be available. This involves scrambling the data at one end of the line, transmitting the scrambled data, and unscrambling it at the receiver's end of the line. **Authentication** is another technique that could be used. This makes sure that a message has come from an authorised sender, by including an extra field in a record derived from the data in the record by applying a previously agreed algorithm.

Measures should also be taken to **protect data from physical threats** such as a fire that destroys communications equipment or damage to cables, resulting in the loss of data being transmitted.

Computer **viruses** are a real danger: they may be accidentally or deliberately released onto the network by WAN users or ARG customers and do immeasurable damage both to ARG's systems and to those of other users.

Virus control software should be constantly in use and should be regularly updated.

ARG employees

(1) Care should be taken over the **selection of personnel** to administer the WAN, since these people have large opportunity to impair data security if they choose to do so, or if they are not competent to do their jobs. Obvious measures include taking up references, providing training as necessary, and operating termination procedures restricting access to sensitive data for people about to leave the organisation. Other personnel measures may include **division of responsibilities.**

(2) **ARG's employees should be prevented from gaining access** to the data or systems of WAN customers, by means such as those described above. Controls must be especially strict if access is necessary for maintenance purposes.

(3) **Separate facilities** such as servers could be used to operate different parts of the system. If this is a feasible option it is clearly a more secure approach than sharing resources.

55 JTK LTD: DAILY BREAD

Examiner's comment. In part (a) candidates lost marks if they did not consider external sources of information and if they did not explain why the source of information was relevant to the question. In (b) some candidates failed to provide any commentary on JTK's system and some did not identify a sufficient number of problems. In (c), very few answers provided the type of detailed application of knowledge expected on this level, instead concentrating on providing their own calculations (not required) and problems with market surveys in general, rather than on the limitations of **using** the information in this survey. Very few candidates achieved a pass for part (d). The question asked for **financial indicators.** Most candidates provided a lot of irrelevant information.

(a) **Sources of information to monitor quality**

Information that could be utilised by JTK Ltd to monitor the quality of bread can be gathered from the **internal systems** and from **external sources,** particularly the stakeholder groups that are closely related to JTK Ltd.

Quality control department

JTK Ltd currently only takes samples at the **start** of the production run. It is not gathering sufficient information about the **whole** system.

The quality of bread should be checked **throughout** the production process by sampling the inputs of ingredients, taking **samples** at intervals during the process, and at the end of the process. Samples should be taken at receipt of raw ingredients and also during storage.

This will help to identify problems at source, for example potential problems in storage of ingredients.

Production department

The production department should be monitoring quality and reporting any **problems on the production run** that could have implications for quality of the end product, such as the difficulty of **controlling the mix** towards the end of the run. This will be necessary to ensure the **consistency** of product quality.

Customers

Customers are an important source of information on quality and their views will determine future demand for the product. **Customers' perceptions** of the quality of the finished product are **influenced by a wide variety of factors**. A customer **survey** would provide useful information on the customer view of quality and how the product matches that perception.

Monitoring and subsequent analysis of **complaints** would also provide a useful measure of customer satisfaction. As JTK Ltd has experienced adverse publicity in the past this is an important area for the company to monitor. The view held by JTK Ltd is that bread is price sensitive; however, research could indicate a swing towards quality.

Suppliers

It is important to monitor the **quality of ingredients**. This might be done on arrival at JTK by the QC department, but efforts could be made to ensure that good relationships are developed and **quality standards agreed** for ingredients and delivery.

Suppliers should be monitored in terms of performance and regularly visited to maintain good relationships and observe quality control procedures in operation at the suppliers' premises.

Alternative sources of supplies could also be identified to ensure **continued supply** in the event of problems arising. JTK Ltd uses ingredients that could be subject to changes in quality through storage and therefore liaison with the supplier on delivery schedules and storage conditions is essential.

Competitors

Comparison with competitors is an area where **relative quality** can be assessed, perhaps linked to the customer surveys in identifying preferences.

JTK Ltd has a relatively **strong market presence**: it produces 15% of the total demand for bread. This could put the company in a good position to conduct **benchmarking** exercises against industry members. Competitors may also be amenable to this for reasons of **mutual benefit**.

In particular, production methods and ingredient mix could be benchmarked since this is likely to give rise to **new ideas** and provide valuable **cost comparisons.**

Intermediaries

JTK Ltd should be concerned about the quality of its product as it is presented to the customer and therefore the impact of distributing the product to **retail outlets** and **standards of storage by retailers** need to be monitored.

Information about this could be collected by **'mystery shopper'** testing of matters such as the condition of the product on the shelves and retailers' adherence to sell-by dates.

There should also be **feedback from the retailers themselves**, reflecting either complaints from final customers or problems that the retailer has experienced (difficulty in storage, handling, delivery etc).

Industry standards

Often there are standards laid down by an industry body that can be used for monitoring purposes. In the food industry there are quality standards connected with **hygiene and health and safety** of the product. **Ingredients** of the product would need to be clearly stated and quality checks should ensure that these are correct and as stated, particularly as regards any **claims that are made on the packaging**.

Consumer groups

Consumers are becoming well represented as a body and health concerns are increasing in importance. Therefore current issues could be identified by a review of **health and food magazines,** and issues affecting concerns over quality could be flagged for attention: these will indicate consumer preferences for the future.

Establishing regular **contact with consumer groups** is often beneficial as it allows the company to influence, if not directly control, media messages about its product.

(b) **Weaknesses of the system**

A closed loop system is a system where part of the output is fed back, so that the output can initiate control action to change either the activities of the system or the system's input.

Closed loop systems **do not take account of external influences** and therefore, over time, they have a tendency to deteriorate in performance, perhaps due standards becoming out of date.

Inflexibility

The JTK Ltd quality system shows elements that are **inflexible** and therefore detract from the effectiveness of the process.

For example the EOQs have remained unchanged for 15 years, in spite of the fact that the company has experienced a small but marked increase in average raw material stocks over the last five years. If the system had taken account of this the company would have been prompted to **adjust the EOQs** to reflect the improved efficiency of supplier delivery systems.

Also, the **machinery is old,** and this is likely to make input difficult to manage. The system itself is not taking this into account as the QC checks do not monitor the end of the process.

Timing of control points

The production run takes place overnight finishing by 4.00 am whereas the QC department works from 12 noon to 10.00pm. The control loaves are only taken from the start of the production run. The scenario states that inputs become difficult to manage towards the end of the production run. Therefore the current system will **not pick up any quality problems that occur in the middle or at the end of the run**. There are therefore **no controls over consistency** of quality produced.

The standards are amended on a monthly basis but this may not take into account any issues that had been identified on a **particular run** that needed prompt action Likewise the company can only be sure that it meets the **legal requirement** for artificial additives at the beginning of the month: changes shortly after this will not be reflected until the next month.

The **time delay inherent in the closed system** is evident here and could have a significant impact upon the reputation of JTK Ltd if problems were not identified and acted upon quickly.

Value system

As the control is internal there is no check through the value system. For example goods are sold the day after production but **no feedback is received from the retailers**. This is a particular problem of the closed loop system.

Quality of materials in store are not checked and neither is delivery of ingredients. The **source of problems may be difficult to identify quickly** and potential problems are not flagged. It is difficult to see how JTK Ltd would identify problems arising from its suppliers and customers (retailers) at all, using the closed control system.

Quality checks.

The actual quality check appears to be in relation to ingredients and legal requirements and **does not take account of texture, colour, freshness etc**, those wider aspects of quality that are easily identified in the overall consumer impression. It would be possible to measure texture and colour by reference to standards that were tested by sight or machine measurement.

The quantity of loaves sampled is extremely small in comparison to the total produced, and so only provide a **very small level of confidence**.

The actual control information is derived from **historical** information and **professional knowledge** generated **internally**: it does not recognise **external** information.

(c) **Limitations of market research information**

The market research obtained by the Management Accountant has one problem already identified in that the extent of the increase in demand for speciality breads and fewer artificial additives cannot be quantified. Any forecast into future demand carries an element of uncertainty with it and there is therefore **a risk involved in taking the research results as a certain prediction of the future**. At best, market research is often only an indicator of the likely future trend.

One way of reducing the risk is to **obtain corroborative data** from other sources such as complementary research or general trends in the economy, perhaps linked to trends in other food products. The **probabilities** used will add an element of refinement to the survey, but again these can only be estimates.

The survey shows that there is a strong possibility that demand for cheap breads will decrease, but JTK Ltd have 15% of the market. Does this mean that their **relative share will also reduce** or that there will still be a strong chance that JTK can consolidate its position in the market place and **increase its market share** to retain the same volume production? The research does not necessarily indicate that JTK Ltd should jump into the speciality goods market if there will still be a market for cheap bread.

There are other questions that need to be asked about the research. For example **who carried it out** and did they have a **vested interest** in the result? In other words is there any bias built into the end result of the survey? **How big** was the sample? **What time period** was it taken over? Were there any significant **health issues with a high public profile** when the survey was carried out? **What groups** were surveyed: the end consumer or the industry members?

The **timescale** of the forecast is three years, and this may be shorter than any payback period required to warrant the investment in the new plant that the Management Accountant is suggesting.

These are all problems inherent in any secondary data obtained by a company.

It is clear that the data is **only part of the information required** to make the investment decision under review.

(d) **Critical Success Factors and performance indicators**

Return on investment

One of the key financial Critical Success Factors for any investment is that it **generates sufficient future returns** to justify the investment. Returns must be measured both in terms of profit and cash generation, since additional finance may have to be raised to finance the investment, and this debt will have to be serviced.

It is very often difficult to isolate the returns that are derived from any one particular investment in a manufacturing industry where that investment is producing previously produced goods.

A critical success factor of **adequate return on investment** could be used, with the proviso indicated above, and possible performance indicators could include, **Internal Rate of Return, Return On Capital Employed** or **payback period**.

These all have **limitations** in their use individually.

(i) The **IRR** requires the internal rate of return to be compared with an internal hurdle rate to ascertain whether the return is adequate. This is often compared with a cost of capital figure for the company, but over a period of time this can change and therefore, a project that appears in one period to be a good investment may turn out to be a wrong decision in the long run due to the difficulty in estimating the future cost of capital.

(ii) The **ROCE** is also often used to compare with a hurdle rate, but it is difficult to define what is an adequate return and what values should be included in the capital base.

(iii) The **payback period** is also difficult to use in isolation as no account is taken of the timing of the cash flows.

A common approach used today is a **weighted ranking** and scoring method which takes into account several measures. However, although this may take more account of the difficulties than using the performance measures in isolation, there is still the inherent difficulty of projecting the benefits into the future with any **certainty,** particularly as some of the benefits may be **intangible**, such as improved staff morale through the introduction of new technology.

Profitability

Another possible critical success factor would be one based upon the **ability of the new investment to generate increased profit in the future**, either via satisfying new demand or through improved efficiency. As stated above it is difficult to isolate the profit and some elements of improved efficiency will also be difficult to isolate or attach directly to the new investment.

Sales volume and revenue could be used as performance indicators to assist in measuring the profitability or **business generated** by the new investment, but problems of isolating the appropriate figures are also present here.

Costs may be identifiable, such as cost of maintenance, running costs, changeover time and associated costs, the financial effect of downtime and so on. These may all be useful indicators if they are compared with previous figures and show an improvement.

(e) **Notice board v bulletin board**

Communication in a Quality Control department would ideally be professional in nature and become part of the job by habit. Difficulties that could arise through using a notice board for communication of control information include the following.

(i) The problems of **legibility** and **format**. Hand-written messages may differ in format and readability depending upon the care with which they were prepared and who prepared them.

(ii) The degree of **completeness** of messages may also vary in the detail contained, assumptions may be made about the knowledge of the recipient that are false.

(iii) Messages may become **overcrowded** and the notice board may fill up with **out of date** messages making it difficult to identify new messages.

(iv) It may **not be possible to ensure that the intended recipient does in fact read the message** unless it becomes habit to check the notice board upon arrival for the next shift and unless some form of procedure exists to clear the notice board of messages that are no longer applicable. This in itself presents problems of finding out whether all staff are aware of the information before it is removed.

(v) It is unwise to leave **confidential** messages that on a public notice board!

A computer bulletin board can be used to make information more user friendly

(i) Many bulletin boards on computer systems are **easy to use** and can be set up so that the message is completed in a **standard format**, with predefined input boxes to ensure that all pertinent data to QC are entered.

(ii) It could be linked to the logging on and change over of operator so that they are **automatically provided with any new messages**. A record could then kept on the computer that the message was opened (however this does not guarantee that the person who opened the message did actually **read** it).

(iii) Recording and retrieving could be made much more user friendly by utilising common screens and **graphical user interfaces** with prompts for key items and useful **help messages**.

(iv) Messages may be able to be **attached to relevant production batch information** so that a problem with a particular batch can be isolated, recorded and stored for future reference.

(v) **Confidential** messages could be coped with via the use of a **password**.

The use of a bulletin board presents a much more professional image and staff may take a pride in utilising the benefits of the system.

56 SPK PLC: MOTOR VEHICLES

> **Pass marks.** Part (a) tests knowledge that should be very familiar to you and gives you plenty of material to apply it to. For part (b) you need a certain amount of imagination, since the system is not described in much detail in the case study. Part (c) offers an unusual angle on data security. A variety of answers are possible, depending upon how much weight you gave to the topic of data protection. Part (d) again requires imagination as well as good knowledge of hardware and software.
>
> **Examiner's comment.** Answers where fewer marks were obtained tended to concentrate on the attributes of information in very general terms. Although the mnemonic ACCURATE ensured that the general characteristics of information were included in the answer, there was unfortunately no attempt to differentiate between the characteristics of information at each of the three different levels. Some answers gave a long list of information that would be provided at each level but the characteristics of that information, such as 'detailed' were not discussed.

(a) (i) **Characteristics of information**

(1) **Strategic information** is used to plan the objectives of the organisation, and to assess whether the objectives are being met in practice. Strategic information is therefore:

- derived from both **internal and external** sources;
- **summarised** at a high level;
- relevant to the **long term;**
- concerned with the **whole organisation** (although it might go into some detail);
- often prepared on an **'ad hoc'** basis;
- both **quantitative and qualitative;**
- **incapable** of providing **certainty,** as the future cannot be predicted.

(2) **Tactical information** is used to decide how the resources of the business should be employed, and to monitor how they are being and have been employed. Tactical information is therefore:

- derived from a more restricted range of external sources, so is thus **primarily generated internally;**
- **summarised at a lower level** - a report might be included with summaries and raw data as backup;
- relevant to the **short and medium term;**
- concerned with **activities or departments;**
- prepared **routinely and regularly;**
- based on **quantitative** measures.

(3) **Operational information** is used by 'front-line' managers such as foremen or head clerks to ensure that specific tasks are planned and carried out properly. Operational information is:

- derived almost entirely from **internal sources;**
- highly **detailed,** being the processing of raw data;
- relevant to the **immediate term;**
- **task-specific;**
- prepared **constantly,** or very **frequently;**
- largely **quantitative.**

(ii)

Examiner's comment. Only a small minority of answers took the 'middle ground' and showed how the reports were actually good in places, but needed improvement in others. Candidates who were prepared to query whether the information was actually useful and relevant obtained good marks. However, the majority of answers did not contain the depth of analysis required. Candidates should not take information at face value. In an examination, as in the business world, they should always treat information received with healthy scepticism until it has been checked to ensure its reliability.

Information in the reports

The following comments should be read with the proviso that we are not told what information the writers of these reports were **asked** to provide.

(1) **The Chief Executive's memo**

The information is provided very **promptly** (on the same day as the Board meeting) and it is **well laid out**. The memo is highly **summarised**, and it is also **forward looking**.

However, the information is **not sufficient** to help the Board to make a decision. Criticisms include the following.

- The estimate 'between £5m and £20m' is **far too vague**. Does this mean 'about £7m' or 'about £19m'? Does it mean that more extra space will be obtained the more money is spent? More explanation is needed.
- **No figures are given for any other costs**, although these too are likely to run into millions.
- **It is not explained why it can be assumed that the market will expand by 20%.** What information is this based on? Why not 10%? Why not 75%? How much of the expanded market can SPK plc expect to capture? More useful would be projections of likely sales and profits under a number of different scenarios.
- **The CAD/CAM system is not explained.** Presumably the production manager would be best placed to give an explanation, and we might expect the Chief Executive's memo to refer to information that will be produced by him.
- **Information about competitors is needed.** Is this tailoring service already available from other manufacturers, and what impact has it had, if so? If not, for how long can SPK expect to have a competitive advantage, before others respond with systems of their own?

(2) **The Production Manager's memo**

This memo leaves a good deal to be desired.

- The manager has **taken six days to respond**, yet the memo contains **very little information.**
- **Little attempt has been made to summarise** the information for the use of the Chief Executive. In fact the manager even goes so far as to suggest that the Chief Executive reviews the detailed data himself. Detailed information is **difficult to review on screen**.
- **No reason is given for the assumption as to annual production level.** An analysis of the costs at **various different levels** would be more useful.
- **No totals** are given.
- Is the automation expenditure a **one-off capital cost** or a **recurring annual revenue cost**?

- Does the sales forecast assume that **all units produced will be sold**? Is it reasonable to use **average selling price**? If customers are getting an improved service they may be willing to pay more for it. **Have the marketing department been consulted**?
- **Can the Chief Executive open files** produced with the new spreadsheet package? He may still have the old package.

(3) **The memo from the Assistant Operations Manager**

This too leaves a good deal to be desired.

- It is described as a **'best guess'**, yet some of the figures are **stated to the penny.**
- **No indication is given of when** the Operations Manager is likely to return to work and produce the **'more detailed report'**.
- The information about **personnel** is **confusingly presented** in **narrative** form, whereas a table of figures would be much easier to understand.
- If the probabilities, labour turnover figures and absenteeism rates are relevant, the **financial implications need to be calculated and set out clearly,** not merely stated. In fact (even multiplied by 1,500) the amounts involved seem to be barely material to a decision involving millions of pounds.
- The **recruitment company costs** are presumably **one-off costs,** but this seems **not to be taken into account.**
- The **materials figures could be totalled**, and there is probably no reason to present them to the exact penny, especially as they are averages. An average cost is fine, but it would also be useful to know what the **extremes** (maximum and minimum) are.
- Reservations about the '£5m-£20m' cost are expressed in the notes above on the Chief Executive's memo (assuming this is referring to the same £5m-£20m!). In any case **this information would not be expected at the operational level.**

(b)

> **Examiner's comment.** The requirement to 'appraise' was not always fully addressed. Most answers assumed that the technology was essential to the company's production system. Although this was certainly correct, the provision of further explanation to show what alternatives were available, and whether they could work, would in most cases obtain additional marks.

Information technology and the new system

Clearly there is **no** part of the new system that could **not** work without the use of IT, since other manufacturers are able to tailor vehicles to precise requirements in non-automated factories.

However, this approach is **not practicable** for SPK because it would take **too long** and **cost too much** to build a typical SPK model using manual methods.

The service that SPK is planning to offer is only possible at an acceptable cost and rate of output because of the use of **manufacturing** technology in the form of robots. These in turn will be controlled by new **information** technology.

(i) Customers will use IT in the **showroom** to design their vehicles, and showroom computers will be linked via telecommunications directly to the **production line**. However, the telecommunications link must be secure and reliable.

This could be done in other ways (for instance by filling in a **questionnaire**), but this would **delay** the process unacceptably.

(ii) Computers can make use of **3D colour graphics** to show the customer exactly what they will get, inside and outside the car. This would be virtually **impossible to do using conventional brochures.**

(iii) Depending on the number of options available it might be possible in theory for a customer to design a car that **broke safety regulations** or regulations on emissions, or even was impossible to build in engineering terms. A computer will be able to perform an **automatic check** that a particular permutation meets with the rules and with practical possibility.

Again, this would take an **unacceptably long time** if done by other means, and **human error** might literally be fatal.

(iv) **Scheduling of production** is likely to be done using production planning software, which will help to **batch together variations chosen by customers** and keep interruptions to a minimum. Once again, given the number of permutations, it would be very difficult to do this by other means.

(c)

> **Examiner's comment.** Most answers tended to focus on the various computer controls that could be implemented to protect data in the company. This approach missed the main point of the question, which was to explain the **responsibilities of each management level** and not just to provide a list of the controls that could be implemented.

Data security at different levels

Data security involves protecting data from accidental or deliberate threats which might cause its modification, disclosure or destruction. There is a British Standard **Code of Practice for Information Security Management** (BS 7799). The ten sections of this standard give a good indication of the areas that need to be considered.

(i) **Security policy**. A written document setting out the organisation's approach to information security should be available to all staff.

(ii) **Security organisation.** It should be clear who has responsibility for the various aspects of information security.

(iii) **Asset classification and control.** Information is an asset, just like a machine, building or a vehicle.

(iv) **Personnel security.** This covers issues such as recruitment of trustworthy employees, training and also reporting of security-related incidents.

(v) **Physical and environmental security**

(vi) **Computer and network management.**

(vii) **Systems access control**

(viii) **Systems development and maintenance**

(ix) **Business continuity planning.**

(x) **Compliance** with any relevant legal requirements and also with organisational policies.

Strategic level

At strategic level, the Board will be responsible for developing the **overall** security policy, and for dealing with major (organisation-wide) compliance issues.

The Board would **delegate responsibility** for drafting **specific procedures** to **tactical** managers and would periodically **review policy** in the light of breaches of security. They might also initiate a review of policies to ensure compliance with **new legislation** such as the Data Protection Act 1998 and its provisions regarding manual records and sensitive personal data.

Board members themselves would theoretically have unlimited access to the system, and they therefore need to **exercise personal diligence** to ensure that they do not breach any of the security procedures (although in practice many non-IT-literate directors deliberately ask to be given low-level access, in case they damage the system).

Tactical level

Tactical managers are likely to be the ones who actually **devise practical policies** to deal with issues like backing up, access control, and so on, who **monitor their operation** and who **take appropriate action** to deal with breaches of security. Actions might include disciplining staff or authorising the restoration of a back-up file to recover data that has become corrupted.

Tactical managers are most likely to have access to sensitive personal data about employees, and they need to **respect the rights of individuals** regarding protection and privacy.

Operational level

At the operational level, managers will be responsible for **operating the controls** put in place by higher levels of management. They will do tasks such as performing **back-ups**, observing **access procedures**, day-to-day **systems maintenance**, taking appropriate action when **verification or validation checks** give rise to exceptions, and so on.

(d)

> **Examiner's comment.** A significant minority of candidates failed to notice that the emphasis of this question was on the Human Computer Interface itself. Purely technological details (eg '450 MHz') obtained very few marks because the candidate did not show how they were relevant to the use of the HCI. Many candidates would be advised to actually imagine themselves using the computer system as a means of helping them to consider what is important. For example the examiner wrote this using a Pentium processor running at 200 megahertz. This information is actually **irrelevant** to the use of the HCI unless the processor cannot cope with the speed of keyboard input.

Hardware and software elements

Software requirements are as follows.

(i) An **operating system**, most probably Windows 95/98 or Windows NT Workstation.

(ii) **Software drivers** for the various hardware components such as the sound card.

(iii) **Communications software** to enable data to be transmitted from showrooms to the production line.

(iv) A program (probably **written specially** for the purpose) to **display graphics** and present options for customers to choose. This is likely to be GUI driven. Typical Windows components such as menus, help prompts, toolbars, buttons, and scroll bars **may** be used and (in spite of the assumption in the case study) probably **will** be familiar to many potential customers (since they are likely to use Windows-based software in their own jobs). On the other hand it may be felt that an even easier, **'idiot-proof' interface** is needed, requiring no familiarity with computers at all. An interface resembling those found with simple computer games may be most appropriate.

(v) Possibly, **voice recognition software**, if it is felt to be desirable to avoid any keying-in of data by the customer. However, voice recognition is not 100% reliable at the moment.

(vi) **Browser software**, to enable showroom staff to download small updates to the vehicle information. In fact, if telecommunications links are fast enough it may be possible to run the entire presentation package across the Internet within a browser.

The following **hardware** elements are likely to be required.

(i) An **SVGA screen** (probably at least 17') capable of displaying **high quality graphics** so that the customer can see what is being designed clearly.

(ii) A **keyboard** to enable the customer to type in their name, address and so on. It may be possible to avoid typing by using voice recognition equipment (a microphone and speakers), although, as already mentioned, this cannot be relied upon 100% at present.

(iii) A **mouse**, since most other interaction with the system will be pointing and clicking on options.

(iv) A **sound card and speakers**, over which to play voiceovers, car engine sounds and so on.

(v) A **fast Pentium III processor**, to ensure as little delay as possible, so that customers are not left waiting too long for a response from the computer.

(vi) A **modem**, unless **ISDN** links are to be established between showrooms and the production line, or SPK has its own **private network.**

(vii) A **fast CD-ROM drive**, again to minimise delays in response.

(viii) A **comfortable and well-lit space** for the equipment. Showrooms may have to be furnished with point of sale desks and chairs. SPK will not, however, have full control over the siting of equipment, since this will depend upon space available in different showrooms.

In fact, **a high-spec business PC** is likely to be more than adequate. The vehicle-tailoring software would most probably be issued periodically to dealers on **CD-ROM** and would mainly run from CD-ROM in the showroom, perhaps in conjunction with small **updates,** downloaded onto hard disk from SPK's **website**.

57 TEP PLC: THEME PARK

Examiner's comment. The two areas of this question which caused candidates most difficulty were explaining the relevance of the information sources and providing a sufficient number of information sources.

(a) **Sources of information**

TEP plc needs information to help it choose between the following options.

Option 1	Invest in a hotel, more shows and rides suitable for younger children, and a specialist travel agency offering a complete holiday package
Option 2	Invest in a major new ride (a virtual reality simulator)

The difference in **cost** between the two options is **immaterial** (£200, 000, or around £3% of the total amount to be invested investment).

Information sources **mentioned in the scenario** are as follows.

Internal	*External*
Internal policy documents about objectives	Market research into the theme park market
Cost information about maintenance costs	Cost information about future investments
Total visitors entering the park daily	
Information about stock and sales of retail outlets on a daily basis	
Total visitors per ride, daily	

Information could possibly **also** be obtained from **other internal and external sources** that are not mentioned.

Internal sources

(i) **Information systems**

Internal information systems **do not provide any information** that is relevant to **Option 1.**

As for **Option 2,** TEP plc's **sales information** (merely summarised into totals by the EIS) is highly **undeveloped.** At best it can provide information on matters such as the numbers of visitors on different days, which retail items are selling well or badly, and the pattern of usage of current rides.

Since back-ups are kept, however, it is likely that this information is available for a **seven year period,** which would enable further analysis of matters such as, say, **trends by date.**

Further analysis of the information could be done (assuming it is exportable into an easily analysable form such as a spreadsheet) and may yield interesting and meaningful results that would help inform **Option 2.** For instance the number of visitors that go on a new ride, on its introduction, seems likely to be significantly higher than for a ride that has been in operation for some time. **Suitably analysed** the figures should show whether **expectations** for a ride were **realised.**

Since several new rides have been introduced over the period for which data is available it may also be possible to correlate the popularity of a ride with standard **accounting information** (which must be kept by law) about matters such as spending on advertising and promotion of that ride.

Historical **internal** information from information systems could also be correlated with historical **external** information, such as weather patterns, public 'scares' about the safety of theme parks, features about theme parks on TV holiday programs or newspaper/magazine coverage.

(ii) **Accounting information**

This is not mentioned in the scenario, but must, by law, be available for a number of years, since TEP is a plc.

Further analysis could be carried out to provide information such as the following.

(1) Although a **net profit margin** of 10% has been maintained, the increase in competition presumably means the actual net profit margin has been **eroded** over recent years. This should be investigated and any **declining trend** cross-referenced to external information about **competitors activities.**

(2) Similarly, a large number of **other trends** could probably be identified by a year-on-year analysis, and the reasons for **significant variations** investigated in the light of **internal** (eg operational problems) **and external** (eg poor weather) **information**.

(iii) **Other information that could be collected**

(1) **Hearsay**

A representative sample of managers and operational staff could be consulted for word-of-mouth information about the success or failure of different rides. Although such information is necessarily impressionistic and subject to bias, such employees are in close contact with visitors, and are likely to have gained an insight into visitor satisfaction levels.

(2) **Formal research**

Visitors could be asked to fill in questionnaires or take part in focus groups to yield additional information about levels of satisfaction, for instance what they like most about the park at the moment and what they would like to see there in the future

(3) **Staff/Visitor feelings about the options**

A similar (interview/questionnaire) approach could be taken with both staff and visitors to the park to determine their feelings about the specific proposals being considered by management.

A problem with this is that most staff will be used to the 'young adult' visitors, and have no feeling for the 'families with small children market'. Families with small children will not have visited the park in significant numbers so their views will not be known.

(4) **Enhanced information systems**

Existing information systems could be enhanced to provide **additional information** (such as **age profile** of visitors, **average waiting times** per ride, what **type of visitor** 'bought the T-shirt' or any other souvenir and what type didn't). Technology is available in the form, say, of temporary identification badges with **bar-codes**, which could be read whenever a visitor enters into a new transaction. Such information can then be **correlated against information already collected** to provide more detailed analyses of a large number of TEP's services.

External sources

External sources of information will be the chief means of assessing **option 1**, since the company does not have any direct experience of offering this sort of service. External information will also provide further assistance with **option 2**.

Much of the information described below should be available from the **website** of the relevant organisation.

(i) **Demographics**

Demographic information will be available from central and local government sources (eg *Social Trends*), and from commercial bodies. This will help TEP to build up a **broad picture** of likely future **trends in demand,** changing **tastes** and **habits, income** patterns, **age** profiles, **education** and so on, and help the company to tailor its current and future services accordingly.

(ii) **Economic information**

The economic outlook in TEPs country is important: an impending **recession**, for instance, would probably mean that people reduced their expenditure on leisure activities, adversely impacting on TEP.

Sources of economic predictions include the government, newspapers and more specialist publications, trade bodies and consultants on the leisure industry.

(iii) **Market research**

Some market research has already been carried out, indicating that families tend to avoid the park because it is **not suitable for small children**. This seems to be the chief impetus for the **hotel initiative** that is under consideration (**option 1**).

A more detailed picture can be obtained if **further research** could be carried out now that a firm plan has been drawn up, to see whether the hotel proposals appeal to the market segment that TEP is trying to attract (and to existing customers and other segments, such as active older people).

The ultimate decision will be highly dependent upon the results of market research. For instance it may well be that young adults, who tend to be very image-conscious, will be **deterred from visiting the park** if there is an increase in the number of older adults and young children. This may lead TEP to the conclusion that it would be best to maintain its existing market and choose option 2.

(iv) **Business partners**

Additional information may be obtained from **other businesses that deal with TEP**, all of which are likely to have views on market trends. Examples include booking agencies, providers of local transport, suppliers of retail items, and local hotels. Depending on confidentiality requirements such partners could be consulted for their views about the proposed hotel development, how it will affect them, whether they can offer anything else, and whether they will support it. If TEP is perceived to be **going into competition with local suppliers** of accommodation, or with existing booking agencies, for instance, this could have an adverse effect upon the existing market.

If detailed **costings** of the proposed options have not already been obtained then this should be done, in collaboration with builders, suppliers, manufacturers, surveyors, the target travel agency and the like. There may be hidden costs in addition to the ball-park figures given in the scenario and these may be sufficient to sway the decision one way or another.

(v) **Competitors**

TEP appears to have carried out some analysis of its direct **competitors**' activities already. Such research should be on-going, should look at issues such as **pricing**, **quality** and **relative popularity** of rides. This is easily done simply by visiting the competition as a customer, although some competitors may be prepared to co-operate more fully and **benchmark** with TEP. Research should perhaps be broadened to include theme parks (such as DisneyWorld) in **other countries**, which may be even more technologically advanced than TEP.

(vi) **Other external information**

As indicated above a certain amount of **external information** (such as historic weather patterns) is needed to help interpret the existing internal information. This should be obtained from appropriate sources (such as the meteorological office, in the case of the weather), as necessary.

(b)

> **Pass marks.** In our answer we have based much of our comment on the analysis and design issues that are considered in SSADM, as applied to TEP plc. This is a way of helping focusing on the relevant issues rather than trying to write an answer that covers every aspect of the SDLC. However, this is a difficult question, not least because we are given very little information about TEP's system or the Travel Agency's system, but also because the detail of analysis and design is a rather abstract subject for most accountants.
>
> **Examiner's comment.** Following the SDLC to the letter was a major hindrance to many candidates. Candidates tended to explain the whole of the SDLC rather than apply that knowledge to the specific question situation.

Investigation during the analysis and design phase

Systems analysis examines why current methods are used, what alternatives might achieve the same, or better, results, what restricts the effectiveness of the system and what performance criteria are required from a system. It employs a variety of fact-finding techniques to determine what the system actually does or is supposed to do, what document flows occur, what work processes are involved, and what personnel are involved. This phase concludes with the construction of dataflow diagrams.

Systems design is a technical phase which addresses in particular inputs, outputs, program design, dialogue design, file design and storage matters, and security. The conclusion of this phase is a detailed specification of the new system.

However, there is **no clear-cut distinction** between analysis and design, and indeed some of the investigative work of systems analysis is usually done in preceding phases leading up to the initial **feasibility report**.

(i) **Investigation of the current environment**

In this stage the current system is **investigated**, described and analysed using the techniques of observation, questionnaires, document description forms and so forth. Some of the work may have been done already during the feasibility study.

A major requirement of this phase is that the current system is properly documented in **dataflow diagrams (DFDs)** and the **logical data structure** is described (the latter shows the relationships between the **entities** in the system (customers, rides etc) and their **attributes**).

One of the most important products of this stage is a detailed **problems/requirements** list.

(1) **Problems** are likely to relate to the age of TEP plc's existing system, and the compatibility of TEPs system with that of the travel agency.

(2) **Requirements** may simply be the **solutions** to the problems identified in the current system, but could also imply a completely **new way** of doing things. For instance it may be decided that the existing system should be dispensed with entirely.

(ii) **Business system options**

The **new system** requirements, in outline, are for hotel accommodation to be booked directly by the travel agency via an Internet connection, to provide details of special events from TEP's web-site, and to provide on-line booking and payments facilities through the travel agent's web-site.

The next stage is to discover **in detail** what data will have to be dealt with and what information is required as output.

There will normally be a number of possible solutions and those considered the best will be put forward to users as Business System Options. For each option on the shortlist there is drawn up a level-1 DFD, descriptions of the basic processes that transform data, a logical data structure, a cost/benefit analysis (in brief) and an assessment of the impact of the proposed system. Users are then asked to make a choice.

(iii) **Requirements specification**

This stage has several steps.

(1) Detailed DFDs etc are drawn up, and the **required** system matched with the **current** system to ensure that all necessary processing will be performed. The DFDs are modified by the solutions to the problems/requirements identified earlier.

(2) Specifications for **input** and **output** from the chosen system are prepared. These detail what appears on screen, or on documents. An input/output description of a **booking confirmation**, for instance, will list what should appear on the confirmation (customer number, name, address, date of confirmation, dates of stay, type of accommodation required and so on).

(3) Relational data analysis (**normalisation**) is performed on the input and output descriptions. This is to identify any entities that might not have been noticed, or drawn in enough detail, in the existing **logical data structure.**

(4) **Entity life histories** are drawn up, indicating what happens to each entity, ie what functions (processes) it is subjected to, and so forth.

(iv) **Technical system options**

Given that it is seven years old, it is likely that TEP plc's hardware will be unable to run the new system without a significant upgrade.

TEP will therefore be asked to make choices concerning the means by which the system should be **implemented.**

There might be a number of ways of implementing a system physically. These can include:

(1) **hardware configuration** (for example mainframe, mini, PC; centralised or distributed processing); and

(2) **software** (use of a database or a conventional file structure).

The technical system will need to be capable of **communicating** over quite a wide area and managing **Internet connections**.

Performance objectives for the system are then specified in detail so that these can be followed in the actual design of the system.

(v) **Logical design**

In this stage, the data and file structures for the entire new system are designed.

This stage includes the development of **output formats**, and specifying the type of **dialogue** that users will have with the system, to ensure that it is consistent with what has been prepared so far. This applies both to systems used **within TEP** and to the **Website**, where an attractive and easy-to-use interface is essential.

Prototyping may be used so that users can actually see what the system will look like and get a feel for how it will work.

(vi) **Physical design**

Physical design involves the following tasks.

(1) **Initial physical design** (obtaining the design rules from the chosen database, and applying them to the logical data design drawn up in the previous stages).

(2) Further define the **processing** required. For instance requirements for **audit, security and control** are considered, such as **controls over access** to the system; controls **incorporated within programs** (eg data validation, error handling); and **recovery procedures**, in case processing is interrupted.

(3) **Program specifications** are created. These provide in detail exactly what a particular program is supposed to achieve.

(4) Program specifications are assessed for their **performance** when implemented. For example, it should be possible to make some estimate of the times that some programs will take to run.

(5) **File and database specifications** are designed in detail

(6) **Operating instructions** are drawn up (user documentation). These will include such items as error correction and detailed instructions for operators and users (eg the sort of screen format that will appear).

(c)

Examiner's comment. A significant majority of answers did not achieve a high standard because they only provided lists of information rather than explaining **why** the information was needed by the directors, and did not explain any of the other changes that could be made to the EIS.

Changes that need to be made to the EIS

The current EIS is **hardly ever used** by the directors. The only information it provides is daily totals. The system is seven years old, so it will reflect few of the developments that have taken place in computing in the 1990s, notably with regard to **user-friendliness**.

An entirely new **GUI-based** system is needed as the font-end for directors, and this needs to be linked to an **enhanced database** that includes the information described in the answer to part (a).

The EIS should provide managers with **key internal and external data** and the facility to '**drill down**' to the detailed transactions, and **analyse and manipulate** the data in new ways, as required. It should include easy-to-use **graphical facilities** which will help directors to detect **trends** and **correlation** between variables, and tools for other kinds of analysis such as **ratio analysis**, **forecasts**, and **what-if** analysis. The most informative representation is a 'cubic' view (**Rubik's cube** is a good analogy).

Because of the newness of the hotel venture it will be useful if the EIS includes **project management** facilities, which will help with controlling costs and making sure that the hotel development is completed on schedule.

When the hotel development becomes operational the EIS will need to provide information such as **room occupancy** rates, **running costs,** average **spending by guests** and so on. The development will also have an impact on existing operations, and **comparative figures** should be available.

The EIS should also provide access to **environmental data** on the political and economic environment, and competitor and market intelligence. An **intranet** with links to appropriate Internet sites such as Reuters, the Financial Times, the sites of competitors and so on, may be an effective way of providing this facility.

(d)

Examiner's comment. Almost all candidates could have increased the number of marks obtained by providing more alternatives. More than half of the candidates failed to give a recommendation.

Back-ups

The company currently backs up its EIS and information system on a **daily** basis. The back-up medium is disk: presumably this means **floppy** disks. Disks are kept in a **fire-proof safe on site.**

Storage of back-ups on site is a dangerous policy. Although they are stored in a fire-proof safe, this does not offer complete protection. For instance the **safe itself could be stolen**.

The following changes or enhancements are **recommended.**

(i) Back-up onto **tape using a tape streamer.** Tape can store a much larger amount of data. At present it is likely that several disks are needed, and the physical process of backing up is laborious and time-consuming.

(ii) Back-up on a weekly basis as well as daily. This means that even if a daily back-up fails, no more than a week's transactions are ever lost.

(iii) Back-ups should be **stored off-site.**

(iv) Conduct a formal **risk analysis** to identify the sensitive aspects of the system and then draw up a **contingency plan** covering standby and recovery procedures, defining responsibilities and establishing priorities.

Back-up alternatives

Other possible approaches to back-up are as follows.

(i) **Hard copy**

Daily transactions can be printed and paper copies can be stored off-site. The disadvantages are that it takes a **long time** to print out the data and it consumes a **lot of paper**. Moreover, although the information is saved it is not in digital form and will have to be re-input.

(ii) **Standby arrangements**

These offer some protection in case of damage to the organisation's **hardware,** but not its data.

Computer bureaux can agree to make their own systems available in the event of an emergency. Such an arrangement has to be specified in advance, as there might be other demands on a bureau's resources.

Co-operating with **other organisations** in the locality, through a mutual aid agreement, may be a way of pooling resources. However, these other organisations themselves might not, in the event, be able to spare the computer time.

Disaster standby companies typically offer office premises with desks, telephones and storage space which are equipped with hardware of the same type as that used by their customers. In the event of a disaster, the customer can 'invoke' standby procedures and load back-ups of software to carry on essential business.

The provision of stand-by arrangements tends to be quite **costly**, particularly where these systems have no other function. In the event of a disaster **TEP plc** could probably record essential information **manually** until the system was back on line.

(e)

> **Examiner's comment.** From the content of the answers it appears that most candidates had given some thought to their answer, and the average mark obtained was quite high. Some answers were hurried and provided insufficient explanation. Some tended to focus on just one or two points, limiting the number of marks that could be awarded.

Internet booking and society and working practices

The impact on society

Society is taken to mean the customs of a group of people and the way they organise what they do. In this case we are discussing the way in which people do business with commercial organisations.

Most transactions at present are done either in shops, via mail order or via the telephone. The Internet offers an alternative way of doing business, and as e-commerce increases the following social phenomena are likely to be observed.

(i) **Travel**

Rather than visiting shops and people can obtain what they want without leaving their desk. This should make shops and roads less crowded and more pleasant for those who still use them. In the long-term it may affect where people choose to live.

(ii) **Consumer choice**

A computer search for an item or service can be done in seconds, whereas it could take hours, days or weeks to find exactly what was wanted by more conventional means. Consumers are also not restricted to local providers: they can do business with any company in the world that has a website. On the one hand this increases choice for consumers, but on the other it may make the purchase decision more difficult, because there are more options.

(iii) **The 'size' of society**

Following on from point (ii), society itself becomes global. People do business in places and with organisations that they would never have considered or even known about before.

(iv) **Time management and quality of life**

Rather than being restricted to business hours people can obtain what they want 24 hours a day. This helps people to manage their time and do what they want to do at their own convenience.

(v) **Interaction**

Instead of dealing face-to-face or voice-to-voice with others, people interact with their computer. If human contact is valued, this makes the experience a poorer one. On the other hand it removes possible sources of conflict.

(vi) **Work opportunities**

There will be fewer opportunities for people to work in sales roles that involve direct contact with others, but greater opportunities to work in distribution and transport. In the long-term this could be a major change since both sectors employ large numbers of people.

Demand for people with web-site programming skills and computer graphics skills will increase.

Working practices

(i) **Marketing**

Companies will need to develop new means of promoting their wares through the medium of the Internet, as opposed to shop displays or motionless graphics. Web-sites can provide **sound and movement** and allow **interactivity**, so that the user can, say, drill down to obtain further information or watch a video of the product in use, or get a virtual reality experience of the product or service (a particularly attractive option for TEP plc).

For many companies this will involve a rethink of current promotional activity.

Companies will be able to **collect information** about their customers that they would not obtain by means of a conventional transactions, and this will allow them to tailor their products and services more closely to customers' requirements, and target new products and services at customers who are likely to be interested in them.

(ii) **Administration and security**

New **systems and procedures** will need to be set up to manage Internet transactions, and in time existing systems, such as sorting and distributing mail, will become less important.

Customer confidence needs to be gained in the **encryption methods** used to protect sensitive data such as credit card numbers.

There is a danger that **staff** will **download** files that damage their organisations' systems or waste disk space. A common management concern is that staff will waste time **surfing the net** instead of working. This is possibly rather insulting to the majority of working people, who have a sense of responsibility, but it is worth mentioning.

(iii) **Skills**

As mentioned the **mix of skills** required by organisations will change. There will be less need for staff with people skills, because there will be less direct interaction with the public. There will be more need for staff who can present information attractively and interestingly on computer screen. The distribution function of organisations that sell physical products will become more important.

58 KJ PLC: OFFICE SUPPLIES

Pass marks. To answer it well this question requires you to refer extensively to the information provided in the scenario, rather than relying upon book knowledge, and so it is an excellent opportunity to practise your high level application skills.

Examiner's comment. The Information within the question itself provided an outline for the structure of an answer. Specific areas that were omitted from most answers included:

- The lack of past transaction data, the lack of trend analysis for individual customers and the problems of producing the financial statements.
- The motivational impact of Alternative Two on the managers and the consequent effect on customer service.
- The need to provide upgrade paths for the future, and in particular the advantages of including Internet access in Alternative Two.

(a) **Comparison of the two new systems**

(i) **Alternative One**

(1) **Goal congruence**

This system offers a **centralised** structure with a **common database** storing information concerning **all** of the company's activities. This implies that all managers will have access to data about the activities of their colleagues, which ought to facilitate common understanding and goal congruence.

(2) **Customer service**

The system will enhance the service given to customers because **delivery** will be faster and instances of **non-availability** of stock will be reduced. These factors are ranked, respectively, first and second in importance by customers.

If **historical data** is important in maintaining good customer service, a **problem** with this alternative is that existing data will cease to be available after six months. Any **analysis of trends and sales patterns** needs to be carried out in this timescale and it may not be long enough to do the job fully. **New ideas** that ideally require reference to past data if they are to be developed will be deprived of this luxury.

(3) **Transaction Processing System**

The current system has received very **few complaints**, so there is no reason to suppose that a system provided by the same supplier would be any less effective.

The fact that the systems provided by this supplier are **not industry standard** may be problematic, however. Future developments, such as EDI links with customers and suppliers, may not possible because of incompatibility of systems. The supplier may in time move across to industry standards and cease to support its current offerings.

(ii) **Alternative Two**

(1) **Goal congruence**

Under this alternative each department maintains its own computer systems and information sharing is restricted. This allows for the possibility that systems could be **developed in divergent ways** in the future and may end up unable to talk to each other. It may mean that **sub-optimal decisions** are made on the basis of **inaccurate information** about the position in another department.

In this situation it is likely to be difficult to maintain goal congruence.

On the other hand this alternative does offer **better communication** facilities between employees (e-mail) which may help to enhance understanding of issues facing other departments.

(2) **Customer service**

Customers will be able to place orders by **e-mail** and over the **Internet.** The convenience of this means that it is something that customers are likely to demand more and more **in the future,** although the recent customer survey suggests that ease of ordering is one of the least important issues as far as customers are concerned at present. The IT strategy stresses that good service must be good service **from the point of view of the customer.**

KJ's **own branded products** are to be offered as first choice. However, again this is **little valued by customers,** being last in importance.

Speed of delivery, the most important single factor, will be **adversely affected.**

On the plus side with this alternative, **historical information** can be made available, and sophisticated **query tools** and this will be helpful on occasions in dealing with customers, and for developing new products and services more closely **tailored to individual customer needs.**

(3) **Transaction Processing System**

Each department will have its own system and managers will have full responsibility for running them. This may bring about **improvements to the functionality** of the system in some areas, via specialised applications that cannot be, or have not been, developed under the current system.

However, rather than being directly linked to each other systems will share and **transfer information** via an intranet. The intervention of a third party system may cause problems: for instance the indication is that the time taken to transfer information will increase.

Since IBM-compatible equipment is to be supplied it is likely that **compatibility with other systems** (for EDI links, say) will be possible and there should be no problems with future upgrades and continuing support, whether from this supplier or from another one.

Recommendation

Neither system perfectly meets the requirements of KJ plc. Perhaps the biggest drawback in the case of **Alternative One** is that the system is **not industry standard,** while **Alternative Two** will result in a **poorer service** (slower deliveries) being offered to customers.

It is recommended that the company seek **other alternatives** or go back to each supplier and ask whether the drawbacks can be eliminated.

The **IT strategy itself** needs to take account of the MD's recognition of the need to enhance the decision-making opportunities of managers. This conflicts somewhat with the desire to ensure goal congruence.

(b)

Pass marks. Ensure your answer to this part of the question focuses on the extent to which the two options will facilitate organisational change.

Examiner's comment. Good answers hinged on candidates understanding:

- The information requirements of different levels of management.
- That the authoritarian nature of the MD meant that normal management information requirements probably don't apply in this particular company.
- That the two alternatives would change not only the information being provided to management but also required the MD to change his management style for at least one alternative to be implemented effectively.

Most answers would be improved by:

- Providing a clearer structure for the answer;
- Focusing on the information needs of managers rather than on the attributes of the processing system itself;
- Additional consideration of the role of the MD and the aspirations of long-serving managers.

According to the scenario very **few complaints** have been received about the information supplied and on the face of it this suggests that the current system almost fully meets manager's requirements.

However, managers do not take a very active role in decision making at strategic and tactical levels, and so their information requirements are likely to be **fairly modest** at present.

There is a hint of **some dissatisfaction** with the system in that there have been requests to **modify** the system which have been refused by the MD.

Alternative One

Alternative One maintains the status quo. All staff will have access to the database, but the new system will merely provide the **same information as the current system**, so there is no improvement at all.

Historical information will soon cease to be available. Whether or not this impairs the information provided depends upon **how historical information is used** at present, for instance whether managers need to monitor trends such as **seasonal** stock requirements or seasonal volume of orders to be processed.

The system will be centralised, which may mean that it can be **more closely controlled** than the current system, possibly improving the **accuracy and consistency** of information available.

The only manager who will see an improvement in the information available is the Managing Director, who will have exclusive access to a **strategic planning module**. Strategic plans will most probably be formulated on a better-informed basis, and this could result in new information being available to enable other managers to **implement the plans.**

Alternative Two

Under this alternative managers have control over their own computer systems and in theory can therefore devise systems that will collect, and allow analysis of, **any information they require**. They will **need** improved information because they, rather than the MD, will have the responsibility to take all **tactical decisions** relating to their area of the business.

The information provided should therefore improve significantly, although of course this depends upon **how well they set up their own systems**, a task of which they have **not had previous experience** within KJ plc.

Information flows will improve because managers will also have **e-mail** and are likely to use it to exchange more information, more speedily with their colleagues in other departments than was previously the case.

Managers will presumably be amongst the employees who have **Internet** facilities, giving them a gateway to the vast information resources of the world wide web.

There will also be improved **data analysis tools** which will enable managers to get new, and hopefully revealing, views of data that they had not had before.

On the downside, it will be **more difficult to get access** to other departments' information, which will presumably be restricted to what each department chooses to post onto the intranet. The information posted **may not be in a readily-analysable format** for all departments.

Although **historical information** can be made available, this is subject to budget pressures, and some managers may be **reluctant to spend** in this area and so choose to go without information that they might ideally like to have.

(c) **Strategic and operational advantages of payment methods**

> **Pass marks.** Your answer should be clearly structured around the requirement to discuss the issues in terms of **strategic** and **operational** advantages.
>
> **Examiner's comment.** Candidates who take note of the requirement to show the benefits of each option to the company will have the chance of obtaining high marks; general answers which simply explain the finance options available will score less well.

(i) **Cash purchase**

From a **strategic** point of view cash purchase has the advantage that the organisation **owns** the asset and can do what it likes with it. For instance it can **modify it** in the light of changed strategy, or dispose of it and replace it at a time that fits in with **other corporate needs** and demands from other projects for cash investment. There is **no danger** that an asset that is essential to the running of the business will be **repossessed** if the company gets into financial difficulties.

Funding for the purchase can be from a variety of sources, depending on what is most advantageous from the point of view of the overall **cost of capital** of the company.

From an **operational** point of view cash purchase offers the flexibility to add small items of equipment from time to time, as required. **Day to day costs** such as maintenance costs can be better controlled, since the company can simply choose not to maintain the equipment if it so desires.

Greater **operational stability** may be achieved through this financing method, since the assets are likely to be kept for some time, users are not constantly expected to learn how to use the latest piece of equipment, and there is not a constant need to transfer data from an older machine.

(ii) **Operating lease**

Under a leasing arrangement the lessee uses the equipment for a defined period of time, for the payment of a fee to the lessor. It **remains the property of the lessor**, usually a specialist leasing company which has purchased the equipment from the manufacturer. An **operating lease** is a **rental** arrangement, usually for a short term.

Possible **strategic advantages** of this approach are that it does not involve the outlay of a large sum of money (which may not be available or may be needed for other corporate projects), up front. It offers **certainty**: the company knows exactly how much it will be expected to pay each month for the foreseeable future. It **avoids risking** a large commitment to a system that may turn out not to meet requirements, or may become obsolete due to technological developments.

Operational advantages are that **maintenance costs,** and the costs of rectifying faulty equipment, are generally **included** in the payment. **New equipment** can be included in the arrangement as required, so users can always have the **most up to date** model which, in some organisations, may be perceived as a particular benefit given the pace of change in IT.

(d) **Management motivation and responsibility**

> **Pass marks.** The CIMA suggested answer deals with part (i) of the question under the headings communication, participation, delegation, decision-making, planning.
>
> **Examiner's comment.** Candidates must show how a revised IT configuration can assist in the motivation of managers in the company. Answers that explain features of the new system in the context of the benefits that would be brought to managers tended to score well.

(i) **Improving motivation**

Alternative Two recognises the concerns of the majority of managers about the authoritarian approach of the MD.

Of particular concern is their lack of involvement in **higher-level decision making**. Alternative Two addresses this because it means that all of the tactical decisions (as well as operational decisions) necessary to run their departments will be made by them. A major cause of discontent is therefore removed.

In general the new system would give managers more **control over their own destiny**, and would offer them greater opportunities to **do their jobs well.**

Specifically, some ways in which the system may help are as follows.

(1) **Communication** throughout the organisation is likely to improve because of the introduction of e-mail. Improved communication not only has social benefits but also allows managers to see a bigger picture and understand how what they are doing contributes to the work of the organisation as a whole.

(2) The **intranet** offers managers the opportunity to **present** what their department does to others in the organisation **in a favourable light,** almost forcing them to think about their work in positive terms.

(3) The system offers a good deal of potential for learning **new skills,** both of a technical nature (eg using the database query tools) and in management terms (decision-making, setting up systems). It is therefore likely to be regarded by most as a **career-enhancing** development, improving job prospects both within and outside the company.

(4) It offers opportunities that have not been available before for **creativity.** The facility to generate **new views of internal information** is likely to stimulate **new solutions** to company problems and identify **customer**

needs that have not been recognised before and need to be met. The availability of information about other organisations via the **Internet** will show managers **what is going on in other organisations** and they will no doubt find ideas that can be adapted for the purposes of KJ plc.

(ii) **Encouraging managers to accept more responsibility**

A **minority of long-serving managers** have hitherto been quite satisfied to let the MD make most of the major decisions, and they are **unlikely to welcome** the extra management burden that Alternative Two places upon them.

The following steps may lead these managers to feel differently.

(1) **Communication.** Ensure by means of frequent formal and informal meetings, presentations and discussions that managers understand what is happening and why.

(2) **Gradual change**. Introduce change gradually for managers who are resistant to it. The MD is unlikely to object to retaining control over some departments in the short term.

(3) **Champions.** Many managers welcome the changes and they and their efforts can be used to demonstrate, by means of their actions, to managers who are less keen what benefits are to be had from the new system.

(4) **Training.** All managers are likely to need training, both of a technical nature so that they understand how the new system works, and of a management and personal nature (allocating resources, negotiation skills and so on).

(5) **Rewards.** Financial incentives or promotion may encourage managers to take a positive view of the changes, especially if they feel that they are being asked to take on extra work for no personal gain.

59 JHG: FINANCIAL SERVICES

> **Pass marks.** Use the SDLC as a framework for your answer, but **concentrate on the parts of the SDLC that are relevant** to the question requirement. Simply explaining the various stages of the SDLC will not gain marks – the relevant part of the theory must be identified and **applied** to the situation.
>
> **Examiner's comment.** The overall standard of answers was poor. This was disappointing given that there were plenty of pointers in the case to indicate why the project might fail. Most candidates would gain more marks by making more direct reference to the case study information, and explaining why these specific points could result in project failure.

(a) **Why the project may fail**

The System Development Life Cycle (SDLC) provides a framework for the development of information systems. JHG does not appear to be following best practice in some areas of the SDLC. As a consequence the likelihood of project failure is increased:

(i) **Planning. A lack of planning** is evident from the factors below.

- Implementing the new system **just prior to a busy period**. All information systems can be expected to experience some initial problems. It is sensible to implement the system during a quiet time, so the impact of any teething problems is minimised.

- Training materials and user guides are not expected to be available until three months **after implementation**! Some very costly errors could occur while staff 'learn on the job' for three months.
- The program **should be built around user requirements** yet user input is not being obtained until nine months after writing has commenced. By the time JHG obtains user input it is unlikely user requirements will be able to be built in to the system. A system that does not meet user requirements is likely to be either misused or by-passed.
- The **laws and financial regulations** of the 26 countries that JHG will operate in may **vary greatly**. The local tailoring required is therefore likely to be significant, and should not be expected to be completed in a few weeks.

(ii) The **Analysis** stage of the SDLC examines why current methods are used, what alternatives might achieve the same or better results, what restricts the effectiveness of the system and what performance criteria are required. JHG was formed in July 1998. The writing of the software to provide a standard service to 21,000 people in 26 countries was started only five months later. This **short amount of time** would not have enabled a detailed analysis process to be completed, and a viable system proposed.

(iii) **Design** is a technical phase which considers inputs, outputs, information flow, program design, file design and security.

- **Inputs and outputs**

  To establish what will go into, and come out of the system, an understanding of **day-to-day operations** is needed. This can only be provided by users. The lack of a detailed specification is not surprising given that user involvement has so far been non-existent. Building a system without establishing in detail what users require the system to produce is unlikely to produce a program that is as efficient and helpful as it needs to be. The system produced may hinder rather than help staff and clients.

- **Performance criteria**

  The only criteria mentioned are very general – 'employees will easily be able to share work' and 'to provide an enhanced service to JHG's international clients'. The new system seems to **ignore non-international clients**. This may be a valid strategy if clients that operate in more than one country is the only market JHG wishes to target. However, if JHG has a significant number of clients that do not operate in more than one country, the basic premise of the system is flawed.

- **Information flows**

  How the company proposes to **change information flows** to facilitate the change from 26 development centres to a centrally directed one has not been explained. There is no evidence of adequate system analysis taking place. The hardware and software requirements are scheduled to be addressed in July 1999, yet programming, which should not commence until the system design is finalised, commenced in December 1998.

- File design

  Each of the original businesses have their own systems. Transferring data efficiently and accurately from these **widely varying systems** (both manual and computerised) is vital if the project is to succeed.

Compatibility issues may arise during this process. Again the project timetable does not appear to have built in time for this task to be performed methodically.

(iv) **Implementation.** This stage carries development through from design to operations. For JHG it involves the writing of software, program testing, file conversion, the acquisition and installation of hardware and finally 'going live'. JHG seems to have **concentrated almost exclusively on this stage,** with writing of the software assuming top priority before any analysis and design procedures have been carried out. This means a system is being built that is unlikely to prove useful.

Further faults are apparent in the way the software is being written. The 24-hour working of the three development centres leaves **no time to test** what has been written, and **prevents overall responsibility** for the software being taken by a single centre. Also unless the development documentation is first class, control over the software will not be achieved and time scales will slip even further.

The neglect of the SDLC design stages outlined above has led to the project following a path that seems to have been **pre-determined by senior Board members** from the international committee. Board members can not be expected to have sufficient knowledge of day-to-day operations to take a leading role in this project. Planning and analysis seems to have been sacrificed for speed. The likelihood is a project that maybe comes in on or close to time (to an unrealistic timetable), but fails to achieve its objectives.

(b) **Proposed screen layout**

> **Pass marks.** A useful approach is to briefly explain the concept of the HIP and then **apply** the concept to the screen design itself. Be sure to review the whole screen – there are sufficient issues score well.

A **Human Information Processor** (HIP) is simply a person who processes information. An understanding of how humans process information is useful when designing the **Human Computer Interface** (HCI). The interface between human and computer is probably the most critical component of an information system. The interface is the part of the system which is visible to the user, and is what the user depends on to use the system efficiently. (For example screen layout and design, dialogue boxes etc.)

People use their senses to take in information and then process this in accordance with established patterns. As processes are learned the time taken to complete tasks improves. In the context of a HCI this means that **consistency of design** across different programs will enable users to become proficient users more quickly.

Applying these principles to the JHG screen layout shows the following **deficiencies.**

- The size of the 'information area' is too small and irregularly shaped. The information area is the main area of interest to the user – other features on the screen should support the information area not 'swamp' it. The danger is that users miss important information, as it is not displayed prominently or clearly enough.
- The arrows at the left-hand side and on the bottom of the screen are not standard icons. If these icons have an essential purpose and are to remain, they should be accompanied by a **label** stating their purpose. They are also far **too large** causing an unnecessary distraction.

- Graphical User Interfaces usually position icons on the top or bottom of the screen and the maximise and minimise buttons are traditionally located in the top right corner. Placing the icons on the right of the screen, and the buttons at the top centre, will **waste user time** as they have learned to look for these features in their traditional locations.

Other non-standard features that would **confuse the HIP** are:

- There is no vertical scroll bar.
- The bar with 'JGH Information systems' on serves no purpose, wastes space and prevents the menu items occupying their expected place at the top of the screen.
- The use of flowers is distracting and unnecessary. HIPs require a clear unrestricted view to process information efficiently.
- It is likely that within the 26 countries JHG operates in many are non-English speaking. Expecting HIPs in these countries to use this English screen would be completely impractical.

The purpose of the buttons on the bottom right hand corner is also unclear. eg what does 'Office' mean, what other functions are available by selecting the 'More' option and could these options be placed on this screen if the flowers and arrows were either smaller or removed altogether? The clearer the information presented to the user is, the more efficiently the HIP will perform. In summary, the proposed screen layout looks like it was designed more to satisfy the programmers sense of creativity rather than the requirements of the HIP.

(c) **Information needs of local managers**

> **Examiner's comment.** Many answers appeared to be inadequately planned and focussed on characteristics of information or the type of information that can be obtained from a MIS. Only a small minority of answers considered the possible benefits of using international software. Students that produced a balanced answer scored highest.

JHG may be pursuing an unrealistic and unhelpful IT strategy by attempting to implement a common software system across all 26 countries it operates in. Many of these countries will have their **own local financial regulations**. Local adjustments to the software could therefore be expected to be significant – resulting in software that by necessity is not the same company-wide.

A worse scenario is that the required local modifications are not made, meaning **manual adjustments** are required to output. This would lead to frustration and staff may avoid the new system altogether, and go back to using their old system that satisfied their local needs.

Local managers will also require **management information** that may be different than that required in other countries. The new system would require a **flexible** report writer that would enable local manager to tailor management information to meet their needs. The source data that would feed such reports must first be captured, which again may require local customisation of the software.

Another concern is that as the environment JHG local managers work in changes their information **needs will change too**. With the proposed amalgamation and rationalisation of system development departments the local expertise may not exist to generate new reports or queries. Urgent requests to a **centralised systems department** may find that **staff are not available** due to time zone or national holiday differences. Language and cultural differences could also prove a barrier to resolving problems.

An international system could lead to the incorrect application of local regulations and consequently could lead to **wrong decisions** being made. There is also the need to consider the compatibility with other local systems. Cultural and language issues would require local modification of the HCI.

If an international system was viable for JHG it would provide **some advantages.**

An international system could be expected to give local managers **access to world-wide information** on subjects such as interest rates, inflation, exchange rates and financial and commodity markets. This would enable local managers to provide a **more informed service** to their international clients. A standardised international system would facilitate the sharing of knowledge across the organisation.

A single system should provide assurance to clients that their **global interests** are being taken care of even in the remotest of branches, and would enable JHG to promote itself as a truly global organisation.

The implementation of international software does have some advantages but the amount of local modification required is likely to result in a non-standardised package. The best option may be to introduce standard procedures and standards that must be followed by all offices in the use and development of information systems, but let local managers operate with a certain degree of autonomy rather than imposing an impractical system on them.

(d) **Controls over transferring client data**

> **Examiner's comment.** Most candidates mentioned the main areas of risk in data transfer. The answers that progressed and explained some relevant controls achieved a good pass standard.

Transferring client information between its branches worldwide will require JHG to send data over a **telecommunications link**. This is likely to be either an international telephone line using appropriate hardware (eg modems), or via dedicated ISDN lines. (The ISDN link would be more expensive to set up). When transmitting data over a network or telecommunications link JHG exposes itself to the **risks** outlined below.

- **Viruses** on a single computer will have the opportunity to spread through all JHG offices.
- Accidental **data loss or damage** through poor procedures. For example, a file may be transferred from one location to another overwriting a file with the same name.
- People with a grudge such as disaffected employees or competitors will have increased opportunities to gain unauthorised access through '**hacking**'. They may then view or copy confidential information or do deliberate damage to data.
- Information transmitted from one location to another may be **intercepted** or **damaged.**
- The communications link itself may break down or **distort** data Transmitted data is only as secure as the medium through which it is transmitted.
- Infringement of **data protection legislation.** Data protection legislation varies across international boundaries. Data that is legally held in one location may be transferred to a location where it is illegal – leaving JHG open to embarrassment and, most likely, a fine.

To minimise these risks JHG would need to implement appropriate **controls**. These should include the following measures.

- To prevent or at least detect the possibility of accidental distortion or data loss during transmission, an appropriate **communications protocol** should be implemented eg TCP (Transmissions Control Protocol).
- To protect against 'eavesdropping' or deliberate interception of data during transmission, data should be '**encrypted**' (scrambled). Encryption is the only secure way to prevent eavesdropping (since eavesdroppers can get round password controls, by tapping the line or by experimenting with various likely passwords).
- JHG systems should have **firewalls** at each location (which disable part of the telecommunications technology) to prevent unwelcome intrusions into company systems, but a determined hacker may well be able to bypass even these.
- **Authentication** techniques could be used to ensure incoming data has come from an authorised sender. Authentication involves adding an extra field to a record, with the contents of this field derived from the remainder of the record by applying an algorithm that has previously been agreed between the senders and recipients.
- JHG should implement automated **logging** of all attempted violations of security.
- To control staff members or others with **physical access** to JHG premises only certain terminals should be capable of receiving or copying confidential data, by user-identification procedures (different users have different levels of access), and password procedures. Access control logs should be maintained, recording unauthorised attempts to gain access.
- To reduce the risk of infringing local data protection information local managers should ensure that **local requirements are known**, and that JHG meets them.
- JHG must implement procedures that provide the ability **to recover from mishaps** however they occur. Back-up and correction mechanisms should enable 'roll backs' and the re-creation of correct information. Contingency plans (including hardware) should be made at all locations that could be used to provide backup in the event of a complete system failure.

Stage 4 **MOCK EXAM**

Paper 15 *November 1999*

Information Management

IFM

INSTRUCTIONS TO CANDIDATES

You are allowed three hours to answer this question paper.
Answer the ONE question in section A. *Answer TWO questions ONLY from section B.*

DO NOT OPEN THIS PAPER UNTIL YOU ARE READY TO START UNDER EXAMINATION CONDITIONS

SECTION A - 60 MARKS

ANSWER THIS QUESTION

1

Brief organisation history

LT plc provides telecommunication services ranging from residential telephones to large corporate Intranets. The organisation has 20 million customers and a turnover of several billion pounds. Most customers are satisfied with the level of service received. The main area of concern for customers has been that pricing structures are not always clear and appear to favour individual corporate customer needs rather than residential markets.

Over the past few years, LT plc has built up an unparalleled analogue telephone communication network which it owns and maintains itself. Most other telecommunication companies, including new entrants into the market, lease or rent at least part of their communication network. LT plc has been able to offer more reliable services and fault-fixing times than any other company.

In recent years, LT plc has also been the dominant market leader with over 90% market share in all of its business sectors. However, deregulation of the telecommunications market from 1 January 1998 has meant that its monopolistic power has been significantly weakened in many areas. The Board of LT plc has tended to see this as a threat rather than an opportunity. The view arose partly from a fear of losing market share and partly because information systems were internally focused and so could not provide the necessary competitor information.

One way the Board of LT plc sought to maintain market share has been by forming strategic alliances with similar telecommunications companies in other countries. This strategy has been largely successful, with profits being maintained from these international ventures. However, as a result of IT strategy and information systems being focused on overseas markets, very little attention was paid to the domestic competition or investment during 1998 or the earlier part of 1999.

Other competitive challenges

LT plc is now facing intense competition in its home market from a small number of new companies which will be able to offer new services including:

- digital television
- Internet on TV, and
- films on demand

All these services are being provided over new fibre-optic telephone lines which LT plc has not invested in significantly. However, no one organisation currently offers all services as a comprehensive package and LT plc currently is considering providing this service.

LT plc is also finding it difficult to obtain information on the home market. The development of its Executive Information Systems (EIS) has followed the strategy of the company, providing summary and detailed information about overseas competitors. This has had the effect of losing focus on the home market.

LT plc is facing competitive challenges not only from additional services that are being offered, but also from a significant amount of cross-selling of services. For example a competing company recently offered a telephone service including access to the five main satellite television channels for the price of LT plc's domestic telephone service. LT plc's market share is now being eroded in all areas partly because the company cannot match the offers on price terms and partly because of the time taken to make strategic decisions to offer competing services.

Integrated digital service

In the near future it is expected that telecommunications companies will be able to provide a fully integrated service of traditional telephone, digital cable TV, Internet access and home shopping. This service should be available by 2001. The system effectively means that consumers, in the domestic and overseas markets, could order their shopping, browse the Internet, view films on demand and make telephone calls, possibly with integrated video, from their living room.

LT plc's response to the competitive challenge

In an attempt to provide more timely decisions and meet the expected demand for new services, in August 1999 the Board of LT plc set up four autonomous business units within the organisation.

Each unit was to focus on a specific market such as large corporate organisations, domestic users etc. Each unit was to report back to the Board by December 1999 with an indication of the problems faced by that unit and recommendations for resolving those problems. Early indications are that there are common problems facing all units. These problems include:

- A lack of information on how to set prices for new services.
- Lack of understanding on how to set the existing IT system to stop the fall in market share.
- Lack of available capacity in the existing IT infrastructure (bandwidth) to provide enhanced services to domestic customers.
- Lack of key critical success factors for each business unit.
- Lack of understanding on the social and economic impact of the enhanced services on society.

The Board of LT plc is starting to consider these issues and has requested more information.

REQUIREMENTS:

(a) Explain the sources of information that can be used to assist in the setting of prices for the future integrated digital service. Show why each source of information is required by LT plc. **18 Marks**

(b) Discuss the possible effects that an Integrated Digital Service, as outlined in the scenario, could have on employment and society. **16 Marks**

(c) Discuss the problems that LT plc is facing because its systems are not sufficiently supporting the business strategy of re-focusing onto the home market. Describe the actions that can be taken to overcome these problems. **14 Marks**

(d) Explain what type of information an EIS could provide and show how this would improve decision making for the Board of LT plc. **12 Marks**

Total Marks = 60

SECTION B - 40 MARKS

ANSWER *TWO* QUESTIONS ONLY - 20 MARKS EACH

2

CC plc is a company employing 2,560 staff in 20 different offices within one country. The company offers a wide range of specialist consultancy advice to the building and construction industry. This includes advice on materials to be used, relevant legislation (including planning applications) and appropriate sources of finance.

The information to meet client requirements is held within each office of the company. Although most clients are serviced by a single office, a lot of the information used is duplicated between the different offices. This is not surprising given that legislation and other standard information such as details of materials used are the same for the whole country.

In the past there has been no attempt to share data because of the cost of transferring information and the lack of trust on the part of staff in other offices. Some senior managers tend to keep part of client data confidential to themselves.

The company has recently provided all employees with e-mail for communication within CC plc and to clients. Software with internet access is also available so that staff can obtain undated planning information from appropriate websites. The hardware in the company is quite old and only just meets the minimum specification for these purposes.

The Marketing Director has suggested that an Intranet should be established in the company so that common information can be shared rather than each office maintaining its own data. This suggestion is meeting with come resistance from all grades of staff.

REQUIREMENTS:

(a) Explain the objectives of an Intranet and show how the provision of an intranet within CC plc should result in better provision of information **8 Marks**

(b) Comment on the organisational and human reasons why information may not become more widely available in CC plc, and suggest methods for overcoming these problems. **14 marks**

Total Marks = 20

3

The directors of DS are not satisfied with the GDC Ltd facilities management company which was contracted two years ago to run the IT system of the company. At that time, the existing in-house IT development and support department was disbanded and all control of IT systems handed over to GDC Ltd. The appointment of GDC Ltd was relatively rushed and although an outline contract was agreed, no detailed Service Level Agreement was produced

Over the last few weeks the number of complaints received from staff regarding the service has been increasing and the provision of essential management reports has not been particularly timely.

A recent exchange of correspondence with GDC Ltd failed to resolve the matter. Staff at GDC Ltd recognised the fall in standards of service, but insisted that it has met its contractual obligations. DS's lawyers have confirmed the GDC Ltd is correct.

Key features of DS's contract wit the GDC Ltd facilities management company:

> The contract can be terminated by either party with three months' notice
>
> GDC Ltd will provide IT services for DS, the services to include:
>
> - Purchase of all hardware and software
> - Repair and maintenance of all IT equipment
> - Help desk and other support services for users
> - Writing and maintenance of in-house software
> - Provision of management information
>
> Price charged to be renegotiated each year but any increase must not exceed inflation, plus 10%.

REQUIREMENTS:

(a) Explain, from the point of view of DS, why it might have received poor service from GDC Ltd, even though GDC Ltd has met the requirements of the contract. **12 Marks**

(b) Explain the courses of action now available to DS relating to the provision of IT services. Comment on the problems involved in each course of action. **8 Marks**

Total Marks = 20

4

LMC plc provides advice to a wide range of clients. This advice is based on the internal and external information systems maintained by LMC plc.

As a newly-appointed management accountant at LMC plc, you have been reviewing the information produced by the different systems in the company.

A first evaluation shows that the information produced from the older systems, including the EIS, is incomplete at best. However, more recent systems including Internet monitoring produce a considerable amount of information.

The directors are always interested in the actions of competitors. LMC plc has a 24-hour on-line Internet link which monitors over 100 different websites which are either maintained by competitors or provide information maintained by specialist companies. Any changes in the sites are recorded and reviewed by analysts on a daily basis.

REQUIREMENT:

(a) Explain how the analysts can check whether the information obtained from the monitored websites is accurate. **8 Marks**

(b) The directors have been concerned that the 24-hour on-line web monitoring mentioned above is expensive to maintain.

REQUIREMENT:

Explain how you, the management accountant for LMC plc, can determine the costs and benefits of information produced form the web monitoring activities. **12 Marks**

Total Marks = 20

SUGGESTED ANSWERS

DO NOT TURN THIS PAGE UNTIL YOU HAVE COMPLETED THE MOCK EXAM

The Examiner of IFM offers to future candidates and to lecturers the following background and guidance on the questions included in this examination paper.

Section A - compulsory

Question 1

Question 1 investigates the current state of the telecommunications industry. While the concept of obtaining both internal and external information will be familiar to candidates, the question holds a complication in that the service will be provided in the future.

Section B - two questions from three

Question 2

This question demonstrates the forward-looking nature of the IFM paper by allowing candidates to utilise their knowledge of Intranets. The question examines the 'power and privacy' area of the syllabus – an area somewhat neglected in previous examinations.

Question 3

Question 3 uses the common scenario where the IT function has been outsourced, and things have not gone to plan.

Question 4

This question focuses on the role of the Management Accountant in determining the use and value of information. Candidates are required to show how the cost and benefits of one information source could be determined.

1

(a)

> **Pass marks.** You may find it convenient to split your answer into internal and external sources. The concept of obtaining information from a wide range of sources should be familiar to you. Ensure you chose sources appropriate to the scenario.

To assist in the setting of prices for the future Integrated Digital Service LT plc should gather and analyse information from both **internal** and **external** sources.

Internal sources

(i) **Executive Information System (EIS)**

It is stated in the scenario that LT plc's EIS contains 'summary and detailed information about overseas competitors'. It is probable that at least one overseas competitor is either already providing or has plans to provide a similar integrated digital service.

Although differences in local market conditions would have to be taken into account, the overseas competitor information would help LT plc establish a competitive price. For example it may be possible to establish the estimated cost of providing the service to each subscriber - vital pricing information.

(ii) **Other accounting information**

Other information systems have been internally focused. It is likely therefore that, even though LT plc is new to digital communications, costing data is available on at least some of the individual services that will make up the integrated service. This information should help establish the cost of providing the integrated service. When cross-referenced with other information (such as the number of subscribers expected over the next ten years) a 'break-even' price may be established.

(iii) **LT plc's strategic plan**

Any price setting exercise will need to consider the overall strategy of LT plc. What type of 'image' does LT plc wish to portray – and would this fit best with a high quality service at a premium price, or with a lower level of service and budget pricing.

The internal information gathered will help ensure LT plc sets a price that is sustainable given expected cost levels, is consistent with overall organisation strategy and maximises returns.

External sources

External sources of information that would assist in the setting of prices for the integrated service would include:

(i) **Economic information**

Sources of economic predictions include the government, newspapers and specialist economic agencies and publications. The economic outlook in LT's country would influence the number of customers that would subscribe to the service and the price potential customers would be prepared to pay. Key indicators would include predicted interest rate, inflation and unemployment levels.

(ii) **Market research**

Some market research should be carried out to establish an expected take-up rate of the new service. The number of customers expected will impact significantly on price setting and profitability. The research should include questions that establish consumer pricing expectations for such a service.

(iii) **Competitors**

LT plc is facing intense competition from companies offering very similar services. Price will therefore be a major consideration of consumers when choosing (or changing) supplier. LT plc will be unable to attract a significant number of subscribers to its service if prices are set significantly higher than those of competitors.

As the integrated service will include a range of services, prices of other integrated service providers as well as telephone companies, Internet Service Providers and pay television companies will all need to be considered.

The external information gathered will help ensure LT plc does not set a price significantly higher than competitors. Economic conditions will also give an indication of what price the market could be expected to bear, while interest rates and inflation expectations will influence the cost of investing in new equipment – which would in turn affect pricing decisions.

(b)

> **Pass marks.** If you are struggling, apply (and adapt) knowledge from the effects of similar technological changes such as television or home computers.

An integrated telephone, digital cable television, Internet and home shopping service has the potential to impact on employment and society. The extent of any impact will depend on the popularity of the service.

The **effects on employment** would include those discussed below.

Redundancies at traditional telephone companies. Companies that provide solely telephone services are likely to experience a reduction in demand as consumers are attracted to integrated services. This would cause a fall in profitability, which may lead to redundancies. These companies are likely to either diversify or go out of business.

Reduction in 'high street' retail staff. The number of website and home shopping transactions will increase, causing a reduction in demand in traditional shopping outlets, and a reduction in the number of staff required. However, this is likely to be at least partially offset by an **increased need for distribution staff** - processing orders received through digital channels.

Increased opportunities in all areas of television. As cable television expands, the number of 'small' cable television companies increase. These stations will require staff.

Increased **demand for IT literate staff.** For example, marketing staff are likely to need some **knowledge of websites,** as the importance of web-based information and transactions increases.

More opportunity for **homeworking/teleworking.** As the number of people with access to the Internet increases, organisations may consider employees working from home - particularly for 'screen-based' tasks.

'**Society**' describes the habits and customs of a group of people and the way they organise what they do. The integrated service could have the following **effects on society**.

Reduction in shopping journeys undertaken. If more people obtain the goods and services they require without leaving their home, this should reduce the number of shopping trips. This should benefit society as a whole as pressure on public transport and total car exhaust emissions should both be reduced.

Increased consumer choice. Consumers with Internet and/or digital home shopping access are able to source goods and services from all over the world. This leads to a truly **global society** in which people make purchases, send e-mails and have traditional phone conversations with people and organisations from all around the globe.

The growth of a 24 hour society. People will be able to place orders and enjoy on-line leisure pursuits 24 hours a day. This helps people to manage their time and do what they want to do at their own convenience.

Reduced human contact. Instead of dealing face-to-face with others, people will increasingly interact with their PC or television screen and keypad.

The amount of information available to a large percentage of the population will increase significantly. People may experience **information overload** when making a previously simple decision such as 'what shall I watch on television tonight.' At the same time the **value placed on information and knowledge** will increase.

(c)

> **Pass marks.** The importance of systems adapting to support current corporate structure and goals is a regularly examined theme. Again, you will score well if you apply the knowledge you have to the situation LT plc is facing.

The systems at LT plc have not been adapted in line with the re-focus on the home market, resulting in a mismatch between current strategy and the systems used. This has led to a number of **problems.**

Information required to make informed decisions about the domestic market is not readily available. Time and effort has to be spent gathering and analysing this information in an ad-hoc manner. The end result is that decisions are taking too long to me made. Not only is decision making slow, but the ad-hoc nature of the information they are based on increases the risk of making a bad decision. This could erode market share and profitability, and damage consumer perceptions of LT plc.

There is confusion on how to set prices for the new service. Price is likely to be key in the fight for market share, and in profitability. Information regarding the cost to LT plc of providing the service, and about competitors pricing polices is vital to the development of a realistic pricing strategy.

LT plc it is taking too long to react to competitor initiatives. This is causing an erosion of market share is being eroded because of the time it is taking to react to competitor initiatives. There is a lack of understanding on how to stop this fall. This problem must be addressed immediately. The customers leaving LT plc are unlikely to return in the short to medium term. New customers will also be hard to attract, as unsatisfied customers will harm LT plc's reputation.

There is insufficient bandwidth available to domestic customers. This is a major factor in the loss of market share and a major barrier to the growth of the integrated service. Customers will not tolerate 'slow' data transmission or being unable to access the services they want because of overloading.

To address these problems LT plc should take the following actions.

Key targets need to be identified that must be achieved if the re-focus on the domestic market is to prove successful. (ie **critical success factors.**) Systems need to be developed that monitor and report the status of these factors, and staff need to be trained so they are able to perform tasks to the required standard.

LT plc therefore needs to implement **an EIS that provides information that supports decision-making in the domestic market.** This EIS should include competitor intelligence showing how IT is being exploited in the home market. Results of market research relating to domestic market consumer perceptions and expectations should also be available within the EIS.

To **stop the fall in market share,** either **significant investment** in hardware or the **purchase of additional bandwidth** from an outside source, will be required to improve the service available to current and future customers. An **aggressive pricing policy** may also be needed to re-establish LT plc in the domestic market.

The detailed data that is held on overseas competitors should be analysed to see if any have faced **similar situations**. If they have, lessons may be able to be learnt from their experience. **Data mining** tools may be useful in analysing the data to reveal previously hidden relationships.

(d)

> **Pass marks.** Do not simply explain the type of information the EIS would provide - you must explain clearly how this information would improve decision making.

An Executive Information System (EIS) should provide senior executives and the Board of LT plc with **easy access to high-level summarised data,** obtained from internal and external sources.

At the heart of LT plc's EIS will be a **corporate model** containing information such as the LT plc corporate structure, critical success factors etc. The model will also contain rules (developed in consultation with the Board and senior executives) as to how the information should be **presented and aggregated.**

The EIS will **summarise information** from all LT plc's transaction systems, with the ability to '**drill-down**' to view underlying data in greater detail. The Board will therefore be able to **select and view** information relating to a single business unit such as telephone services, a combination of units, information for geographic regions or for the organisation as a whole.

Whenever possible, **competitor data** should be gathered and incorporated into the EIS. For example the Board of LT plc should be able to compare the (estimated) profitability of a competitors integrated service against services provided individually. When analysed against competitors pricing information, LT should be able to make **more informed pricing decisions.**

Data manipulation facilities should enable comparison with budget, prior year data, other business units, competitors and trend analysis. These features should give the Board a **clearer picture of the environment, allowing more informed decision-making.**

For example, the EIS could include market share data for LT plc and competitors, and show when LT plc's market share falls or rises above predetermined limits. The board could then use the data manipulation facilities to cross-reference this information with pricing and marketing expenditure data. Over time a greater understanding will be gained of the **relationship between different variables** affecting the market, **reducing uncertainty in decision making.**

By highlighting results outside pre-determined limits the EIS **focuses management attention where it is most required.** The EIS information is initially screen-based, with printouts only for matters requiring further investigation. This will **prevent information overload** and **improve decision-making.**

2

(a)

> **Pass marks.** This question demonstrates the Examiner's commitment to including questions on new technology where appropriate. If you have revised the Intranet material from the BPP Study Text, you should find this question reasonably straightforward.

An **intranet** uses software and other technology originally developed for the Internet on internal company networks. An intranet comprises an **organisation-wide web** of internal documents that is familiar, easy to use and comparatively inexpensive. Each employee has a **browser** enabling him or her to view information held on a server computer and may offer access to the Internet.

The main objective of an intranet is to **provide easy access to information** that helps people perform their jobs more efficiently. Many roles require increased access to knowledge and information. An intranet is a way of making this knowledge readily available.

Other objectives are outlined below.

To encourage the use of reference documents. Documents on-line are more likely to be used than those stored on shelves, especially if the document is bulky (for instance procedure manuals).

To create a sense of organisational unity. An intranet 'pulls together' in a co-ordinated fashion information from disparate parts of an organisation. It may be the only visible way some parts of a large organisation are linked.

The provision of an Intranet within CC plc should result in **better provision of information** by:

Ensuring consistency in information held and provided to clients. The intranet will enable one set of data to be held and accessed by all 20 offices.

Providing easy access to a larger pool of data. Information that managers previously 'kept to themselves' will be available to others.

The intranet-Internet link will ensure the most up-to-date planning information is available. It would be useful to develop an intranet page complied from appropriate websites. (This must be kept up to date.)

(b)

Even after an intranet and e-mail have been implemented at CC plc organisational and human reasons will hinder the process of making information more widely available. Steps need to be taken to overcome these barriers to information sharing.

Human reasons that will need to be overcome include the following.

Information is only available if people know how to find it. The people at CC plc who could use the information held on the intranet must be told that the information is available, and trained so that they are confident enough to access it.

Efficient **communication** (including a company-wide e-mail explaining the intranet) and staff **training programmes** demonstrating intranet use will help overcome this problem.

Some staff will not choose to share information or knowledge. People may protect the information they have to boost their own performance relative to their colleagues. A culture change within CC plc is required before staff will be willing to share knowledge and information so that the organisation as a whole can benefit.

To tackle this problem techniques and processes to **encourage the sharing of information** could be included as part of a communication and knowledge management programme.

Organisational reasons that will need to be overcome include the following.

The **hardware** used by CC plc is too old to support the new communication tools. This is likely to lead to user frustration with slow response times and problems gaining access to various systems. Unless the systems provided are efficient, users will abandon them.

To overcome this problem CC plc will need to make a **significant investment** in new hardware.

Work practices that do not involve or encourage the sharing of information have become established. A significant number of CC plc staff are likely to have a building and construction background, and not be enthusiastic towards computing developments. These staff may see these new communication tools as an unnecessary waste of resources by IT staff who do not have a feel for the business.

This problem could be minimised by **involving staff** in the design of systems from the outset. Staff should be asked what information would make them more efficient. A tool that helps them do their job better will be welcomed by even the most sceptical.

Staff training programmes and a **user friendly human-computer interface** should also reduce staff resistance.

3

(a)

> **Pass marks.** The absence of a Service Level Agreement is obviously a major factor in the poor service being experienced. Remember in Part (b) that there are always some disadvantages in terminating a relationship with a supplier – even when the supplier is performing poorly.

GDC Ltd appears to have met its legal obligations even though the level of service it has provided to DS has been poor. There are a number of reasons for this.

DS rushed the appointment of GDC and did not insist on a **detailed Service Level Agreement (SLA)**. The contract does not specify the level of service that GDC will provide.

For example, GDC is obligated to provide 'management information', but there is no detailed definition of what this information will entail, and no deadline for the provision of the information. (eg '...within 5 working days of month-end').

DS handed **complete control** of its IT systems to GDC Ltd. The absence of IT expertise within DS puts it at a **disadvantage** when arguing its case with GDC Ltd.

For example, GDC could spend significant amounts of DS money on sub-standard hardware and software. DC Ltd would **not have the expertise to question** or challenge this purchase, resulting in poor use of DS funds and a poor level of service. However, even when purchasing sub-standard hardware GDC would not have breached the requirement of the contract to 'purchase all hardware and software'.

GDC Ltd is also responsible for the writing and maintenance of in-house software. **Unless GDC has a detailed understanding of DS the software written may not be suitable**. As GDC receives a set annual fee, it may be tempted to produce software as quickly and cheaply as possible. As the contract has no mention of software standards, GDC would be meeting its legal obligations.

Another reason that could be contributing DS receiving poor service is that **the agreement is now two years old**. Changes could have taken place inside DS within the past two years that an outside organisation such as GDC does not understand. The nature of management information required now may be different to that required two years ago.

Service levels could also be suffering because **GDC has no financial incentive to provide a good standard of service.** GDC Ltd has the right under the contract to increase the annual fee, above the rate of inflation, without any consultation and with no reference to the satisfaction of DS.

(b)

The courses of action now available to DS relating to the provision if IT services, and the problems involved in each, are outlined below.

- **DS could carry on under the existing agreement**, protecting the knowledge that GDC has built up on the provision of IT services to DS, **but applying 'moral' pressure** (in the form of complaints and meetings with GDC management) to obtain a better level of service. The main problem with this course of action is that the level of service may not improve at all.
- DS could terminate the existing contract by giving three months notice, and **negotiate a new contract with GDC with a well-defined SLA**. Possible problems include the fact that GDC may not wish to negotiate a new SLA leaving DS with no IT services, or GDC may agree a new SLA but still provide the old shoddy service.
- DS could terminate the existing contract by giving three months notice and **look for a new supplier** of all its IT services. However, this would mean 'starting-from scratch'. Even an efficient provider would take time to develop a feel for the requirements at DS, and build up their expertise. There is no guarantee the new service provider would be better than GDC, although a more detailed SLA would help.
- **DS could establish its own in-house IT team**, probably using a combination of contractors and 'permanent' employees. The main problems with this option are the time and cost of finding setting up the team and that the team would be 'starting from scratch' and may only receive limited help from GDC during the hand-over.

4

(a)

> **Pass marks.** Use your initiative in Part (a) – think about how you would go about checking information viewed on a website. This question focuses on the role of the Management Accountant in determining the use and value of information, rather than the preparation of information.

The World Wide Web enables a wide range of people and organisations to publish material on Internet websites. Checking the validity and accuracy of information is therefore vital.

The analysts at LMC plc could **check the accuracy** of the information obtained from the monitored websites in the ways outlined below.

Analysts should be encouraged to use their 'common sense' and check any information they feel may be suspect. Some information is likely to be able to be verified by **staff** within LMC plc. Analysts should have a list of personnel they are able to contact on various subjects.

Some information will require checking through **an outside alternative source**. The source(s) used as a check should be as close to the origin of the information as possible. Other information agencies should be used with care in this capacity, as they are likely to obtain their data by similar methods, and could have reproduced the suspect data. Depending on the nature of the information, and the contacts of the analysts, experts such as academics and media commentators could be consulted. Websites from respected operators such as The Financial Times could be used to check business information.

The **credentials of the site-holder** may need to be re-established as the true 'owner' of the site could change without notice. Research should be undertaken to establish who 'is behind' sites. **Phone contact** could be made with the site holder, and company background information requested. Sites from very small organisations with no industry credentials would require a detailed background investigation.

The official sites of large reputable organisations would require a lower level of scrutiny. Sites may have **connections to organisations that encourage a particular bias** that is not apparent from the site name. Companies House records and Industry or Trade associations may be able to provide relevant background information relating to organisation ownership.

If the Internet monitoring is being conducted initially by software ('Net agents'), spot checks should be carried out to ensure the **monitoring software is reporting changes correctly**. Analysts should save a monitored page to disk on two consecutive days, and check the two stored pages against the changes reported by the software.

(b)

LMC plc will incur costs producing the information from the monitoring activities.

To enable all the costs incurred by the Internet monitoring activity to be tracked the process should be allocated a unique code on LMC plc's internal systems, for example WEBMON (assuming a six character alphanumeric coding system). All costs incurred to produce this information should be processed with this cost code.

The main costs would be:

- The wages and other employment costs of the **analysts** employed to check the information.
- The cost of the monitoring **software** is likely to have been capitalised, so the amortisation expense should be allocated to the WEBMON code.
- **Telephone and Internet connection costs**, and the depreciation charge from related hardware.

Costs relating to the provision of the service will be incurred on the payroll, accounts payable and fixed asset systems of LMC. However, as long as the correct WEBMON code has been used on all systems, the Management Accountant will be able to **produce a report** from the accounting system showing the **total cost of providing the service** over a given period of time.

These costs need to be considered in relation to **other methods** of obtaining similar information, and against the cost of not having this information at all.

The **benefits of the information produced** are harder to determine.

The purpose of obtaining the information that results from the web monitoring activity is to **enable better advice to be provided to clients**. Clients pay fees, so the ultimate benefit of the activity is to **bring in additional revenue**, or to **increase the margin** obtained on revenues earned.

Clients pay fees for advice, but the advice will be the result of many sources of information. It is unlikely that a coding system could be used to identify and track revenue earned directly as a result of web monitoring. So, to establish the financial benefits of the information an exercise would have to be undertaken to establish the proportion of client advice that can be directly attributed to information gained from web-monitoring. A reasonable estimate should then be able to be made as to **how much revenue can be attributed to the activity**.

To show the profitability of the web-monitoring activity the management accountant could construct a spreadsheet model showing the income earned from information produced from web monitoring (and the assumptions made), together with the costs incurred producing the information.

Other benefits may even more difficult to measure. For example some clients may pay only a small proportion of their fee for information obtained from web-monitoring, but may cease to do business with LMC completely if this information was not available.

If a long term view of profitability was required, assumptions would need to be made regarding future revenue, and a discount rate applied to ascertain a Net Present Value (NPV).

REVIEW FORM & FREE PRIZE DRAW

All original review forms from the entire BPP range, completed with genuine comments, will be entered into one of two draws on 31 July 2000 and 31 January 2001. The names on the first four forms picked out on each occasion will be sent a cheque for £50.

Name: ______________________ **Address:** ______________________

____

____

How have you used this Kit?
(Tick one box only)

- ☐ Home study (book only)
- ☐ On a course: college ______________
- ☐ With 'correspondence' package
- ☐ Other ______________

Why did you decide to purchase this Kit?
(Tick one box only)

- ☐ Have used complementary Study Text
- ☐ Have used BPP Kits in the past
- ☐ Recommendation by friend/colleague
- ☐ Recommendation by a lecturer at college
- ☐ Saw advertising
- ☐ Other ______________

During the past six months do you recall seeing/receiving any of the following?
(Tick as many boxes as are relevant)

- ☐ Our advertisement in *CIMA Student*
- ☐ Our advertisement in *Management Accounting*
- ☐ Our advertisement in *Pass*
- ☐ Our brochure with a letter through the post

Which (if any) aspects of our advertising do you find useful?
(Tick as many boxes as are relevant)

- ☐ Prices and publication dates of new editions
- ☐ Information on Kit content
- ☐ Facility to order books off-the-page
- ☐ None of the above

Have you used the companion Study Text for this subject? ☐ Yes ☐ No

Your ratings, comments and suggestions would be appreciated on the following areas

	Very useful	*Useful*	*Not useful*
Introductory section (Advice on revision, question practice and exam technique, question and answer checklist, etc)	☐	☐	☐
'Do you know?/Did you know?' checklists	☐	☐	☐
Tutorial questions	☐	☐	☐
Examination-standard questions	☐	☐	☐
Pass marks	☐	☐	☐
Content of answers	☐	☐	☐
Mock exam	☐	☐	☐
Structure and presentation	☐	☐	☐

	Excellent	*Good*	*Adequate*	*Poor*
Overall opinion of this Kit	☐	☐	☐	☐

Do you intend to continue using BPP Study Texts/Kits? ☐ Yes ☐ No

Please note any further comments and suggestions/errors on the reverse of this page or write by e-mail to alisonmchugh@bpp.co.uk

Please return to: Alison McHugh, BPP Publishing Ltd, FREEPOST, London, W12 8BR

REVIEW FORM & FREE PRIZE DRAW (continued)

Please note any further comments and suggestions/errors below

FREE PRIZE DRAW RULES

1 Closing date for 31 July 2000 draw is 30 June 2000. Closing date for 31 January 2001 draw is 31 December 2000.

2 Restricted to entries with UK and Eire addresses only. BPP employees, their families and business associates are excluded.

3 No purchase necessary. Entry forms are available upon request from BPP Publishing. No more than one entry per title, per person. Draw restricted to persons aged 16 and over.

4 Winners will be notified by post and receive their cheques not later than 6 weeks after the relevant draw date. Lists of winners will be published in BPP's *focus* newsletter following the relevant draw.

5 The decision of the promoter in all matters is final and binding. No correspondence will be entered into.

See overleaf for information on other BPP products and how to order

CIMA Order

To BPP Publishing Ltd, Aldine Place, London W12 8AA

Tel: 020 8740 2211. Fax: 020 8740 1184

Mr/Mrs/Ms (Full name)

Daytime delivery address

Postcode

Daytime Tel

Date of exam (month/year)

		7/99 Texts	1/2000 Kits	1/2000 Psscrds	1999 Tapes	1999 Videos	1999 CDs
STAGE 1							
1	Financial Accounting Fundamentals	£18.95 ☐	£9.95 ☐	£5.95 ☐	£12.95 ☐	£25.00 ☐	£34.95 ☐
2	Cost Accounting and Quantitative Methods	£18.95 ☐	£9.95 ☐	£5.95 ☐	£12.95 ☐	£25.00 ☐	£34.95 ☐
3	Economic Environment	£18.95 ☐	£9.95 ☐	£5.95 ☐	£12.95 ☐	£25.00 ☐	£34.95 ☐
4	Business Environment & Information Technology	£18.95 ☐	£9.95 ☐	£5.95 ☐	£12.95 ☐	£25.00 ☐	£34.95 ☐
STAGE 2							
5	Financial Accounting	£18.95 ☐	£9.95 ☐	£5.95 ☐	£12.95 ☐	£25.00 ☐	£34.95 ☐
6	Operational Cost Accounting	£18.95 ☐	£9.95 ☐	£5.95 ☐	£12.95 ☐	£25.00 ☐	£34.95 ☐
7	Management Science Applications	£18.95 ☐	£9.95 ☐	£5.95 ☐	£12.95 ☐	£25.00 ☐	£34.95 ☐
8	Business and Company Law	£18.95 ☐	£9.95 ☐	£5.95 ☐	£12.95 ☐	£25.00 ☐	£34.95 ☐
STAGE 3							
9	Financial Reporting	£19.95 ☐	£10.95 ☐	£5.95 ☐	£12.95 ☐	£25.00 ☐	£34.95 ☐
10	Management Accounting Applications	£19.95 ☐	£10.95 ☐	£5.95 ☐	£12.95 ☐	£25.00 ☐	
11	Organisational Management & Development	£19.95 ☐	£10.95 ☐	£5.95 ☐	£12.95 ☐	£25.00 ☐	
12	Business Taxation (FA 99)	£19.95 ☐	£10.95 ☐	£5.95 ☐	£12.95 ☐	£25.00 ☐	
STAGE 4							
13	Strategic Financial Management	£20.95 ☐	£10.95 ☐	£5.95 ☐	£12.95 ☐	£25.00 ☐	
14	Strategic Management Accountancy & Mktg	£20.95 ☐	£10.95 ☐	£5.95 ☐	£12.95 ☐	£25.00 ☐	
15	Information Management	£20.95 ☐	£10.95 ☐	£5.95 ☐	£12.95 ☐	£25.00 ☐	
16	Management Accounting Control Systems	£20.95 ☐	£10.95 ☐	£5.95 ☐	£12.95 ☐	£25.00 ☐	
						£	

POSTAGE & PACKING

Study Texts

	First	Each extra	
UK	£3.00	£2.00	£
Europe*	£5.00	£4.00	£
Rest of world	£20.00	£10.00	£

Kits/Passcards/Success Tapes

	First	Each extra	
UK	£2.00	£1.00	£
Europe*	£2.50	£1.00	£
Rest of world	£15.00	£8.00	£

Master CDs/Breakthrough Videos

	First	Each extra	
UK	£2.00	£2.00	£
Europe*	£2.00	£2.00	£
Rest of world	£20.00	£10.00	£

Grand Total (Cheques to *BPP Publishing*) I enclose a cheque for (incl. Postage) £

Or charge to Access/Visa/Switch

Card Number

Expiry date Start Date

Issue Number (Switch Only)

Signature

We aim to deliver to all UK addresses inside 5 working days. Orders to all EU addresses should be delivered within 6 working days. All other orders to overseas addresses should be delivered within 8 working days.

* Europe includes the Republic of Ireland and the Channel Islands.